*Books by Fred Allen*

TREADMILL TO OBLIVION

MUCH ADO ABOUT ME

# Much Ado About Me

# Much Ado About Me

by FRED ALLEN

*With Photographs*

*An Atlantic Monthly Press Book*
Little, Brown and Company · Boston · Toronto

ATLANTIC–LITTLE, BROWN BOOKS
ARE PUBLISHED BY
LITTLE, BROWN AND COMPANY
IN ASSOCIATION WITH
THE ATLANTIC MONTHLY PRESS

*Published simultaneously in Canada*
*by Little, Brown & Company (Canada) Limited*

PRINTED IN THE UNITED STATES OF AMERICA

*Again, to Portland*

# Foreword

SOME years ago John Steinbeck offered to help me with a book. I didn't know how to write a book. John listed some rudimentary suggestions for the beginner. I pass them on to you. John wrote:

Don't start by trying to make the book chronological. Just take a period. Then try to remember it so clearly that you can see things: what colors and how warm or cold and how you got there. Then try to remember people. And then just tell what happened. It is important to tell what people looked like, how they walked, what they wore, what they ate. Put it all in. Don't try to organize it. And put in all the details you can remember. You will find that in a very short time things will begin coming back to you, you thought you had forgotten. Do it for very short periods at first but kind of think of it when you aren't doing it. Don't think back over what you have done. Don't think of literary form. Let it get out as it wants to. Over tell it in the matter of detail — cutting comes later. The form will develop in the telling. Don't make the telling follow a form.

Fortified with John Steinbeck's advice I am starting my autobiography.

# Contents

# Contents

# List of Illustrations

# Much Ado About Me

# 1

## My Aunt Lizzie

ON May 31, 1894, the population of Cambridge, Massachusetts, was increased by one. On that day a son was born to James Henry Sullivan and his wife Cecilia Herlihy of that city. In Irish homes in those days there was no idle talk about the stork. When babies arrived in Cambridge they were expected. Poor mothers, who could not afford the luxury of a hospital bed, had their babies at home. On the appointed day, a relative or a friendly neighbor came in to take over the housework. Then the doctor drove up in his buggy, hitched his horse, and hurried into the house with his little black bag. Some hours later, looking a mite disheveled, the doctor walked slowly out the front door and drove away in his buggy; a tiny cry was heard from within the confines of the house. A baby had been born. That was all there was to it.

On May 31, then, this performance was given; the result was John Florence Sullivan. Two years later, on June 27, 1896, the performance was repeated. The doctor drove away again, another tiny cry soiled the neighborhood acoustics, and a second son, Robert, had joined James Henry Sullivan and his wife Cecilia.

One year later Cecilia contracted pneumonia and died.

James Henry Sullivan was left to face the world with his two small sons. After the funeral the usual family councils were held; there was a noticeable lack of enthusiasm among my father's brothers and sister when it was proposed that he and his brace of embryo males join one of their households. Our destiny was finally settled when one of my mother's sisters offered to make a home for James Henry and "the boys," as my brother and I were called.

I was not three years old. I knew that my name was John Florence Sullivan. I knew that my father, my brother Bob, and I were living with my Aunt Lizzie. All these early years are a montage of hazy memories: a house that had grapevines all over the place, another house with a great field in back to play in, and a parlor in which a coffin lay. Through the glass covering at one end of the coffin I could see a man's face; the man was strangely still. Later I was told that the man was my Grandfather Herlihy.

The first thing I recall distinctly is a short walk I took with my Aunt Lizzie. As the walk started I was five years old, and we were living on Bayard Street in Allston. My aunt escorted me to the end of Bayard Street and pointed me towards a red brick building directly across the road. I scurried away, went through the open door, and disappeared into the bowels of the North Harvard Grammar School.

My life assumed a pattern. I was going to school. My teacher's name was Miss Travis. Every morning brought pleasant surprises: new boys and girls to meet, new lessons to study, errands to run, a quota of play to consummate, a given number of meals to be eaten — and suddenly, when my back was turned, night would fall and, exhausted, I would be chased, or carried off, to bed.

I knew that James Henry Sullivan was my father; I didn't remember my mother at all. Even when I tried I couldn't remember what my mother looked like, what her voice sounded like, or anything at all about her. To me, it seemed that Aunt Lizzie had always been my mother. My father was a stranger. He was always in a hurry going off to work in the morning, and many nights he wouldn't be home for supper. When my father came home late we would hear him ascending the front stairs; he seemed to have an impediment in his tread. When my brother and I ran out to greet him we noticed that his breath was dominated by a potent element with which we were not familiar. As my Aunt Lizzie would start to warm up the cold supper dishes we would hear her say, "Henry's been drinking again." Everybody called my father Henry.

My father was a bookbinder by trade, as were all of his brothers. In those days, many young Cambridge boys and girls who had to go to work at an early age went into the Riverside Press or one of the other binderies in that section. My father went all through life binding books and trying to make both ends meet. He was good at binding books. In appearance, he was thin and rather artistic-looking, with brown hair cut in a pompadour style, and his upper lip sporting a well-landscaped mustache. He dressed very simply. His one bid for ostentation was the heavy gold watch chain that hung across his vest, supporting a large elk's tooth. My father had a good sense of humor and enjoyed being the life of the party; when I grew older, people often told me how funny he was. At that time he didn't seem funny to me. He squandered most of his fun away from home. In the house, he was always serious. On several occasions I heard my aunts say that it was after my mother died that he started to drink. When he was even mildly under the influence, if he heard the song "Love Me, and the World Is Mine," my father would start to cry. My aunts used to say that the song reminded my father of Cecilia.

We lived, at that time, in a two-family house on Bayard Street. We lived upstairs, and on the second floor there was a parlor, a dining room, two bedrooms, a kitchen, and a bath; in a sort of large attic right above this, there were four small bedrooms. Here, the ceilings slanted down with the roof. If you had to get up in the middle of the night, you had to get up in the middle of the room — or else.

The house was heated by a coal furnace, and lit by gas. Today, with the oil furnace, the thermostat, and electricity, light and heat are no problem, but circa 1900, things were different. The cellar had to be filled with coal to service the furnace, the furnace had to be adjusted and shaken down at certain hours of the day and night, ashes had to be sifted to salvage pieces of coal and coke that could be used again, and the ash barrels had to be filled and rolled out to the sidewalk to be emptied by the ashman. Then, for light, there were the gas jets and the kerosene lamps. Kerosene had to be transported from the grocery store; the grocer always stuck a small potato over the end of the spout on the can to keep the kerosene from joggling out on the way home. With the coming of the Welsbach mantle, lighting became an even greater problem. The mantle, placed over the gas jet, reduced the yellow glare to a soft white light; the only trouble was that replacing the mantle required a steady hand. The new mantle was set over the jet, and the gas was turned on and lighted. When the gauze of the mantle had burned off, the mantle itself was nothing but a fragile ash. A tiny zephyr or the slightest jarring of the hand would crumple the mantle completely. If you avoided both the zephyr and the jarring, the mantle ignited, and light was available. In those days, I was new at it, but life to me seemed terribly complicated.

Aunt Lizzie dominated the household, and ruled her domestic domain with quiet efficiency. Not so many years before, shortly after her marriage, her husband Mike, who was a plumber by profession, had been stricken with lead poisoning. This left him partly paralyzed and unable to work. To support herself, and to provide a home for her crippled husband, Aunt Lizzie kept house for her two sisters, Jane and Mary, and for her brother, Joe. It was a sort of community project, in which the boarders paid five dollars a week apiece. This princely sum entitled them to a breakfast, a lunch to be packed and taken to work, and a big supper at night. Washing, ironing, and housework were included, and Aunt Lizzie paid the rent. The money she had left was hers to keep. Aunt Lizzie had her hands full, and not with money.

When my father joined the household, he was working for the Boston Public Library Bindery at an annual salary of $1000. When you divided this by fifty-two weeks, you learned that my father's take-home pay — if he was going home on pay day — was $19.23 a week. From this sum he paid Aunt Lizzie eight dollars a week for the three of us. It was a tribute to Aunt Lizzie's skill that we all survived. There was always good wholesome food available. She baked her own bread, and on Saturday nights she made her own baked beans and brown bread. She would start off with a leg of lamb for Sunday dinner, and then, on successive days, there would be lamb chops, cold lamb, shepherd's pie, lamb stew, lamb soup, and finally the lamb bone was turned over to some neighbor who was operating a dog. My Aunt Lizzie never heard of Fanny Farmer, but she could make nourishing dishes by using only a few scraps and the punctuation from one of Fanny's recipes.

As I grew older I never could understand why my Aunt Lizzie took in my father, my brother, and me to further augment her cluttered existence. I felt that she should have turned my father away from her door and thrown his progeny at him. But this would never have occurred to Aunt Lizzie. She was born generous and charitable and had her own simple philosophy. She had implicit faith in the Lord and that He would provide. Aunt Lizzie never let the Lord down, and until the day she died it was vice versa.

With the three sisters living together there were occasional family crises; after a heated exchange my Aunt Mary or my Aunt Jane or perhaps both of them would move out of the house and take a room in town. With her budget curtailed Aunt Lizzie would carry on, sometimes owing a little to the grocer or the landlord. Weeks later, the departed sister would return to take her place in the family as though nothing had happened. Whether blood really was thicker than water, or whether the five-dollar weekly rate was the attraction, I never knew. Usually, in their disputes, the bone of contention was my Uncle Mike. Aunt Lizzie's sisters resented Uncle Mike. They thought that he had ruined my Aunt Lizzie's life, and that she was wearing herself out caring for him while none of his own relatives made any effort to contribute to his welfare. Aunt Lizzie never complained; she took care of Uncle Mike for forty years, the last eighteen of which he spent in bed. She was a wonderful woman.

During the early stages of his illness, Uncle Mike was able to walk. He would visit the shopkeepers in his neighborhood daily, and spend his hours posing as an authority on anything the other person didn't understand. A candy salesman who liked my Uncle Mike thought that he could make some occasional money selling candy. The salesman, an optimist, left a supply of chocolates and hard candies at our house. Whenever my Uncle Mike got an order for candy, my brother and I would make the delivery. When the customers opened up the boxes of chocolates and hard candies, they found that the lower layers were missing. My brother and I had inspected the candy at home; we had decided that if we lifted the top two layers, we could eat most of the bottom layer and nobody would notice it. Uncle Mike wasn't in the candy business long.

When my father first came to live with Aunt Lizzie, he brought a sewing machine and a piano along. The piano was an Emerson: an upright model with panels of copper grillwork in the front. In time I was ordered to take piano lessons. My teacher was a woman named Louise Forest, who charged fifty cents a lesson, and who lived three miles from our house. I had to walk the three miles to Miss Forest's, carrying the fifty cents and a roll of music; by the time I had walked back home, with all the distractions on the way, I had forgotten most of the notes, the scales, and the musical exercises which Miss Forest thought she had just taught me. Eventually I did master two pianoforte gems. One was "Hiawatha" and the other was "Pitter, Patter, Little Rain Drops." Frequently, when company called, I would be asked to render half or all of my repertoire. As time wore on, either the company stopped coming or the requests fell off: I forget which. Today, all I know about the piano is that without it the world would never have heard of Liberace.

Life in Allston in those days was monotony broken by certain regular community high lights. One of these was the nightly still alarm drill at the firehouse. At eight o'clock sharp every weekday night the fire bells sounded, the firehouse doors flew open, and you could see the firemen sliding down the brass pole. The crowd would gather across the street, watching the firemen as they stoked the fire in the engine and hitched the horses just as though an actual alarm had come in. The air would be charged with excitement, and then, when everything was ready, the driver would grasp the reins, the steam whistle would rupture the night with an ungodly blast, and with bells ringing Engine 49 would streak out of the door, the three white horses straining and frothing, a shower of live sparks spewing from the engine as the bedlam on wheels shrieked its way into the distance. It did not go far. After a short run Engine 49 would return, the firemen would dismount, back the engine into the firehouse, and un-hitch the horses. Suddenly the doors would close, the crowd would disperse, and all would be quiet again until the next night.

A juicy tidbit for the neighborhood gossips was always provided when the patrol wagon dashed down our street. The early paddy wagons were not covered, and the unfortunate person being arrested had no privacy. He sat by the side of the arresting officer, the center of all prying eyes. By the time the prisoner arrived at the police station the entire neighbor-hood knew who he was and what he had done.

The arrival of Mr. Harrington, the soap-grease man, was always a great and rancid event. Each week Aunt Lizzie saved all her fat and grease. On the appointed day, if the wind was right, you could anticipate Mr. Harrington and his pungent vehicle long before you could hear his shrill cry: "S-o-o-a-p gr-e-e-e-z!" Mr. Harrington would pull up his fragrant horse, weigh Aunt Lizzie's fat and grease, give her some yellow laundry soap in exchange, and depart, leaving behind a med-ley of odors that hung over the street long after he was out of sight.

A sensation was caused in Allston by the first appearance of the college ice. Howes Drug Store introduced this innova-tion to the soda and straw set. The college ice was the pre-historic sundae, and in its first form was merely a ball of ice cream covered with syrup, fruit, or chopped nuts. On special occasions Aunt Jane or Aunt Mary would treat my brother and me to a college ice. After the ice cream was finished I would sit there with my empty plate and envy my stomach.

One afternoon a week, it was an experience to go over to

Western Avenue to see the cattle being driven to the Brighton
Abbatoir, where they were to be slaughtered. It was about
this time that a doctor who examined my Uncle Mike
thought that his paralysis might be helped if he drank warm
blood, so for many weeks I walked to the abbatoir with my
Uncle Mike and waited while he drank the steer or cattle
blood. It didn't help him. Doctors were puzzled by Uncle
Mike's condition and he was examined by a number of medical groups in Boston. One day he came home with a battery
set that had two handles attached; the doctors thought that
the electric current going through his body would restore
life to his withered arms and hands. Another time the doctors wanted to burn the base of his spine. They said it would
either cure him or kill him. It was an easy decision to make.
Uncle Mike kept the base of his spine intact and outlived
most of the doctors.

During the week, from Monday to Saturday, we didn't see
much of my father. He left the house early in the morning
and would return from work at different hours in various
states of exhilaration or depression. Our back yard ran into
the back yard of a family named Dupee. The Dupees kept
an enormous St. Bernard dog tied up in their yard. The St.
Bernard never bothered anybody; he was content to lie
around and doze off to dream about his younger days when,
wearing his brandy lavaliere, he patrolled the snowy wastes of
the Alps, burrowing into drifts to rescue lost monks and
upended skiers. Some nights, when supper was finished and
my father hadn't come home, I would help my Aunt Lizzie
with the dishes. The window at our kitchen sink overlooked the back yard, and as dusk fell on a routine evening
the yard was quiet and serene. However, there were nights
when we'd hear a crashing through the underbrush; the
Dupees' St. Bernard would then start baying and tugging at

his chain, and in rebuttal we'd hear a human voice mumbling an assortment of oaths to augment the din. My Aunt Lizzie would raise her head from her soapy chore and say, "Your father is taking the short cut again tonight." After Mr. Dupee had shouted out of a window to restore his St. Bernard's confidence, and my father had emerged through a hole in the chicken-wire fence and made our back door safely, my Aunt Lizzie and I returned to the dishes, and all was quiet again.

Downstairs in our house there lived a family named Johnson. Mr. Johnson drove a hansom cab, and at night he met all trains coming from Boston at the Allston station. When my father left the city very late, he would take the train. If Mr. Johnson saw my father quitting the train in a variety of directions, he would assist him into the hansom cab, close the double-breasted doors in front, mount his high seat in the rear, brandish his whip, and drive off to deliver Father to our front door. Some nights I didn't have to be psychic to sense that my father and Mr. Johnson had made a few stops on the way. The hansom would come clopping up Bayard Street with Mr. Johnson shouting encouragement to his horse and my father rendering a madrigal from a relaxed position inside the cab. One night, things were so hectic in and atop the hansom as it turned the corner of our street that it seemed the horse was the only one in the party who was sober. Suddenly Mr. Johnson seemed to master his vision, our house took dimension, he pulled the reins sharply, and the horse reared back; Mr. Johnson, shouting "Whoa!" tumbled back off his seat, clavicle over fritter, and lay inert in the street. I don't know who helped my father into the house that night. It might have been the horse.

These were the week days; Sundays were different. Every Sunday my father had the same routine. After church and dinner at our house, he would take my brother and me to visit my grandfather and grandmother in Cambridge. Leaving our house in Allston, we would walk down North Harvard Street into Harvard Square, then through the Harvard Yard — the closest I ever came to going to Harvard — out past the Fogg Museum, up Emmons Street to Emmons Place. My grandfather and grandmother Sullivan lived here, in the last house on the right. Each week my father and his four brothers visited their father and mother; each boy brought a pint of whiskey to the old folks. They spent the day quietly, discussing the news and playing "forty-fives," a game my grandmother liked to play while taking frequent pinches of snuff. The bottle was also passed around occasionally. My grandmother had open house on Sunday, and all of her sons were welcome to bring their friends to spend the day. These Sundays always came to an end with an early dinner, and as twilight set in, my brother and I knew that the time had come to prepare for our collective departure. We also knew that my father, having spent the day with his family and the bottles, would be a trifle loose-gaited on our way home. After the good-bys had been said, my brother and I would flank my father, and we'd start off. It was a long three-mile walk home, and if you had met the three of us along the road you would have seen a peculiar sight: we looked like two sardines guiding an unsteady Moby Dick into port.

It was in my grandmother's house that I met my Aunt Mame. She was my father's only sister, and a very religious woman. She went to Mass every morning at six o'clock, taking a short cut through a neighboring field; over the months and years she had worn a path through the tall grass in this field. As the years went on, Aunt Mame became increasingly religious, and took to leaving her bedroom window open a little at the top at night to enable the Blessed Virgin to enter and depart if she felt so inclined. Many years later, when my father died, my Aunt Mame managed to conceal his gold watch and to have his piano moved to another house to make sure that my Aunt Lizzie would not get this so-called estate. Religion affects some people strangely.

It was also in my grandmother's house that I attended my first wake, when my grandfather Sullivan died. The wake was an Irish institution. When a member of the family died, the body was laid out in the front room and floral offerings were draped all around. Chairs were borrowed, and the neighbors supplied extra cups and saucers so that there would be plenty of tea and coffee available for the womenfolk. Great mounds of tobacco were piled up on the kitchen table, surrounded by clay pipes which were called "T.D.'s." Also, there was plenty of whiskey for the male mourners. For the two days and nights the wake was in progress the members of the immediate family rarely slept. When the neighbors called, they first went into the front room to pay their respects to the deceased; then the men would gather in the kitchen, fill their clay pipes from the mounds of tobacco, take their glasses of caper juice, and join the general conversation. The exploits and achievements of the departed were embellished, his sense of humor was extolled, and his loss to the community was overly evaluated. As the night wore on, the tobacco fumes cast a blue haze over the kitchen, glasses were filled and refilled, the talk changed to other subjects, stories were told, occasional laughter rang out, and a good time generally was had by the many friends who had gathered to see the host off on his final journey. The women assembled in the dining room for tea and coffee and perhaps a snack. Memories, encomiums, and anecdotes involving the departed were exchanged and intermittent tears were shed. In every neighborhood there was a group of old women who thrived on wakes. They would descend on the house in their glory, sitting through the night swilling gallons of tea, stimulating the wailing and the mournful small talk. In the morning they would join the family for the church services, and if there was room available in a carriage, the old crones would go along to the cemetery for the ride.

Not only the women loved funerals. On our street we had a retired old gentleman named Tom Carpenter. Every time Tom saw a funeral wreath on a door he thought nothing of bursting into the house and taking over. It didn't make any difference to Tom that the next of kin, or those who had assembled for the weeping, had no idea who he was. He would bustle around the stove making tea and coffee, send out for food if it was needed, wash the dishes, and keep things humming in general. Tom would stay on for two days and nights with no sleep, happy at his chores. He would be the last one out of the house. After the body had been taken to the church and the crowd had gone, Tom's work was still not done: he would remain to give the rooms a few licks with the broom so that the family could return to a clean house. Every few weeks Tom would show up at our house to report to my aunt on his most recent ghoulish peccadillo. He would be exhausted, with long dark bags hanging under his eyes. "Mrs. Lovely," he would tell my aunt, "I don't know what they'd have done without me. The widow went to pieces. I had to make forty pots of coffee and God knows how many sandwiches." When my aunt asked him whose funeral it was, Tom would answer, "Gosh, I was so busy crying and working I didn't find out!"

On these Sundays in Allston, before we went to my grandmother's house, we went to St. Anthony's Church. After the Masses the priests always stood outside the church, ostensibly to greet the parishioners, but I am sure they also had another motive. They were always pouncing on the parents of small boys. After some nondescript talk about the weather, the parents were made aware of the opportunities available for their small fry as either altar boys or choirboys. One Sunday, Father McNamara stopped my Aunt Lizzie when she had me in tow. A few Sundays later I was wearing a cassock and a surplice and posing as a choirboy. For years I told a joke about this experience: "The first Sunday I sang in the choir two hundred people changed their religion." It was not quite as bad as that. The congregation was protected; the choir boasted some twenty other raucous small vocalists who could easily smother my nasal soprano.

Shortly after my debut as a choirboy I made my first appearance as an actor. The church presented a Christmas pageant. I was cast as one of the Wise Men (I was then about seven) bringing gifts to the Christ child in the manger. Dressed in a toga my aunt had made which looked like a long mess jacket, I came on the stage, and I can still remember the first lines I ever spoke to an audience:

> Myrrh is mine — its bitter perfume
> Breathes a life of gathering gloom
> Sorrow, sighing, bleeding, dying,
> Sealed in a stone-cold tomb.

I didn't stay up for the notices and consequently never learned the critics' reaction to my first performance.

The church was also responsible for my second appearance as an actor. Before the coming of Bingo, the churches had to raise money by promoting lawn parties, bridge evenings, field days, travel talks with magic-lantern slides, and other forms of mild entertainment. As was its winter custom, St. Anthony's announced that an annual minstrel show was to be given by the children of the parish. When the rehearsals started, I found that I was not cast as the star. I was an undersized nonentity, just a member of the chorus: my doubtful contribution was to be confined to ensemble singing. This minstrel show, however, made parish history. On the big night, some fifty parents delivered their children to the hall in which the show was to be held. This insured a full house, because the parents and relatives had to wait around to take the cast home, and instead of loitering around outside, they bought tickets and prepared to sit through the show. My Aunt Lizzie had made me a minstrel shirt with long pointed collars, and deposited me with the other kids in a large dressing room in the back of the hall. In order to make this a real minstrel show, the pastor had engaged a make-up man to blacken up the little minstrel girls and boys. This make-up man was a local smalltime actor who had seen better days. He had an over-all bloodshot look, and appeared to be a hang-over with a suit on. After he had blackened up his last small charge, the minstrel show proceeded, and as soon as it did, the make-up man stepped out into the night and an adjacent saloon to test his nonexistent will power. When the minstrel show was over and the parents came backstage to pick up their sprats, the make-up man was nowhere to be found. There were fifty-odd black-faced little minstrel kiddies and nobody knew how to remove the black. When, after a reasonable length of time, it became obvious that the make-up man was not planning to return, the parents started home with their soiled progeny. The trolley cars and the streets were filled with crying tiny troubadours who were convinced that they were destined to go through life in blackface.

Apparently the series of scrubbings required to restore my normal pasty hue cured me of any desire to invade the minstrel field again. Instead, I turned to music. Through a bit of snide bartering, I had come into possession of a harmonica.

With a little practice, I mastered a folio of *Southern Folk Songs*. Wind of my prowess spread through the grammar school like bad news at a pessimists' convention, and I was tapped to appear in a variety show to be given by the school. The teacher, a Miss Bancroft, arranged my act for me. Miss Bancroft gave me a joke to tell, and some definite instructions. I was to walk out on the stage, tell this one joke, and then proceed with my harmonica. In her haste Miss Bancroft didn't analyze the joke. It required two people to tell it. This forced me to walk on stage alone and start a conversation with myself. The joke was this: "If the people in Poland are called Poles — why aren't the people in Holland called Holes?" If this joke had come off, I would have gotten my first laugh from an audience. I have often tried to recall how my harmonica concert was received that day. Memory has mercifully failed me on each occasion.

One other grammar school teacher I have tried to forget down through the years with no success was Miss Boynton. Miss Boynton was a mountainous spinster who, when she sat at her desk, looked as though she had just made a parachute landing and the parachute was all skin. Her pupils called her "Sally Fat." Every morning Miss Boynton drove to school with her horse and buggy. The walk from the stable to the school was too great a physical chore for the pneumatic Miss Boynton, so when she plopped down from the step of the buggy in front of the school, she would ask one of the boys to drive the horse around the corner to the stable. The stable owner would unhitch the buggy and turn the horse into a stall where it could stand all day and wonder why it was that people had to go to school and horses didn't. This left Miss Boynton with a problem to solve each day. It wasn't a dilemma in education; it was simply that when school was over, somebody would have to go and bring the horse and buggy back from the stable. This meant that every day one boy, preferably a big boy, would have to be kept after school. When class was dismissed, the boy would be summoned by the flabby schoolmarm and be told that his punishment would be overlooked if he would step around to the stable and drive Miss Boynton's rig to the front of the school. I was too small to manage the horse. When I was kept after school, Miss Boynton meant business.

At home, I took things for granted. My Aunt Lizzie seemed to do everything. Occasionally, my other aunts would bring us presents or take my brother and me to the beach or on a picnic, but in any emergency or in sickness I always turned to my Aunt Lizzie. When my tonsils had to come out, Aunt Lizzie took me to the hospital to stay overnight. Dr. Fitzgerald arrived and looped little wires over my tonsils and nipped them off. Many years later, I learned that Dr. Fitzgerald had left both tonsil ends in my throat, and they are still in there today. When my throat was healing I could have ice cream. I would lie in bed at home, waiting to hear the tinkle of the bells on the horse's harness that announced the presence of Bushway's Ice Cream Wagon coming up the street. When I had a stomach-ache Aunt Lizzie would pack me into bed with a hot flatiron wrapped in heavy cloth. With Dr. Fitzgerald, hot flatirons, and Aunt Lizzie, I survived.

In an effort to augment Aunt Lizzie's income, my father hinted that a man who worked with him at the bindery was looking for a room out of the city. The man's name was Mr. Geyer. My father gave him an excellent character reference and said that Mr. Geyer would be no trouble, since he could share my father's room and bed. Apart from two meals, according to my father, the income provided by the new guest would be clear profit. Mr. Geyer subsequently arrived: a big-bellied Teutonic gentleman with a cardboard suitcase.

He seemed to be agreeable and no trouble at all. However, it soon developed that Mr. Geyer was not perfect; he had two weaknesses. The first was that he consumed great quantities of beer when awake. The second was that he had no control of his kidneys when asleep. It soon became obvious that we were going to have to strap pontoons on my father or petition the Coast Guard to open a station in the room. The final straw was when Aunt Lizzie discovered that the new guest had ruined the feather mattress. He was asked to leave. Mr. Geyer, being a gentleman despite his organic shortcomings, hauled his acid presence out of our midst.

We lived on Bayard Street for over ten years. One rainy spring night, as we were all eating supper, my Aunt Lizzie announced that she wanted everyone to come home early the following evening. She said that it was very important. I sensed something ominous. The next night my Aunt Jane, my Aunt Mary, my Uncle Mike, my Uncle Joe, my brother, and I all assembled in the living room. Aunt Lizzie opened the session tersely. She said, "Henry has something to say." My father rarely had anything to say. Something told me that if my father really had something to say, we were all facing a crisis.

Apparently too embarrassed to face the others, my father hung his head and said what he had to say to the elk's tooth that lay dormant on his vest. He spoke slowly. *Rigor mortis* seemed to have set in on every sentence he uttered; each word appeared to lie in state on his lips before it tumbled out into space. When my father had finished, the little group sat staring at him, stunned. My father had informed us abruptly that he was going to remarry. He was also going to move out of the house and take his piano and his sewing machine with him. My Aunt Lizzie didn't mind losing the piano, but she did mention that she really needed the sewing machine. My father was adamant. Addressing my brother and me, he told us that we could either come with him and his new bride, whom neither of us had ever seen, or we could stay with Aunt Lizzie. My brother Bob decided to go with my father. Young as I was, I felt that I owed something to a wonderful woman who had been a mother to me for some twelve years. I said that I would stay with my Aunt Lizzie. I never regretted it.

# 2

## My Library Routine

ON May 31, 1908, I was fourteen; it was a memorable birthday. At breakfast that morning Aunt Lizzie told me that, after school, I was to put on my best blue suit and go into Boston to meet my father. My best suit was always a blue serge two-piece ensemble consisting of a Norfolk jacket, with pleats down the front and a belt around the waist that buttoned over the navel, and a pair of knickerbocker pants. Each year, the week before Easter, my Aunt Lizzie took my brother and me to the Jordan Marsh department store in Boston where we got our annual wardrobe. Our suits always cost five dollars each, and, with the suits, we also received a fried-egg cap. We called them fried eggs because that is what they looked like. The fried egg sat very tight on top of the head. The blue serge in the cap was quite thin, and a phrenologist could have read a small boy's head without troubling him to take off his fried egg.

My Aunt Lizzie told me that I was to meet my father at Con Keefe's on Dartmouth Street. Con Keefe's was a popular alcoholic shrine, a cheer chapel with all the routine accouterments: the swinging doors, the five-cent beer, the free lunch, the starched bartenders, and the inevitable quota of frowzy thinkers draped along the bar. Riding in from Allston on the trolley car, I wondered why my father had summoned me. True, it was my fourteenth birthday, but I had had thirteen other birthdays on which my father had never sent for me to meet him in town. Something was up and it was my curiosity.

When I arrived at Con Keefe's I pushed back one of the swinging doors and peeked in. My father was waiting at the end of the bar with another man; each had a whiskey glass within easy reach. My father, after checking his watch and complimenting me on my punctuality, introduced me to the other man, who turned out to be a Mr. Billy Hempstead. Mr. Hempstead was an austere-looking gentleman with a bulbous nose, a tall forehead that went over the top of his head, and an over-all boiled complexion. If I had been old enough to attempt character reading, I would have judged Mr. Hempstead to be the custodian of a thirst and, as acting custodian, to be fulfilling his every obligation to his charge.

As my father talked, he kept lubricating his throat, taking little sips from his glass. He divulged that since I was now fourteen years of age, I could go to work. That was the law, my father said, and since it was the first law I had ever heard him mention, something told me he was going to see that it was enforced. In the good old days in Massachusetts, manual labor was performed by the untutored and the young; it was necessary for the state to protect the child. But at fourteen it was all right for him to go to work.

My father continued to talk. I learned that, during the day, Mr. Hempstead worked at the book bindery with my father. At night, however, he worked at the Boston Public Library. Mr. Hempstead each night dropped in at Con Keefe's for a light supper with some liquid embellishments. Insulated against elements that might ruffle his complacency, Mr. Hempstead stepped gingerly out of Con Keefe's down Dartmouth Street to the library, where he changed from his street clothes into a blue uniform and became a police officer from 6 P.M. until the library closed. Mr. Hempstead walked

from room to room exuding authority and silently implying
that readers had better keep order if they knew what was
good for them. The library employed a number of small
boys in minor capacities, and, taking advantage of Mr.
Hempstead's contacts, my father had arranged to have him
drag me into the presence of the man who hired these small
boys.

The minute my father had explained my status and the
reason I was the only one of my age in Con Keefe's, Mr.
Hempstead was galvanized into action. He and my father
drained their glasses, took some cloves to chew so that in case
one breathed on the other he would not be suspected of
drinking, and, calling the bartender's attention to their departure, pushed me ahead through the swinging doors and
off towards the library. When we arrived at the employees'
entrance, my father waited in the vestibule and Mr. Hempstead said that he would take me upstairs. Following Mr.
Hempstead up an iron spiral staircase, I finally reached a
room that appeared to be fraught with books and people.
Girls were putting slips into round carrier pouches and popping the pouches into a pneumatic device that snapped shut;
wire baskets containing books were coming down on an elevator arrangement from some place upstairs; small boys were
taking the books out of the baskets, checking the slips, and
rushing off into the yonder. In a corner, obviously in control
of this tome tumult, stood a dapper man. He took our entrance calmly; he seemed to be expecting Mr. Hempstead.
After I was introduced to the dapper party, I could now
number among my acquaintances Mr. Pierce Buckley. For
my information, and to fill in a lull, Mr. Hempstead whis-
pered that Mr. Buckley hired the boys who worked evenings. After inspecting me, and apparently evaluating my
potential, Mr. Buckley told Mr. Hempstead that I would

have to take a civil-service examination; if this hazard could be surmounted, Mr. Buckley would find a place for me. This seemed to conclude the business at hand. Mr. Buckley beamed and withdrew. Mr. Hempstead and I went back down the spiral staircase. My father was waiting, and a full report was turned over to him on the meeting with Mr. Buckley. Mr. Hempstead, having served his purpose, then left to don his policeman's uniform, and my father and I started home.

Some weeks later, after I had taken the examination, I was notified that I had passed. Then a card came, telling me to report to Mr. Buckley. The library, at that time, was open from 9 A.M. to 9 P.M. seven days a week. The day staff finished at 6 P.M., while the night employees worked the three remaining hours. To augment their incomes, many of the day workers stayed over and worked two or three nights a week, or all day Sunday. These day workers had the key positions when they were on at night. The small boys, all of whom were going to school, were used only as runners or stack boys. The runner was activated by a series of circumstances. The reader, entering the library to obtain a certain book, looked the book up in the catalogue room, then noted its number on a slip of paper. Also on this slip the reader put the number of his seat in Bates Hall, the large reading room where he would await the book. The slip was turned in at the desk, placed in one of the pneumatic carrier tubes, and dispatched to the proper stack. If the book was on the shelf, it was sent down in one of the wire baskets I had seen in Mr. Buckley's department. The runner was then given the book and told to deliver it to the reader at his seat in Bates Hall.

The stack boy had the better job. He sat up in his stack alone. He had a small table, lighted by a green-shaded bulb that hung from the ceiling; at his right was one of the pneumatic devices that delivered the pouches containing the book slips. During the night, if things were dull, the stack boy could do his homework or read. The arrival of a slip was announced by a rush of air and the plopping of the pouch in a padded receptacle. The boy put down his homework, opened the pouch, looked at the number on the slip, and disappeared down the dark, narrow corridor. If the book was not in, the slip was stamped "Out" and returned to the reader. Otherwise, the boy took the book, placed it in the wire basket, and sent it downstairs. The stack boy had one other chore, that of seeing to it that all books sent back to the stacks from the reading room were put back in their places before he left at 9 P.M.

When I reported to the dapper Mr. Buckley, I was told that I was to be a runner, and that I was to work regularly, Tuesdays and Thursdays. Mr. Buckley told me that some nights boys were ill or didn't report for work, and if I wanted to take a chance, I could come in on any of my off nights and see if there was a job open. I did that quite often. It was sort of a contest. If there were two places to be filled, and five boys hoping to get them, Mr. Buckley would line up the applicants, look them up and down until he had built up the proper amount of suspense, and then, with a dapper finger, he would point at the two lucky winners. The three losers would slink out into the night.

All summer I worked as a runner. The runner's qualifications presented no problem for me. All I needed was a sense of direction and enough wind to last me through the night. There was no school, and I only had to work at night. During the day there was time to swim, play baseball, and participate in the seasonal antics that a fourteen-year-old boy is supposed to enjoy. That summer I ran in a junior marathon held as a feature of the church field day. As the starting gun was fired

I saw my father standing in the crowd. As the race progressed and I ran through the neighborhood streets, trying to keep up with the pack of kids, it seemed to me that my father suddenly started coming out of every saloon we passed, shouting encouragement. While I was trying to figure out how my father was able to come out of a number of saloons in different sections, and virtually simultaneously, I lost the race. Later, I found out that my father knew the route the race was to travel, and had been taking short cuts to the various saloons to be able to give me vocal encouragement en route. Also during this summer I made weekly trips with an enterprising boy named Raymond Young who owned and operated a Punch and Judy show. On Saturdays I helped Raymond transport his dummies and paraphernalia to field days, lawn parties, and children's entertainments. Raymond did the entire Punch and Judy presentation alone: I merely took tickets and helped him pull the wagon back and forth.

In September, all this changed. I continued to work at the library, but I began to go to high school, the Boston High School of Commerce, which had been opened four years earlier as the pet project of the then mayor of Boston, John F. Fitzgerald. "John F.," or "Honey Fitz," as his supporters called him, was a very popular mayor whose hobby was singing. His vocal prowess was known as far as his high tenor voice had reached, and his high tenor voice had reached every nook and cranny in which a voter might conceivably be hiding in the wards and precincts of the city of Boston. Mayor Fitzgerald's favorite song was "Sweet Adeline." The Mayor sang "Sweet Adeline" at every political rally, public function, and private gathering to which he lent his august presence. There was a rumor that Mayor Fitzgerald had sung "Sweet Adeline" in office for so many years that the City Hall acoustics had diabetes.

While the Mayor knew that through his efforts his loyal constituents were being surfeited with song, he also knew that there were other more important things that they were being denied. John F. realized that if all he was going to do was sing for his salary, it would be cheaper for the taxpayers of Boston to turn their City Hall into a bird cage and elect a nightingale as mayor. Examining a number of ideas to improve the conditions of the faithful and their families, the Mayor kept returning to one: figures showed that thousands of Boston boys of poorer families had no opportunity to go to college. Because their families needed the additional income, the boys had to go to work as soon as they finished grammar or high school. The Mayor felt that Boston should have a school that would equip these boys for definite jobs, or give them an opportunity to enter a specific business.

The Mayor's abstract thought shortly became a concrete reality. The High School of Commerce opened its doors on September 6, 1904, with appropriate ceremonies and the blessings of John F. Fitzgerald. Possibly the Mayor sang a chorus or two of "Sweet Adeline." The records are vague on this point.

The Commerce student had a variety of subjects not available at other high schools to gird him for the eternal fray. Shorthand, typing, salesmanship, French, German, and Spanish were at his disposal. The Commerce boy was told what New England had to offer him with its wool and leather marts; he learned about the opportunities to come with the development of South America. He was given courses to prepare him to talk on his feet and acquire confidence in himself. Outstanding businessmen gave weekly talks to the Commerce student body, each tycoon explaining his particular business, the circumstances that had led him into it, and the opportunities for the student in it. Excursions to local industries were held for Commerce classes; in one school year I remember treks to the Walter Baker Chocolate Company factory, the Customs House, the docks of the United Fruit Company, the Waltham Watch Company, the United Drug Company, the Hood Milk Company, an investment and securities office, and many others. Through the variety of these trips, the High School of Commerce did everything it could to stimulate the student's interest in business. Through its employment bureau it tried to launch him into some branch of endeavor that not only appealed to him but promised him a future.

As it turned out over the years, the hopes of Mayor John F. Fitzgerald were fulfilled. Forty years later, on May 29, 1945, a testimonial dinner was given Dr. James E. Downey, who was retiring as headmaster after guiding the destinies of the school for more than thirty-five years. On the dais with Mr. Downey were Commerce graduates who had been successful in almost every known business and profession. The then governor of Massachusetts, Maurice Tobin, was there; Arthur O'Keefe, president of the First National Stores; George Hansen, president of Chandler's, one of Boston's leading women's shops; and bankers, lawyers, doctors, dentists, singers, actors, leather and wool barons were all on hand. All were Commerce graduates; all had become successful in totally different fields.

As toastmaster, commenting on this, I said (and I quote myself), "You have probably noticed, on the first page of the testimonial program, that Mr. Downey is hailed as a Builder of Men. Tonight, he will have an opportunity of seeing how some of his earlier models have weathered the years. We Commerce students were indeed fortunate in our choice of school. Years ago, if a boy went to Latin School, at the end of four years he could read, write, and speak Latin. All the boy knew was Latin — he had no choice. He either had to go to Harvard — where even the janitor speaks Latin around the cellar — or he had to get a menial job reading prescriptions in one of the Rexall Drug Stores. If a boy went to Mechanics Arts, at the end of four years, instead of a diploma, he was given a tool chest, a hammer, and the right of way. A boy who went to the average high school found that his course was charted and he was doomed. BUT — not the boy who went to Commerce. The great advantage of a Commerce education was that it wouldn't interfere with any plans you might have for the future. After four years in Commerce — you were just four years older. A Commerce graduate was not bound by custom or hampered by tradition. He could become anything he pleased. A Commerce education merely siphoned the dew from his ignorance. A Commerce diploma was simply a passport to tomorrow."

This was said on May 29, 1945. On September 11, 1908, I had no such lofty thoughts. I was walking down Winthrop Street in Roxbury, on my way to enter the High School of Commerce for the first time. I was fourteen years old, and I wasn't looking ahead to the day when the school could find me work. I had a job. I had heard of students' working their way through college. In the library, I was working my way through high school.

Now that summer was over and I was in school, things were different. On Tuesday and Thursday nights I had to work at the library, and on these days my Aunt Lizzie had to pack two lunches for me. As a runner, I couldn't do my homework during working hours; I was too busy running. After school, where I had eaten my first lunch, I would walk from Roxbury into Boston, to the library — a distance of about four miles. Sitting in one of the reading rooms, I would finish my homework; then, at five o'clock, I would go down to my    locker on the employees' floor, eat my second lunch, wash, and be ready to assume my runner's role at six o'clock.

If I had gone through life as a runner, I would have died winded rather than rich. A runner was paid twenty cents an hour. Working three hours a night, I earned sixty cents. Working two nights, my weekly salary was $1.20. This, however, was not my take-home pay. I was now a city employee. I had to go into Boston every Saturday and report at the City Hall. There I signed the payroll at the paymaster's office and took possession of my $1.20 salary. The trolley fare each way was five cents; ten cents deducted from the $1.20 left me with $1.10 net. Some weeks, if I was fortunate enough to get an extra night or two, my income zoomed up to $1.80 or $2.40, but in addition to the trolley expenses, there were other frequent deductions. Many nights, after finishing at the library, I was hungry. On my way to the trolley stop, I had to pass a Waldorf Lunch. Looking in through the window at the white-tiled walls, the inviting chairs, the smiling waiter standing behind the glass counter with the tempting foods on display, my eyes seemed to communicate with my stomach. My stomach instantly took over and overpowered my mind. Before I knew it, my legs were taking me in through the Waldorf Lunch door and up to the counter; my stomach, through some strange ventriloquial magic, was compelling my mouth to say to the waiter, "A trilby sandwich and a glass of milk." A trilby was a fried egg served à la mode with a thick slice of onion. Encased in a large bun, well seasoned with salt and pepper, and doused with ketchup until the ketchup flowed down the sides of the bun onto the plate to be dunked in later, the trilby was guaranteed to fend off malnutrition indefinitely. The trilby was five cents and the milk five cents. This ten-cent expenditure reduced my night's earnings to fifty cents. Many nights, after demolishing my trilby down to the final ketchup-soaked crumb, my body would restore itself to normal. My brain would subdue my stomach, and my legs would celebrate the victory by walking me home. Saving this five-cent trolley fare rocketed my earnings back up to fifty-five cents.

My duplex lunches, afternoon homework sessions, night work, and my eternal walking from school to library to home must have overly diversified my interests. My scholastic record was never mentioned audibly either around the halls of Commerce or at home. I had no time to go out for sports, although during my last year I did play on the second basketball team representing our class. I had only one close friend at school. His name was Ernest Lally, and for some reason the fellows called him "Tug." Why, I don't remember. Tug and I were embryonic Merry Andrews, and our didoes in class drove the various teachers to plumb the alphabet, dredging up new letters to allot us for deportment on our report cards.

When my father remarried, Aunt Lizzie had to retrench. There was a major family upheaval, and when our forces were consolidated once again, we had lost my Uncle Joe and my Aunt Mary. As a result, we moved from Allston, and now my Aunt Lizzie, my Uncle Mike, my Aunt Jane, and I were living in close proximity in an attic apartment atop a two-family house in Dorchester. This rookery, in the Savin Hill section, was a sort of indoor penthouse. After we had been living there for a few months, my Aunt Lizzie, who had been worried about my brother Bob contracting beriberi in his new home with my father and his bride (there was a rumor that the bride was far from abstemious), managed to return Bob to her fold. Bob and I seemed to fit into the adolescent group at Savin Hill. We made friends and enjoyed life as it was being lived by our *hoi-polloi* set in that section during that era.

The library still kept me busy. I got to know the Bates Hall tattered literati who were a constant annoyance to the runners. They were a set of old people. Nightly, in their threadbare dignity, they would arrive and order ten or fifteen books for the runner to carry to their seats. For hours these frustrated pedants, men and women, pored through the mound of books right up to closing time. Some were supposed to be doing research for books that would never be written. Others were sedate cranks or harmless demented specimens who had literary delusions.

To counteract these petty annoyances, the runner was eager to join in an occasional occupational prank. One of the department heads, a Mr. Chevalier, was reputed to speak and understand Chinese. He was constantly being put to the test. Whenever a runner could find a Chinese loose in the library, looking for something, he immediately brought him to Mr. Chevalier's desk and stood by to await developments. The developments were two: one frustrated Mr. Chevalier, and one baffled Chinese.

Most library employees, toiling in a world of everlasting quiet, eventually assume the characteristics of the mouse and take on the small rodent's attitude towards life. They seem to shrink in size, acquire a frail look, walk with silent tread, convene in corners, and converse in whispers. In our library we did have one exception. He was a man named Mr. Forsyth. As Mr. Forsyth wafted zephyrlike from place to place, a small gust with a suit on, you knew that he was a library man. Something told you that Mr. Forsyth had gone through the best years of his working life without ever hearing or making a sound. One day Mr. Forsyth suddenly raised a gun to his head, pressed the trigger, and, following a loud report, left the library and his small circle of tranquil friends forever.

Also in the library was another employee who seemed to me unusual. She was a middle-aged lady who walked around expectorating in a small receptacle that looked like a compact. It was said that she had some lung problem and couldn't use the public cuspidors that were located in convenient corners on all of the library floors. To the runner set, she was a lady of mystery and the subject of much conjecture.

As I became a trusted employee at the library, I was given Sunday work. The Sunday hours were from 2 to 9 P.M. When a number of readers petitioned to have the library opened at noon, a trial period was inaugurated, and I was part of it. I was posted in the outer lobby, right off the street. It was in the middle of winter; my assignment was to stand in the draft, shiver, and count the people who came in during the first two hours. At two o'clock promptly my figures were turned over to Mr. Blaisdell, the acting librarian. For two months I turned over my findings every Sunday, and finally, since the number of early arrivals increased to the point where it justified the additional expense, the library added the extra two hours to its day and opened at noon.

On occasional weekday nights I functioned as a stack boy. These nights I enjoyed. If there was no work, I could roam around the stacks after I had finished my homework and browse through the books. On one browsing expedition I found a schoolbook. It looked familiar. After close inspection I found it was an English translation of a French storybook we were currently studying in the French class at school. I brought the translation to school. It was passed around, and suddenly, to the amazement of the French teacher, the entire class started to turn in perfect translations in the written homework. When we went on to a different French book to be translated, the French teacher was again amazed to discover that the class that had been progressing so well had suddenly lost its grasp of the language.

One night, going through the library shelves, I found a book that told about the origin and development of comedy. It explained that the early jesters were deformed people. Many of the kings had collections of bowlegged, knock-kneed, humpbacked, big-mouthed, cross-eyed or long-nosed specimens kept at the castle. Different jesters were called for different occasions. On a day when the king was depressed and felt in a knock-kneed mood, he would send for his knock-kneed jester. The knock-kneed jester would enter the court and walk around knocking his knees until the king was reduced to hysterics. Having concluded his grotesque performance, the jester would exit to the echo of the royal guffaw. The book traced the history of comedy from Vice (the comedy character in the religious plays that taunted the Devil by hitting him over the head with bladders and slapsticks) down through the ages. To me, all this was new and very interesting.

It also gave me an idea for a classroom assignment. In the High School of Commerce, there was one course called the Salesmanship Course. Once a week, every student in this course had to prepare and deliver a five-minute talk on any subject he cared to select. The teacher of this course would often demonstrate the proper approach and technique. During his demonstration the teacher hinted that if the potential salesman prefaced his sales talk with a funny story it would tend to relax the customer and soften his resistance. To illustrate, the teacher had a set of stock jokes he told. One screamer was about a man who met a friend who was carrying an expensive gold watch. Some time later, they met again and the man noticed that his friend was now carrying a cheap silver watch. He said to his friend, "Why is it the last time we met you had an expensive gold watch and today you are carrying a cheap silver watch?" The friend answered, "Circumstances alter cases." I often suspected that if the teacher had started out in life as a salesman and had tried that joke on his customer, he must have been forced to turn in his sample case, complete with joke, and find another profession.

Most of the talks by the students in this Salesmanship Course were pretty deadly. The subject matter, culled from the editorial columns, ran the gamut from "The Dangers of Log Jams in Minnesota" to "Flora and Fauna Peculiar to Putney, Vermont." I remember that the title of one student's talk was "Should the Abolishment of Billboards Be Done Away With?" Another embalmed few minutes I recall were laid to rest by a student telling about an experience he had had on a picnic with his mother. They had eaten at a teahouse in the country. The teahouse was built like a pagoda. After finishing their tea, the boy and his mother had gone up to the roof of the pagoda to admire the view. The owner of the pagoda had charged them ten cents extra. The gist of the student's diatribe was that men who operated teashop pagodas in this country should permit patrons to go up on their pagoda roofs free of charge.

It seemed to me that a talk on comedy would be a little livelier and a welcome change from the customary dreary recitals the teacher and class had to endure. Accordingly, with my recent reading in the library in mind, I prepared my talk. The class received the story of the kings and their deformed jesters very well, but the teacher lit into me in no uncertain terms the minute I sat down. He said that there was a time and place for everything; he added that the schoolroom was no place to discuss comedy, and so forth. I

didn't mind his criticizing my comedy, but I could have
made a few snide remarks myself, for this teacher was the
same one who was forever telling the joke about the gold
watch, the silver watch, and "Circumstances alter cases."

One night when I came home, my Aunt Lizzie gave me
news of another domestic change. My Aunt Mary was coming
back to live with us again; as a consequence, we were going
to leave our attic in Savin Hill and move to Columbia Road,
in another section of Dorchester. This new domicile proved
to be a bright and airy second-floor apartment in a three-
family house. In this new neighborhood I had few friends; I
was away so much at school and the library that at first I
didn't have time to get to know the kids my own age. Left to
my own devices, I started to learn how to juggle; I did this
whenever I had an odd hour or two alone at home. Whatever
possessed me to want to learn how to juggle, I will never
know. I taught myself to juggle three tennis balls and three
tin plates, and I practiced balancing feathers, broomsticks,
and heavier objects on my chin and forehead. Whenever I
saw a juggler, I tried to duplicate his easier tricks. I was able
to go to the theater now, because my income had improved.
At the library I had been promoted: on Sundays I was now
the assistant in the children's room. The head of the children's room on Sunday was a young man named Con-
stantine E. McGuire. Today he is an economist of great
renown, but in 1910 he was a brilliant student attending
Harvard on a scholarship and earning a few needed dollars
tutoring and working in the library. "Connie," as we called
him, was very helpful to me. After I had been his assistant
for two years, and he was about to leave the library to study
in Europe, he told the librarian that I knew the children's-
room catalogue better than anyone else on the Sunday staff.
The result was that I became head of the children's room on

Sundays. The salary was thirty-five cents an hour, and as the library was now open from noon until ten at night, on that one day I was earning $3.50. Added to my other night work, this meant that some Saturdays I was walking away from the paymaster's window in City Hall with a cool five or six dollars in my pocket.

Every week I walked around and looked at the lobby photographs in every vaudeville theater in Boston. When I found a picture of a juggler, I would manage to see his act during an afternoon after school, on my way to work at the library. If the juggler had an unusual trick or routine, I would study it and try to duplicate it when I got back home. My juggling was gradually improving. Moreover, I had heard one or two jugglers telling jokes, and now I started saving jokes that I thought were funny. My Saturday routine was always the same. After I collected my salary, I would squander ten cents or a quarter to go to a vaudeville show, and then I would take the rest of my salary home, set aside carfare for the following week, and give the rest of the money to my Aunt Lizzie.

When the time came to graduate from the High School of Commerce, I was sixteen, about to try for seventeen. One June afternoon, our class teacher, Mr. Laird, announced that pictures of the graduating class would be taken the following week, and that those who wanted copies of the picture could leave their names with him. As I passed his desk on my way out of class, Mr. Laird said, "Sullivan, I want to talk to you." My blood turned to cement. I stood there, all of my thoughts congealed into one. And that one thought was: "The Class of 1911 is going to graduate without Sullivan!" When all the other students had left the room and Mr. Laird had finished packing some work papers into a green cloth schoolbag, he looked up and said, "Sullivan, I wanted to talk to you before this class picture was taken. You are still wearing short pants." "Yes," I replied. Pulling the string in his green bag tight, he said, "All of the other students have long trousers. How is it going to look in the picture with everybody in long trousers and one student in the graduating class wearing short pants?" I agreed that it wouldn't look too good. I promised Mr. Laird that I would explain the dilemma to my aunt. Another dilemma to my Aunt Lizzie was like another raindrop to an umbrella. When I had explained matters, she knew that I had to have a pair of long trousers, and she also knew that there wasn't any money available to buy me a new suit. After a short period of meditation Aunt Lizzie arrived at a solution. At Harvard Square, in Cambridge, there was a clothing store owned by a man named Max Keezer. Mr. Keezer did a secondhand business; he implied by his advertisements that wealthy Harvard students were constantly pressed for cash and that, to relieve their financial pressure, they sold their expensive custom-made clothes to him. Mr. Keezer, in turn, was eager to turn these secondhand garments over to the general public at the right price.

At my Aunt Lizzie's suggestion, she and I visited the Max Keezer moth mart the following evening. When we quit Mr. Keezer's presence, I was carrying a bundle that contained one pair of long trousers that had been to Harvard for the last time. Mr. Keezer assured us that the trousers matched my coat. The next morning, in the daylight, we found that my coat was blue and that my new long trousers were a dirty Confederate gray.

The class picture was finally taken out of doors, on the school steps. As things turned out, Mr. Laird could have

saved my Aunt Lizzie and Mr. Keezer all of the trouble. In
the picture I am seated on the fifth step, completely surrounded by the class; I am on display only from the torso up.
I might just as well have been sitting there with no trousers
on at all.

After graduation, I worked through the summer at the
library. I continued to practice my juggling. I watched every
new juggler who came to Boston and kept trying to master
new tricks. The weeks flew by, and one day I received an
unexpected invitation. The library employees were planning
a show, with the talent to be supplied by the employees
themselves. Some busybody had heard that I could do some
juggling tricks, and I was invited to perform. I had been a
library employee for over four years; I couldn't very well
refuse. After I had agreed to appear, I started to worry. I had
never juggled in public, and as the date of the show grew
closer I became panicky. I knew that I had to have some sort
of an act. I arranged a routine of the various tricks I could
do with the tennis balls, the plates, the cigar boxes, and the
silk hats. I even memorized a few jokes ("I had a dream
last night. I dreamed I was eating flannel cakes. When I woke
up the blanket was half gone." And "How can you stop a
dead fish from smelling? Cut off its nose.") to tell as I did my
tricks.

The eventful night arrived. As the show wore on, it became
evident to those assembled that the talent of the library
employees was limited to two types of endeavor. Every girl
was a singer or a dancer. Every boy was vice versa. After an
hour or so of amateur chanting and clogging I made my
appearance with my juggling act and my attempt at comedy.
I was a great success. When the show was over, I was surrounded by enthusiastic admirers. I stood there treading adulation for a time. As I started to pack up my cigar boxes and

hats, a girl in the crowd said, "You're crazy to keep working here at the library. You ought to go on the stage."

I often wonder who that girl was. If she had only kept her mouth shut that night, today I might be the librarian of the Boston Public Library.

# 3

## Piano Movers

AT the time of the library show, a new complication had entered my life. I was no longer going to school, and when September made its annual appearance, I had to get a steady job; despite my Commerce education, none of the New England businessmen were begging me to join their organizations. Before I started begging them, my Uncle Joe, who was now a piano salesman, told my Aunt Lizzie that there was an opening for a boy at his place of business. I accepted the job. It paid eight dollars a week. I was now an errand boy at the Colonial Piano Company.

The Colonial Piano Company, unlike most of the Boston piano institutions, was not an old established firm. The company did have a few aged, respectable-looking employees on view, but these were mainly to instill confidence in any unsuspecting prospect who, having left home early in the morning to buy a piano, found himself later in the day caught in the tentacles of one of the Colonial Company's salesmen. The enterprise was situated on Boylston Street, in "Piano Row." The "Row" was appropriately named, for in one block, from Tremont Street to Park Square, there were six piano companies competing for business. The Colonial was the first one in the "Row" coming from Tremont Street. It sold pianos almost exclusively on the installment plan.

The store consisted of two front windows, each containing

a brand-new piano, and a street floor which was used as the main showroom; at the back of this showroom was a short flight of stairs which led down into a basement. The basement was divided into a workshop and a storeroom. As the customer entered the main showroom, he saw a small office on his left. The office was furnished with a hall tree, a small black iron safe, two high desks, two high stools, and two bookkeepers — Mr. Kennedy and Miss Bentley. The office space was isolated by a neck-high wooden enclosure with an opening at the side to admit the bookkeepers; around this wooden enclosure ran a collar of frosted glass eight or nine inches high. Two small windows in the glass, one in front of each bookkeeper, enabled the piano purchaser to make his monthly payments or to engage either one of the bookkeepers in conversation. The small office appeared to be cowering in the corner, afraid that the columns of shiny pianos that surrounded it would march ahead some day and trample the office and its occupants into rubble. Near the front door was a grand piano for demonstrating purposes. The rest of the floor was filled with upright pianos, all standing in glittering rows. Keeping the pianos company in the main showroom were three gentlemen: Mr. Avery, Mr. Morse, and Mr. Leonard.

Mr. Avery, the manager of the Colonial Piano Company, always stood silently at the door. All through the day Mr. Avery looked out at the people scurrying by on Boylston Street, waiting for someone to slacken his pace and stop in front of either window. As soon as anyone paused to admire the piano, Mr. Avery would quietly open the door and join the stranger on the sidewalk. Through the glass you could see Mr. Avery engaged in earnest conversation. Furtively, Mr. Avery's left hand would slip under the prospect's arm, his right hand would open the door, and before you could say "down payment," Mr. Avery and his prey were back inside the store. Mr. Avery lived the life of a buzzard, and considered people carrion to be pounced upon and dragged into his nest.

If Mr. Avery was engaged, the piano prospect who entered the store of his own volition found the other two salesmen eager to serve him. Mr. Leonard, a fleshy gentleman with a large head and red face, always seemed to be concealing himself behind the pianos. His body was never in view; he was always peeking over the uprights off into space. Seeing Mr. Leonard for the first time, you had the impression that someone had left a fat head on top of one of the pianos. The other salesman, Mr. Morse, was a fine musician who was often busy in a corner composing music. He composed mostly marches and hymns. Whenever Mr. Avery or Mr. Leonard had a prospect wavering, Mr. Morse would be summoned to play something to demonstrate the superior tone of the instrument and clinch the sale. Mr. Morse would arrive, be introduced to the person, adjust the piano stool to his liking, and sit. After relieving the pressure of his pince-nez, flexing his fingers, and engaging in a series of vibrant chords and nimble runs, Mr. Morse would launch into a classical rendition or a ragtime potpourri, depending upon the appearance of the prospect. When Mr. Morse concluded, he shook hands with the prospect, congratulated him on getting such an unusual instrument, and left him to the salesman who had first snared him.

When the warm weather arrived, Mr. Avery threw open both front doors and had Mr. Morse sit at the grand piano to perform. As Mr. Morse ran the gamut from popular tunes to nocturnes and sonatas, crowds would gather on the sidewalk. To the musical background, Mr. Avery scanned the faces meticulously, hoping to find one face in the crowd that belonged to the body of a music lover who had a suppressed desire to own a Colonial piano and who also had the money to pay for it. On a really hot day, when Mr. Morse pounded out a crescendo, tramps who were sleeping on the grass on Boston Common awoke with a start, and as Mr. Morse's bass notes rumbled, shoppers three blocks away on Tremont Street looked up at the sky to see if rain would follow the thunder.

Mr. Avery, Mr. Leonard, and Mr. Morse confined their activities to the store. My Uncle Joe and another optimist were the outside salesmen. My Uncle Joe visited prospects who had reacted to the company's advertising, which appeared only in the Sunday newspapers. The advertising campaign consisted of one small ad that read simply FOR SALE. STEINWAY PIANO. SLIGHTLY USED. IN EXCELLENT CONDITION. A BARGAIN. EASY TERMS. The ad always listed a Steinway, an Ivers and Pond, a Knabe, or one of the more expensive pianos of the day. When the reader who was attracted by the ad arrived at the store, he found the Steinway piano, but it was either an outmoded square model or a dilapidated specimen that he wouldn't have in his home. This advertised piano was always kept in a darkened corner of the storeroom down in the basement. To reach the shabby Steinway the prospect had to pass rows and rows of sparkling new Colonial pianos in the main showroom and also in the storeroom. The salesman said nothing on the trip down to the basement, but, when the customer expressed his disappointment upon seeing the advertised piano, the salesman went to work. Before the prospect could get back up the stairs and out into the street, he had seen every Colonial piano in the store. He had heard Mr. Morse play a short showy piece on each piano. He had been told that by paying a small down payment he would find the piano at his home when he arrived there. The prospect might wriggle away, but not before he had left his address with the salesman. With this, the potential piano owner was really in trouble. The instant the company knew where he lived, my Uncle Joe or the other outside salesman started calling at his house on the half-hour until, in self-defense, the prospect weakened. My Uncle Joe was a good salesman. He spoke in a soft, convincing voice. When my Uncle Joe drooled, little drops of honey oozed out of his mouth and trickled down his chin.

When I joined the Colonial Piano Company, Mr. Avery told me that my salary was to be eight dollars a week. My duties were to be flexible. I was to open the store at 8 A.M. I was to sweep the floor of the main showroom. I was to dust all of the pianos on the floor. I was to take a damp chamois, mount a ladder, and clean the front windows inside and out. I was to stand by to run errands that might be required to further interests and improve the financial condition of the company.

When Mr. Avery arrived every morning at nine he checked my work. I could see him going from piano to piano, rubbing his fingers over the tops and across the keys to find a little dust that I had missed. Next he would look through both windows to make sure they had been cleaned. One morning Mr. Avery called me over and said, "John, do you see that man coming across the common?" After I had looked out, I replied, "No, Mr. Avery I don't see any man." He chuckled and said, "I don't either, John. But that window is so dirty that I couldn't see a man if he *was* coming across the common." Mr. Avery had a drab sense of humor that only he seemed to enjoy.

As I perfected and speeded up my work, Mr. Avery found new chores to make sure that if I had anything on my hands it wasn't time. Mr. Bonney, one of the owners of the business, made a weekly trip into the store from his country home in

Newton. Mr. Bonney was very wealthy and quite old. He knew that he couldn't take it with him, and he wasn't planning to go. On one of his weekly business trips Mr. Bonney told Mr. Avery that his hens were laying so many extra eggs that he did not know what to do with them. Obviously, he couldn't put them back in the hens. Mr. Avery had the solution. He said that many of the people working in offices in the building, as well as others who worked in piano stores along the "Row," would be eager to buy real fresh eggs if they were available. I was called into consultation. When the meeting adjourned it was agreed that every week Mr. Bonney would deliver three crates of eggs to the store. I was to open the crates and put the eggs into one dozen cardboard boxes. When the boxes were filled I was to deliver them on foot. Mr. Avery assured Mr. Bonney that he would contact the prospective customers and supply me with a list. It all worked out rather efficiently. When Mr. Bonney heard from the hens, I heard from Mr. Bonney. When I heard from Mr. Bonney, the egg customers heard from me.

During slow afternoons, Mr. Avery would send me down to help out in the workshop. This basement workshop was another world. A Swedish craftsman named Axel Johnson was in charge. He and two Swedish co-workers took the pianos apart, varnished and polished the mahogany cases, cleaned the actions, whitened the keys, and made whatever repairs were necessary. In this workshop there was also a piano tuner who was busy all day striking his monotonous chords, going from piano to piano to make sure they were all in tune. The workshop furbished pianos that had been repossessed; when finished, they looked like new and were put back on the floor in stock. Other pianos came in from old customers who wanted them cleaned, polished, and repaired. I soon learned how to dismantle a piano and place the various parts — the frames, the action, the keyboards, the key block, and the keys — up on the benches to await the workmen's attention. When this was finished I removed the piano pedals and took them out to be replated.

All of the Swedish workmen chewed snuff. They claimed it kept them from inhaling the particles of dust and felt that filled the air in the shop. I was quickly initiated into the snuff-chewing fraternity. The results were anything but gratifying. The snuff chewers placed the snuff under their lower lip and kept it there for hours. The minute I mated the snuff with my lower lip, half of it was swallowed. When my stomach started sneezing I knew that snuff and I had nothing in common. The Swedish workers couldn't understand this. They advised me to chew something else to keep the airborne debris from getting into my mouth and down into my lungs. I settled for medicinal licorice. The licorice was bitter but it was black: the color was important. When my mandible was in action on the licorice I appeared to be chewing tobacco, and this gave me stature with the workmen. Later, I did master chewing tobacco, which was good news for the tobacco interests, and — as I thought at the time — quite an accomplishment at my age.

Early one afternoon, in an effort to keep me occupied, Mr. Avery rose to new inventive heights. I had swept the floor, dusted the pianos, cleaned the windows, completed the errands, delivered the eggs, and finished in the workshop. I thought I had Mr. Avery stymied, but I was wrong. Mr. Avery called me to heel. He told me that Mr. Kennedy, the bookkeeper, was going to give me the name and address of a family in Melrose, and that I was to try to get some information about these people. Mr. Kennedy explained confidentially that these people had stolen a piano. The piano had been bought on the installment plan. After payments had been missing for several months, and Mr. Kennedy's routine dunning letters had been ignored, a salesman had been sent out to the address. The salesman had returned and reported that the family had moved with the piano and had left no traces. It would seem impossible to steal a piano from a piano company, and I'm sure that with most companies it was impossible. But not with the Colonial Piano Company. Colonial not only invited you to steal the piano: to help you get away it would give you a six months' head start.

This was because of Mr. Kennedy and his system of keeping the books. Mr. Kennedy kept the books and handled all the accounts all by himself. Mr. Kennedy had both feet on the ground. He never sat down. He arrived at the office punctually at nine each morning, entered the office enclosure, hung his hat and coat on the hall tree, opened the small black iron safe, and removed one large ledger and two card-index files. Mr. Kennedy then closed the safe, placed the ledger and the card-index files on his desk, and started to work. He had a high desk which came up to his chest, and he leaned against this hour after hour doing all of his writing in longhand. His letters, receipts and bills, and notices were all done in a small neat hand. The flaw in Mr. Kennedy's bookkeeping system was his card-index file. The cards were listed alphabetically, and with hundreds of payments to be entered monthly, Mr. Kennedy rarely knew which families had failed to pay in any given month. At regular intervals he would go through the complete list to check every account, but by the time Mr. Kennedy had started with the A's, a family named Zimmerman could have bought a piano, missed five monthly installments, and moved to California with the piano.

Something like this had evidently happened with the family in Melrose. Mr. Kennedy gave me the address; I rode out in the streetcar, feeling like Sherlock Holmes as I planned my campaign. It was simple. I would merely go to the post office and ask for the family's forwarding address. I wondered why the salesman hadn't thought of that. At the Melrose Post Office, my campaign collapsed: I learned that the family had left no forwarding address. At the police station they had no information about the family. There were no Communists in those days. Even people with stolen pianos came and went at will. When I questioned the two local moving men it developed that neither had been given the moving job, knew anything about or had any interest in the family. As a last resort I started questioning the neighbors. A seventeen-year-old boy, with a sprinkling of acne on his cheeks, can hardly hope to inspire confidence in strangers. Every housewife I summoned to her door was suspicious. Finally, I found a neighbor who didn't like the absconding family. Fortunately for me, this lady's hobby was gossip. When I described how these despicable people had stolen a piano, she knew she had a rare tidbit of dirt for her friends and became enthusiastic. She confided that she had seen the family moving. She didn't know where they had gone, but she did notice that some strange moving men had taken the furniture. With a little more pressing she remembered the name of the moving company, and that it had come from Revere. The rest was comparatively easy. At Revere, calling at the moving company's office, I hinted that transporting stolen pianos could provoke legal unpleasantness. The family's address was begrudgingly divulged. I went to the house and confronted the housewife with my identity. She broke down, claimed that the pianonaping was a misunderstanding, gave me ten dollars to cover two months' payments, and promised that her husband would see Mr. Kennedy the next day and make amends. In subsequent months four stolen pianos were located using my technique. The moral is: "Love your neighbor and make sure your neighbor loves you if you are ever planning to steal a piano."

Mr. Avery was pleased by this. He always reacted to good news in the same manner. He rubbed his hands and looked up with a used glance. If I had been a retriever I am sure Mr. Avery would have patted me on the head. However, Mr. Avery did reward me in another way: he gave me a chance to test my latent histrionic abilities. The Colonial Piano Company had many reluctant payers on its books. A number of piano purchasers were incessantly making excuses to avoid their monthly payments. When Mr. Kennedy's patience was exhausted and no results were forthcoming, dramatic methods were employed. The company did not want the piano back; it wanted to frighten the defaulter and cause him to bring his account up to date. Mr. Avery told me that the company was going to present a dramatic high light the following morning, and that I was to be the star. The subordinate cast of characters, Mr. Avery explained, consisted of two husky piano movers. The property list called for one horse, one wagon large enough to hold a piano, a large coil of rope, and one block and tackle. The next morning, armed with the name and address of the delinquent, I went forth to make my debut. The two husky piano movers had driven out to the scene before me. When I arrived, the Colonial Piano Company's wagon was standing in front of the victim's house. I approached the front door followed by the two movers, one carrying the coil of rope, the other dragging the block and tackle. When the housewife opened the door, I stepped brusquely inside, my supporting cast behind me. I informed the lady exactly how many payments she was behind and how much she owed; I told her that if she wasn't prepared to bring her account up to date, we were going to have to take away the piano. At this cue the husky mover with the rope started to uncoil. The man with the block and tackle stepped to the window and threw it open wide. This produced results. The woman couldn't make a payment on the spot, but she took an oath on the graves of a number of dear departed relatives that she would pay up the balance immediately. Assuring the lady of the dire consequences sure to follow if her word was not kept, the block and tackle man closed the window, the rope man started coiling, and the entire cast made an impressive exit. My debut was so well received I made frequent appearances in this role, usually with excellent results. On rare occasions, when the victim told us what we could do with the piano, we didn't do it. We gave the person one more chance, and withdrew with the coil of rope, the block and tackle, and as much dignity as we could muster under the circumstances. We then came back to the Colonial Piano Company empty handed. This was not good, but it was, we knew, better than the alternative: to come back to the Colonial Piano Company with a Colonial piano.

# 4

## Amateur Nights

MY affiliation with the Colonial Piano Company had not interfered with my library routine. I still worked every Sunday and two or three nights a week. And I continued to practice my juggling. I have never been analyzed, but I suspect that my great success at the library employees' show, and hearing the girl's voice say, "You ought to be on the stage," did something to my subconscious. As I improved my juggling and my monologue I began to feel that perhaps that anonymous girl had something. I decided to find out.

In Boston, and all through New England at that time, Amateur Nights were very popular. Nobody quite knew how they first started. Rumor had it that originally, when the owner of a small theater found that his business was poor, he tried advertising an occasional Amateur Night. He found that people in the neighborhood would flock to the theater to see the local girls and boys perform. The word spread and other theater owners discovered that Amateur Nights attracted audiences. They found, however, that they soon exhausted the neighborhood amateur talent, and they realized that the audiences would not come to see the same girls and boys every week. This was their problem; before they even had time to solve it, it was solved for them. The theater owners were informed that there was a service in Boston which would supply them with new amateur talent every single week.

This service was provided by three men: Sam Cohen, Lippy Huston, and Jolly Ed Price. Of these, the most important was Sam Cohen; he was the most famous impresario in his field. Sam booked three large theaters in Boston: the Columbia Theatre, the Grand Opera House, and the Bowdoin Square Theatre. He appeared in person with his amateurs, and was very popular with the audiences. Mr. Huston was next. He was called Lippy because he had a large lower lip that hung down and rested on his chin. Lippy had no office. Amateurs who were looking for work knew that every afternoon they could find Lippy on the sidewalk across from the Globe Theatre on Washington Street. Lippy's office was in his hat. When an amateur accosted him, Lippy removed his hat and took out some soiled papers on which he had listed the theaters and amateurs he had booked for that night. After scanning the list, Lippy either engaged the amateur or told him to come back the next day. His business completed, Lippy tucked the soiled papers back under the sweatband and put his hat back on. His office was closed. Jolly Ed Price was a former minstrel nonentity. Ed looked anything but jolly. Standing up, Ed was tall and emaciated. Sitting down, Ed was short and emaciated. Lippy and Jolly Ed booked only a few Amateur Nights. These were at theaters that Sam couldn't service or which were in competition with those he was servicing.

Sam Cohen's office was in an old, pigeon-littered building on Court Street. The edifice had been built long before Otis was born or the elevator perfected. Sam's lair was one flight up. When I called, I found that the office consisted of two rooms: a dimly lit waiting room, where the amateurs who were hoping to get work sat around, and another room, with the door marked PRIVATE. As I sat down in the crowded waiting room, I noticed that most of the amateurs were young girls and boys obviously not from sorority or fraternity houses. Three or four of the boys were smoking cigarettes, and one lean dancer was showing an intricate step to a pretty blonde in the corner. The other kids were explaining to each other how their acts had gone at different Amateur Nights the previous evening. Two old men and a dowdy-type middle-aged woman sat quietly ignoring the others. Before I could decide whether the old people were amateurs, the door of the private office opened and a man I assumed to be Sam stepped out. As he looked around the waiting room, he said, "Not too much noise, you kids." Then I knew it was Sam. When his eyes came to me, he beckoned me to follow him.

As Sam closed the door behind us, the phone rang. Sam reached for the receiver, and while he was occupied I had time to appraise his sanctum. In décor, it was apparent that the office had been done by the same interior decorator who had done the Black Hole of Calcutta. The one window, overlooking an alley, was dirty. The walls were covered with faded one sheets showing Sam as a young man wearing a leopard skin and lifting heavy weights and bending iron bars. Large letters at the bottom of these one sheets proclaimed that Sam Cohen was THE STRONGEST MAN IN THE WORLD. The names of the attractions with which he had appeared showed that Sam's might had been exploited by small carnivals and circuses which confined their travels to the New England states. The floor was bare and had not been swept in our generation. Next to Sam's battered rolltop desk sat a tall spittoon that had been missed more than an only child who leaves home for the first time.

Sam, a powerful-looking man who was slowly turning to

flab, didn't look any better than his surroundings. Taking inventory of Sam from head to foot, you had to list one black derby hat, tilted back on the head and exposing Sam's thinning light hair which was parted in the center; then came one large nose, rampant in a pasty complexion. Sam's face was lard white. With his dark beady eyes and the big cigar jutting out of his mouth, Sam looked like an animated but partly melted snowman. His coat and vest were wrinkled and soiled, his pants were baggy, and his shoes unshined. As Sam argued into the phone, I wondered what I was doing there. I had watched some amateur shows. Did I think my juggling act was better than the acts that I had seen? Was it the voice of that girl — "You ought to be on the stage" — echoing through my ego? Before I could answer either question, I heard the click of the receiver; Sam had finished on the phone. Looking through some papers on his desk, Sam said, "You're a new kid around here, ain't you?"

"Yes," I replied.

"What do you do?"

"I'm a juggler."

"A juggler?" Sam said, looking up from the papers with surprise. "What tricks can you do?"

"I have a whole act: balls, plates, hats, cigar boxes. And I also tell jokes."

"Will your parents let you go on Amateur Night?"

"Yes," I lied.

"Next Monday night at eight o'clock. Meet me at the corner of Dover and Washington Streets." Sam marked something on one of the papers and added, "Bring your jugglin' stuff."

"What's the theater?"

"The Hub," said Sam. With this, he readjusted his hat, lit his cigar, and the interview was over.

Monday night, promptly at eight, I arrived at the corner of Dover and Washington Streets, carrying two cardboard suitcases. Sam was waiting, talking to six kids and an old man wearing overalls. Of the six kids, five were rather tough-looking boys I judged to be of about my age, and the sixth, upon closer examination, proved to be a flashily dressed tall girl who seemed to have grown out of the kid category. The man in the overalls had obviously been drinking. He was talking to himself and I knew that he was deaf because he was talking in a loud voice. With my arrival, Sam turned to the others and said, "The show's all here. Let's go backstage."

The entrance of the Hub Theatre, which had formerly been the Grand Dime, was on Washington Street. Sam led the way up Dover Street, and then turned into an alley; halfway down the alley we came to a door marked STAGE ENTRANCE. Sam opened the door and we all followed him in. I had never been on a stage before. Everything was dark. I could hear a piano playing. Sam said, "The picture's on. Step over these ropes, the dressing room's over here." Crossing the stage slowly in the dark, we came to another door; when this was opened, the light from within revealed a large room with mirrors lining the walls. Sam said, "You kids wait in here." Closing the door behind us, he disappeared. Dropping my cardboard suitcases to the floor, I could only think to myself, "So this is the Hub Theatre!"

At that time there were hundreds of smalltime theaters of the Hub category entertaining audiences around the country. They all had the same policy: three acts of cheap vaudeville and a feature picture, three shows a day. The moving pictures were silent, and to supply music for the vaudeville acts as well as to furnish a background for the picture, the larger theaters used full orchestras. The smaller theaters merely used piano and drums.

In a little while, the dressing-room door of the Hub opened again, and Sam reappeared to announce that after the picture was over the vaudeville would go on; then, after the vaudeville, would come the amateurs. He asked if we needed anything; I told him I needed a table to hold my juggling utensils. Sam disappeared again and returned shortly with two men. The first of these was the theater's piano player, who asked the amateurs about their musical requirements. The flashily dressed girl, who turned out to be a singer, had her own music which she handed to the piano player and gave him some instructions that concerned her tempo. Two of the tough-looking boys were wooden-shoe dancers who requested endless choruses of "Chicken Reel." One of the other boys was a harmonica player. When it came my turn, I asked the piano player to play "Comin' Through the Rye" in time when I juggled my cigar boxes, and to have the drummer do some rolls on the drum when I finished my act with the silk hats. The piano player, well briefed, departed. Sam then brought the second man over to me and said, "This is the property man. Tell him what you want." I explained about the table, and the property man dragged a table out from behind some scenery and helped me open my suitcases and arrange my cigar boxes and other things. After we had finished, the property man said, "Don't worry about anything. I'll set the table on the stage before you go on." As he carried the table away I thanked him and went back into the dressing room.

In the room, the others were all busy. Sam was slouched in a chair looking over some slips on which he had a number of jokes he was going to tell as he introduced the amateur acts. Sam always livened things up with some homemade jokes. The singer was flexing her voice. The dancers were trying a variety of steps in their wooden shoes. The others were

straightening ties, brushing shoes, and making other preparations to help them look presentable for the show. The old
man in the overalls sat dozing in the corner. I still wondered
what he had to do with the amateur show. I heard a drum
roll from the orchestra pit, followed by some approximate
martial music on the piano. Sam stood up, put his cards in
his pocket, and announced, "The vaudeville's on. We follow
the third act." As he walked out of the dressing room to the
stage I followed him to the door. The backstage was fully
lighted now. I could see the scenery, the curtains, the ropes
coming down from the flies, the switchboard, the footlights,
and the professional acts, all made up and waiting to go on.
It was too much for me. I started to wish I was home. I
couldn't go home so I did the next best thing: I concentrated
on getting nervous.

By the time the vaudeville was over, things seemed to be
getting hazy. I could hear applause and Sam's voice. Apparently Sam was on the stage, introducing the first amateur.
Then followed a thirty-minute montage of laughter, Sam's
voice, wooden-shoe dancing, applause, a harmonica playing,
applause, a girl singing, laughter. Then I could hear Sam
again. His voice seemed far away. It was saying, "And now,
from Dorchester, a juggler, Johnny Sullivan." Sam came off
the stage. I heard the piano playing. I couldn't move. All of
the iron in my system had become two ingots and they were
my feet. Sam gave me a nudge and said, "That's you, kid."
The next thing I knew I was standing in a glare of light. I
might as well have been in the police line-up. I was petrified.
Somehow, automatically I began my juggling routine, and,
after some hesitation, I noticed that I had started my monologue. During my act there was no audible resentment from
the audience. When I finished juggling the three silk hats,
with the drum rolling in the pit, there was considerable ap-

plause. As I came off the stage I saw the old man in the overalls waiting to go on. Back in the dressing room, as I tried to tremble and pack my suitcases at the same time, I heard one of the dancers say, "That Peter Dooley is killing them." I was to learn later that Peter Dooley was one of Boston's most famous amateurs. He was in his sixties. Peter worked for the street department and came right from work to the theater in his overalls. After a few nips he became Peter Dooley the comedian, ready to take on any audience with his insane limericks, jokes, and burlesque dances.

When the amateur program was over, we all had to line up on the stage to enable the audience to choose its winner. Sam walked up and down behind the line, holding his hand over each act's head. The audience expressed its approval by its applause. Sam went back and forth several times, holding his hand over the two acts that the audience liked best. Finally he announced that the winner was Peter Dooley. The audience was happy. The stage was darkened and we returned to the dressing room. There was a knock on the door, and before anyone could answer, the theater manager stepped in briskly, said, "Great show, Sam," and handed him some money. Sam smiled. "That juggler," the manager continued. "Nobody in the audience could hear what he was talking about. Bring him back some week and tell him to talk louder."

Sam promised he would; I stood there, realizing now that nobody had heard my jokes. Without knowing it, I had done the first ingrown monologue in the history of show business. The manager shook hands with Sam and left. Sam paid each of the amateurs. Good nights were exchanged, and the others left. As I started out, Sam handed me a one-dollar bill and said, "Come up to the office tomorrow."

That single dollar bill finished my interest in the library.

When I stopped shaking from my stage fright, I reasoned that rational economics were involved. Why should I work all night at the stuffy library for sixty cents when I could have a lot of fun and excitement at Amateur Nights and be paid a dollar? For a while, I continued with my two regular nights at the library, but for my free evenings now I had other plans.

The next day, on my lunch hour, I stopped in at Sam's office. He told me that he liked my act. Sam also confided that he had too many singers and dancers, and that he could use a juggler every night if I could work. The piano store now became the base of my operations; my cardboard suitcases were concealed behind a piano in the basement. Every night that Sam could book me I appeared on an amateur show.

My Aunt Lizzie took a dim view of my theatrical activities; she had a poor opinion of all actors. She called them "high flyers." She used to tell about a young man who was in her class at school. He went on the stage and turned to drink. He never supported his mother and finally came to an end in a drunkard's grave. I don't think my Aunt Lizzie ever approved of my career. One time, I went up to visit her in Boston. I had been in show business for over twenty years and was currently enjoying success in radio. As we were having dinner, my Aunt Lizzie said, "You've had enough of it. You'd better come back and settle down."

I had no artistic ambitions. The only appeal Amateur Nights had for me was the dollar, the fun, and the excitement. I enjoyed the company of the other amateurs. Every night there was a new theater and a new group of kids. Before many months I had appeared as an amateur in almost every smalltime theater in and around Boston.

I learned about the amateur's problems. In the early

days of the Amateur Nights, the money prizes were important. Only the winners received anything; the losers merely had the use of the hall. The young singer, dancer, or acrobat knew that he had no chance to win the twenty-five-dollar first prize if there was a "sympathy act" on the bill. A "sympathy act" was an old man, an old woman, a child, or a crippled person who performed and traded on the sympathy of the audience. The "sympathy acts" with no ability won the prizes and talented kids went home with nothing. One hunchback on our Amateur Nights sang "Mother Machree" in a thin tenor voice and invariably won first prize. He was not only a hunchback but as he walked on the stage to sing he bent over farther to wring the last drop of pity from the audience. A middle-aged woman used to hobble onto the stage, leaning on crutches, and sing "Only a Bird in a Gilded Cage." She didn't need the crutches to walk; she carried them to the theater as lumber, and used them only to appeal to the emotions of the audience.

To combat the "sympathy act" competition, one of the amateur dancers used to buy a pair of cheap black socks in the five and ten cent store. He'd cut the heels out of the socks before putting them on for his act. Then, for his last step, the dancer would put both hands in his pockets, raise his trousers up over his socks, and do several steps with his back to the audience. As he turned, the audience saw the large holes in his socks and the bare heels. The people felt sorry for him, and his chances versus the hunchback and the woman on crutches were greatly improved. Another dancer wore a short coat and carried a pair of pants with a long rip in the seat. Before the show the dancer removed his underwear and donned the torn pants. When he turned around and the audience saw that his heels were bare up to his bottom, the sympathy he received was tinctured with laughter.

Through constant work, my act improved. Sam finally booked me into the Columbia Theatre. This was flattering. Only his best amateurs appeared at the Columbia, for this was his best theater. The Columbia presented the biggest Amateur Nights in Boston. It paid Sam more money than any of his other theaters, and the first hilarious Amateur Nights that he produced at the Columbia were responsible for his initial success. I am not sure that Sam invented "The Hook," a long pole with an enormous iron hook on the end of it that was used to pull amateurs off the stage, but I do know that Sam was one of the first to make it popular. Sam also invented a special curtain that was split from top to bottom every few feet. No matter where the amateur stood on the stage, Sam could step through the curtain behind him and clobber him with an inflated bladder. If an amateur suddenly incurred the disfavor of the audience and there was a concerted cry of "Get the hook!" from the balcony, Sam stepped gingerly through the nearest aperture with the hook and accommodated the dissenters. If a singer foaled a flat cadenza, a sign appeared on the curtain reading "He's good to his mother," or "He's flat — he's been standing too long." A dancer, finishing his routine and expecting applause, would see a stuffed fish five feet long fly from one side of the stage to the other, missing his head by inches. An acrobat, in the middle of a difficult trick, might find two hundred old derby hats descending on him from the flies covering the entire stage. If an amateur backed close enough to the curtain, Sam whacked his posterior with a wooden slapstick; the resounding smack could be heard all over the theater. Wearing funny clothes, using such things as comedy signs, slapsticks, seltzer water, the hook, and an assortment of practical jokes played on the unsuspecting amateurs, Sam kept the Columbia audiences in hysterics.

Sam Cohen made the Amateur Night a big business. When the local theater owner started his amateur shows, he had only neighborhood talent, and this made for monotony. Some nights he had all singers, other nights he had all dancers. After sitting through eight acts, all of which were alike, the audience would be inclined to avoid the next Amateur Night. Sam booked shows that had variety. He had singers, dancers, magicians, musical acts, and acrobats. Then, too, in the beginning the local theater owner had the amateurs competing for three cash prizes — twenty-five dollars, fifteen dollars, and ten dollars. Sam eliminated these cash prizes, but continued the contest at the end of each show. He held the prize envelopes over the heads of the contestants. The audience whistled and applauded for its favorites. Sam presented the three winners with their envelopes, but the envelopes were empty. Amateurs who worked for Sam were paid fifty cents or a dollar a head. A routine singer or dancer got fifty cents; a magician, an acrobat, a juggler, or any other unusual act got a dollar. When the theater was out of the city, Sam paid the amateur's carfare. If an amateur show had to go to Worcester, or some other fairly distant city, and had to leave Boston late in the afternoon, Sam not only gave each amateur fifty cents for dinner but gave him the location of a lunchwagon or the address of a cheap restaurant near the theater where he could eat.

Sam had so many theaters to book in Boston and the suburbs that he had no time to travel out of town. At one time he was supplying weekly amateur shows for some thirty theaters. Since it was impossible for Sam to appear on each show himself, Sam did the next best thing. He picked out a few boys he could trust and put them in charge of the suburban shows. I must have looked honest to Sam, for one night he asked me to take out a show. The procedure was simple.

If the Amateur Night was to be presented in the city, the amateurs met at the theater; if a trolley ride was involved, the kids met at Sam's office. The amateur in charge was briefed. Before I started out with my first show, Sam gave all the assembled amateurs their carfare, then took me into his private office and handed me a piece of paper. It was a list of the acts who were going to perform that night, and some instructions for me. Before introducing the first amateur, I was to walk out on the stage and make this announcement: "Ladies and Gentlemen, this Amateur Night is being presented by the Sam Cohen Booking Office, 80 Court Street, Boston. Sam Cohen books talent for any occasion. If you are planning a concert, a smoker, or a stag show, get your talent from the Sam Cohen Booking Office."

Following this commercial for Sam, I introduced the first amateur. On the piece of paper he had given me, Sam had written a joke to be told with each act. A few of the jokes were: "The next act, ladies and gentlemen, is the Wood Sisters — Rose and Mahogany." "And now, Mario Ferris. Mario is a light-opera singer — from the Boston Lighthouse." Opposite my name, I noticed "Johnny Sullivan, the juggler. He isn't seasick, but he's going to throw up." Under the names of two acts, Sam had written the word "lemon." This meant that these amateurs had no talent. When the act appeared, the audience would start an uproar, but if the manager knew the act was a "lemon," he was prepared. Many such acts knew they were "lemons," and didn't mind the jeers and catcalls as long as they were paid.

When Sam had finished explaining how to tell the jokes, and had completed his other instructions, he handed me an envelope I was to give to the theater manager. This was Sam's bill. I was to collect the money, pay all of the amateurs, give them their fares home, and meet Sam after the show.

Things went smoothly at the theater. I did Sam's opening commercial, announced the acts, told the jokes, did my juggling, ran the contest at the end of the show, collected the money, paid the amateurs and gave them their fares, and started off with the residue to meet Sam. When the shows were over, it was too late at night to go back to Sam's office in the city, and so to save everybody the trip, Sam arranged a trysting place: the Dudley Street Terminal, in Roxbury. Trolley cars from Dorchester, Roxbury, Jamaica Plain, Boston, and all of the adjoining suburbs came into the Dudley Street Terminal, or made connections with cars that did. Also, the terminal was not far from Sam's home.

When I arrived with my two cardboard suitcases and Sam's profits, Sam was sitting on a bench, giving off an aroma of malt, and smoking a cigar that looked like a digest bonfire. I handed him the envelope containing the rest of his money. The theater manager had given me thirty dollars; as I had paid out about nine dollars, Sam had little more than twenty left. After he had counted the money, Sam thanked me and asked me how the amateur show had done. I assured him that the acts had gone well. Then he said, "How did the lemons do?" I explained that both lemons had had the audience in a bedlam. Sam laughed and gave me an extra dollar for myself. As I sat talking to Sam, three other boys arrived, reported, and turned over their money. Sam checked his list. All of his nightly shows had been accounted for. Sam got up unsteadily and lumbered down the stairs to get his trolley home.

I was now a Master of Ceremonies and a trusted employee of the Sam Cohen Booking Office. That summer I spent my two-week vacation with a group of amateurs, booked by Sam, at amusement parks and resorts in Maine, New Hampshire, and Vermont. Our expenses were paid, and this was really

an adventure: seeing new places, living at different boardinghouses, doing my act in strange theaters, and knowing the
excitement of the nightly shows. The amateurs were good
company: the younger ones with their hopes and ambitions,
the older ones who were either "lemons" or were doing
nondescript acts to earn the few dollars they needed to
survive. Very few of these younger amateurs went on to success in the theater. Most of the singers, dancers, and
harmonica players wisely remained in Boston and retained
their jobs and their amateur status.

When the amateur vogue started to wane, Sam originated
several new contest ideas: "Can You Walk Like Charlie
Chaplin?" "Does Your Daughter Look Like Mary Pickford?"
and others. None of them ever created the interest or made a
fragment of the money that Sam enjoyed when his Amateur
Nights were the rage. Some people thought that Sam was
crude, but everybody had to agree that he was goodhearted.
Sam was always ready to lend a helping hand. When an amateur needed money, Sam's hand went to his pocket. When an
amateur needed encouragement, Sam's hand went to the
amateur's back with a cheering pat.

After one of the Amateur Nights at an outlying theater, I
made the acquaintance of an actor named Harry LaToy. La-
Toy was one of the professional acts on the show. He billed
his act "Tramp Juggler." I had seen LaToy's act when I
first had juggling ambitions. LaToy had a routine offering.
Almost all of the smalltime jugglers dressed as tramps and
did the same acts: lighting matches on their sandpaper
beards, wearing big shoes and eight or nine vests (so that
when they missed a trick they could stop and take off one of
the vests), blowing up a feather and letting it come down
slowly to balance on the nose, juggling three balls with
comedy pantomime, and juggling plates, Indian clubs, and

silk hats. The original tramp juggler was a man called Harrigan. LaToy and the other tramp jugglers who roamed the smalltime vaudeville circuits owed a lot to Harrigan, which I am sure they never paid.

At that stage in my simulated career, any professional juggler was an idol. After LaToy had watched my juggler act, he seemed to take an interest in me. He asked me if I knew certain tricks. I could juggle only four balls; LaToy showed me how to do five. After he had done a few tricks with my hats, he told me that the following week he was going to be at the Old South Theatre, in Boston, and invited me to visit him backstage. He said that if I would come in he would show me some new tricks that I could do in my act. The next week I stopped in at his dressing room. We talked about all the big jugglers and the difficult tricks they did; he showed me some new hat routines. Between his shows I took him out to eat. In no time at all, it seemed, LaToy and I were close friends. Some nights, on my way home from an amateur show, I would meet him in the city and we'd have a late snack together. LaToy introduced me to the Royal Lunch, a tiny eating place on Hanover Street that featured a meal consisting of one plate of baked beans, three slices of bread with butter, one piece of pie, and one cup of coffee for ten cents.

LaToy also told me where to buy silk hats. I had been buying my juggling hats from an old charlatan named Professor LeRoy. The Professor was a retired magician who had eaten his rabbit in the early days of his retirement and had been existing on the stray customers he caused to appear in his magic shop. I thought that juggling hats had to be weighted and balanced to be manipulated; Professor LeRoy had encouraged me in this belief while he sold me secondhand silk hats for three dollars each. From LaToy I learned that any hat could be juggled, and that all of the professional jugglers

bought their hats at the Salvation Army store. The Army
store had a cellar filled with hats of all sizes that sold for fifty
cents apiece.

LaToy was addicted to the opposite sex and ultimately was
the direct cause of my losing my faith in the birds and bees.
Moreover, although he had never been away from Boston,
he read the *Billboard*, a weekly theatrical publication, and
from this he memorized the cities listed on the Orpheum
circuit. Orpheum theaters were in all of the principal cities in
the western part of the country from Chicago to San Francisco. If we were in a lunchroom, and a pretty waitress was
serving LaToy, he would turn to me and say in a loud voice, "I
was a big hit in San Francisco that week. Then I jumped to
Denver and Salt Lake." After he felt sure that everybody in
the lunchroom knew that he was an actor and had traveled
around the country, he'd look up to see how the waitress was
reacting. Many times it worked. In a crowded streetcar La-
Toy was in his glory. He would improvise in stentorian
tones about his act, the hotel in Seattle, and the girl in
Omaha who was crazy about him. LaToy's travels were all
figments of his tongue. You could go up on top of City Hall
and spit farther than LaToy had been out of Boston. As I
spent more time with my idol, I realized that among his multiple shortcomings he was allergic to spending. I bought all
of the meals and spent any money that was spent when we
were together. LaToy had short arms and he carried his
money low in his pockets. He taught me a few juggling tricks,
but he was well paid.

One Friday, as I started out of the door of the Colonial
Piano Company on my lunch hour, LaToy was waiting. He
had an urgent problem that only I could solve. Any smalltime
vaudeville actor who lived in Boston had a problem. The
men who booked the theaters called the Boston actor a "coast

defender." A coast defender was an actor who never left home. Vaudeville acts which came to Boston from New York, or other cities, were immediately booked into all of the New England theaters. These acts were new faces, and as soon as they had played the theaters in this area, the bookers knew that they would leave Boston and seek work in other parts of the country. The coast defender, on the other hand, was always there, and the bookers used him as a convenience. The Boston actor had to walk from booking office to booking office every day trying to find work. In the morning he started at the Keith office on Tremont Street. The Keith office represented the largest circuit and booked the most theaters. Then he walked to the Loew office on Hamilton Place; this was next to the Keith office in importance. If the Keith and Loew bookers had no work for him, the Boston actor then made the rounds of the smaller offices: Johnny Quigley, Warren Church, Appleby and Donovan, Fred Mardo, Mrs. Merrill, and Pop White. These offices booked two or three small theaters each. If he had walked all over the city and had been turned away from every door, the Boston actor's last resort was Mrs. Mead. Mrs. Mead's husband, Ed Mead, had been a blackface comedian who had died and left an estate of one can of burnt cork, a sponge to remove the cork, and some kinky-haired wigs that he had worn in his act. The widow, to cope with her minimum needs, sat in a form-fitting office on the top floor of a decrepit building in Scollay Square, booking talent for an occasional club and for one theater called the Dreamland. The Dreamland, which was on Washington Street in the South End, was a long, thin theater that looked like a wooden sleeve with seats in it. The Dreamland played split weeks. Single acts working there, four shows a day, received ten dollars; double acts, twenty dollars. That was it, take it or leave it. Late in the afternoon, when the

Boston actor had climbed the three flights of stairs to talk to Mrs. Mead, and found that she had nothing for him, he knew that he had come to the end of a less than perfect day. The Boston actor went home.

On this particular Friday LaToy had started his pilgrimage at the Keith office. There was no work for him. One booker, however, said that the Keith office was holding professional tryouts that night at the National Theatre. The National was a new theater on Clarendon Street, recently opened by the Keith interests. The National played big shows, but for some reason, either because the location was wrong or because the same acts had appeared earlier in the season at the big Keith Theatre, business had been poor. To try to remedy this, they decided to inaugurate a special night. The Professional Tryout was advertised as "Not an Amateur Night"; instead the National Theatre was going to present "Professional Talent New to Boston." The Keith booking office would attend the tryouts, and acts that had merit would be booked on the Keith circuit. LaToy, who hadn't been working, had agreed to appear as one of the "Professional Tryouts." He showed me a little slip of paper; it read: "Paul Huckle. European Entertainer. Salary, $5. National Theatre, 8 P.M." To conceal his identity LaToy had changed his name to Paul Huckle. When I asked why, he explained that after he had left the Keith office and started his trek around to the little bookers, he had been given three weeks' work. These were professional dates, and LaToy knew that if the smaller bookers learned that he had appeared on a tryout show for five dollars, all of his professional dates would be canceled. To protect himself he wanted me to assume the Paul Huckle role and replace him with my juggling act. The minute I agreed to do it, LaToy brought up the question of my fee. He knew that for the Sam Cohen shows I received only one dollar; in a moment of philanthropic abandon, LaToy offered to double my salary. He handed me the Paul Huckle slip with the "Salary, $5." It was a deal. I would do the Professional Tryout show, collect the five dollars, meet LaToy at the Royal Lunch after the show, and give three dollars of it to him.

The National Theatre didn't awe me. For months I had been doing my act at Amateur Nights exposed to a variety of audiences; my tricks were greatly improved and my jokes, too, had taken a turn for the better. The Amateur Night audiences were difficult. They came to enjoy themselves, and while they appreciated talent, they were primarily in the theater to deride and laugh. I had become calloused to all reaction. When my cardboard suitcases and I arrived at the National Theatre at eight, after identifying myself as Paul Huckle, I was assigned to an individual dressing room. The orchestra conductor came up to rehearse my music; I explained about the cigar boxes and the drum effects for my silk hats. The stage manager also reported and, upon learning that I did a juggling act, said that he would have the property man stand by with a table. The Professional Tryouts were to go on after the regular eight-act bill; the stage manager told me to be ready about ten-thirty. I went out to get some coffee, and then came back to the dressing room. To kill time I practiced my tricks and went over my monologue. At ten-thirty I heard the stage manager calling up the stairway, "Paul Huckle! On stage!" The property man came up to the dressing room to help me carrying the juggling props down to the stage. As I walked through the door into the wings, Long Tack Sam, a Chinese novelty act, was finishing the regular vaudeville show. The other professional actors, now dressed in their street clothes, had crowded around the entrance to see the tryouts.

There were five of us in all. I hadn't been able to see any of the regular acts, but I knew the audience was good. There was none of the screaming, whistling, or raucous laughter I had become accustomed to at Amateur Nights. The laughter here was honest laughter, and the applause, minus the whistling and stamping, was sincere. The atmosphere of this theater was different: even the stagehands were considerate. When the stage manager came over and said, "Paul Huckle, you're on!" for the first time as an actor I was being accorded some respect. I walked on. The full orchestra was playing an opening number the conductor had selected to liven my act. I started my monologue. I had never worked to an audience like this. Every joke was greeted with a laugh; every trick, a reaction. When I finished my silk-hat routine, the applause was deafening. Assuming me to be Paul Huckle, a tryout act, the audience was eager to help me get ahead. After taking too many bows, I packed my cardboard suitcases, collected the five dollars, shed the Paul Huckle pseudonym, and started off to meet LaToy. He was waiting at the Royal Lunch. He seemed more interested in the money than he did in Paul Huckle's debut and demise. We ate. I may be wrong, but that night I think LaToy took the check.

The next day, Saturday, I left on my lunch hour again. (This was a long time before the forty-hour week was invented. We worked all day Saturday at the piano store. If Mr. Avery had thought of it, he would have opened on Sunday with the salesmen dressed as ministers trying to sell organs.) LaToy was waiting for me near the door. He was highly excited. On the way to the lunchroom around the corner he kept talking and hitting me on the shoulder. When LaToy finally finished, *I* was highly excited. LaToy's conversation, when distilled, was reduced to a terse but involved story. When he had gone to the Keith office that morning, all the bookers were waiting for him. They had seen the Professional Tryouts at the National, and wanted to know where they could find Paul Huckle. They had liked the act, and wanted to book Huckle in all the Keith New England theaters. Confronted with this sudden turn of events, LaToy had contrived a story. He told the bookers that Paul Huckle was a juggler who had been playing all the leading vaudeville theaters out West. His name, he said, was really Fred St. James. Where he got the "Fred" I never did find out; the "St. James" he borrowed from a hotel of doubtful repute that was thriving in Bowdoin Square. (LaToy approved of fancy names for jugglers. He felt that they impressed audiences, who thought the performers were European. His own name was Shepard; he had taken the LaToy name to sound like LaCroix. Paul LaCroix was a big-name juggler who had originated "the dancing hats." LaToy had borrowed LaCroix's dancing hats and acknowledged this debt by coming as close to LaCroix's name as he could.)

LaToy told the bookers that Fred St. James had just come from the West to visit some relatives in Boston; he had made the Paul Huckle appearance as a favor to LaToy. When the bookers wanted to know if they could see St. James, LaToy said that he didn't think St. James would be interested in working in Boston. He was always booked solid in Western theaters. Before he could extricate himself from the vortex of lies he had told, LaToy had agreed to produce Fred St. James in the Keith office on Monday morning. LaToy was in full charge of my immediate future. He had everything planned. Before I could meet the bookers, I had to have lobby photographs. When I finished work late that afternoon, LaToy and I carried the cardboard suitcases to White's studio on Hanover Street. Mr. White was Boston's official theatrical photographer. Action photographs were snapped of me doing my juggling tricks; straight pictures were taken in which I tried to look like Fred St. James. When we left White's, I promised to flee the Colonial Piano Company premises on some pretext Monday morning and meet LaToy at the Keith office. Carried away by LaToy's enthusiasm, or because he had hypnotized me into thinking I was Fred St. James, I agreed to everything.

In later life, on a number of occasions I had cause to rue the day I permitted LaToy to tuck me under his wing. During a period of unemployment, LaToy at one time moved into our house for a protracted stay and shared my room. We were still living in Dorchester. The theater and I had parted momentarily, and I had gotten a job. I had to get up early in the morning to go to work. LaToy slept late. When he awakened, my Aunt Lizzie prepared his breakfast. At noon, when he met me in Boston to be taken to lunch, he would be wearing my best necktie.

When he finally booked some dates, LaToy moved out of our house. Shortly after his departure, I received a note saying that he was ill. He was out in Medford, in his mother's house, and he asked me to come out and see him. When I arrived, I found LaToy in bed. After we had talked for a while, he asked me to go out and buy him some cigarettes and one or two theatrical magazines. When I told him that I didn't have any money, LaToy sat up in bed, slipped his hand under the bottom sheet, and felt around for something. When his hand returned to view, it held a roll of bills. He gave me some money, and when he replaced the remaining bills, I noticed that he had cut a slit in the mattress. When I asked him about the vent in the Simmons, LaToy said that this enabled him to hide his money where his mother couldn't find it when she made the bed.

Some time later, when I returned to acting and arrived in

Halifax, Nova Scotia, to play the Ackers circuit, I was threatened with cancellation, the reason being that LaToy had played the circuit a few weeks before and had used my photos in all the theaters. He had stolen them while he lived at our house. Mrs. Acker, whose circuit it was, said that since my photos had been seen in all the theater lobbies she couldn't send them out again, because people in the small towns would think the same act was being repeated. After I had explained the circumstances and LaToy's perfidy, Mrs. Acker relented and found some other photos in her office which she loaned me to enable me to play the circuit.

Five years later, when I was playing in Chicago, I learned that LaToy had now taken my billing. I had several small cards printed to mail to the different booking offices and theater managers all over the country. The cards read:

### STOLEN

A smalltime Novelty Artist, calling himself Harry LaToy, has stolen my billing —

### WORLD'S WORST JUGGLER

I, Freddy James, am the Original "World's Worst Juggler." I have made good my claim to the above title from Coast to Coast for the past five years.

FREDDY JAMES

N.B. A recent X-ray taken of Mr. LaToy proves that there is not an original bone in his body.

When I appeared in Broadway shows I received frequent telegrams and notes from LaToy asking for money. He never appeared in person. Then there followed a long period during which I heard nothing. Finally this letter arrived:

November 21, 1944

DEAR FRIEND JOHNNY,

It has been a long time since I have been in touch with you. I want to ask you to try and do me a great favor. I am here in St. Louis very sick with bronchial asthma and in a very run down condition.

Due to this condition it is impossible for me to work either in show business or any outside job, and what few dollars I had laid away, in around the country, has gone to doctors and medicines — including Xrays — which all cost money.

As you know, I am getting along in years — 58 years — and it's growing increasingly difficult for me to breathe. In the past 34 years, when you started, you and I have had differences in which many times I thought I was right. But I can see that I've been wrong in most cases and I want to apologize for anything I may have done or said. As you know, your interests have been above anything else with me. Being now ready to bow out of the picture at any time I want you to know just how I feel.

If you doubt my word get in touch with any booking office, or you can stop off here and check up for yourself through doctors or anyone who knows me.

If you can help me out now, in this last time of need, whatever you can do for me will be sincerely appreciated.

Sincerely yours,
HARRY LaToy

P.S. If you can help me please do it now as time grows short. Your address when I first knew you was Buttonwood Street, Dorchester, Mass. Just to prove I am Harry LaToy.

I mailed him a check, and a few days later I received an ordinary Manila postcard reading:

DEAR FRIEND:

A card of thanks for your kindness. Leaving for Tucson, Arizona.

Sincerely,
HARRY LaToy

At Christmas time, a card sprinkled with holly arrived with this personal message:

Christmas Greetings
from Tucson, Arizona

That was the last word I ever heard from LaToy. In my eternal attempt to get nearer the cheese in the Rat Race of Life, I forgot him. One afternoon, at a radio rehearsal, there was a long-distance call for me. I picked up the phone; the voice at the other end was coming out of a newspaperman in St. Louis. He said that he knew I had been a juggler years ago and that I might be able to help him with a story. There was a vaudeville actor who had been lying in the morgue in St. Louis for a week. Nobody knew who he was. The newspaperman said that he had learned the fellow had been a juggler. When I asked him if he knew the juggler's name, he said "Harry LaToy." I told the newspaperman what he wanted to know about LaToy and assured him that our office would arrange for the burial. Later, when we reached the proper authorities in St. Louis, we were informed that the body had been claimed and buried. A former vaudeville actor, who had become a mortician in a suburb of St. Louis, had read about the case. He didn't know who LaToy was, but, realizing that another vaudeville actor was in trouble, the mortician, living up to the tradition of the profession, did what he could to help a brother performer in distress.

But this was all far in the future. On that Monday morning, as I walked over to the Keith office to meet LaToy, little did I suspect that fate had these cruel surprises in store for us. Our immediate concern was how to turn Johnny Sullivan into Fred St. James. LaToy carried the day. He did all the talking, and his improvised story convinced the bookers. To start Fred St. James on the local Keith circuit, contracts were made out for three weeks, with other contracts to follow. Fred St. James was to open the following Monday for a full week at the Scenic Temple, East Boston. The salary, $30.

When I saw the $30 on the contract, I knew that the Colonial Piano Company, the Boston Public Library, and Fred St. James (formerly known as Johnny Sullivan) had come to a permanent parting of the ways. I decided to resign from both institutions immediately. With the voice of the anonymous girl at the library show echoing in my ears, I joined LaToy and started out for White's studio to pick up my lobby photographs.

# 5

## Scollay Square

I WAS leaving the world of the Colonial Piano Company and the public library for the actor's world and, in Boston, the actor's world was Scollay Square.

Scollay Square was named for William Scollay, a Scotsman who once owned a building there. When a sight-seer who is touring Boston on foot today consults his guidebook, he finds that he has to walk down Tremont Street and pass King's Chapel and the Old Granary Burial Ground to find Scollay Square. If it is night and the sight-seer enters the gloomy and forgotten plaza, he may feel that he has stumbled upon yet another burial ground not listed in his guidebook.

Scollay Square at night is a shabby silhouette bounded on the south by a traffic light; on the north by slowly moving vagrants on their way to, or from, the grubby barrooms and flophouses concealed deeper in the shadows; on the east by a tattooing parlor, an abandoned subway station, and a neon-spattered night club; and on the west, the square is bounded by a large store containing a variety of slot machines, a saloon exuding an aroma of sauerkraut and steam, and a large combination motion-picture and office building, whose denizens have long since fled, and whose entrances are now concealed by heavy wooden planks nailed securely from wall to wall. Scollay Square today is a burial ground which the ghosts of its former inhabitants are ashamed to haunt.

In 1912, Scollay Square was Boston's Tenderloin. It was a diverging point for streetcars, a business and shopping center; a few steps away were Adams Square, Dock Square, the Faneuil Hall and Quincy markets, and State Street — the financial center of Boston. Several famous eating places thrived on nearby Brattle Street; the popular hotels — the Quincy House, Young's Hotel, the Crawford House, and the American House — were within easy reach; and for good measure the square boasted a number of theaters and amusement centers to entertain the throngs who came there on business or pleasure. If the Boston of those days was as proper and conservative as the high-button shoe, the average man's answer to conservatism was Scollay Square. Scollay Square was the hot foot applied to the high-button shoe.

High among the amusement attractions within the square area were the theaters. There were the Beacon and the Palace, which featured smalltime vaudeville; the Comique and the Star, with illustrated songs and motion pictures; the Old Howard, which presented traveling burlesque shows and vaudeville; and the Bowdoin Square Theatre, which had its own stock company. There were also two museums: Walker's Nickelodeon and Austin and Stone's.

Austin and Stone's dime museum, at the corner of Howard Street, had by then been a landmark for thirty years. This dime museum, made famous by P. T. Barnum, gave more for your money than any form of entertainment ever devised by man. Following Barnum's success with his New York museum, similar shows opened in other cities, exhibiting freaks and curiosities, both real and phony, plus varied vaudeville features, and always advertising their "attractions" in the lurid lingo of the circus. Of all these newer museums, Austin and Stone's was the best known. Presiding over the museum's activities was the famous lecturer Professor Hutchings. The

Professor's mouth was an adjective hutch, and his vocabulary was extensive and impressive. The Professor was loath to use one word if eight or nine would do. As a fair sample of Professor Hutchings's rhetoric, here is his introduction of a mediocre contortionist: "Ladies and gentlemen, I ask you to observe the gyrations and genuflexions of the muscles of this peerless athlete as he is about to perform an almost impossible feat! Marvelous! Marvelous!" The Professor always climaxed his verbosities by mumbling, "Marvelous! Marvelous!" as an afterthought.

In opening the museum show, the Professor moved from platform to platform, introducing the freak attractions: "Chang, the Chinese Giant, direct from Barnum's New York museum, and engaged at seven hundred dollars a week; Miss Eva Eversole, the Armless Wonder, who, though born without arms, possesses such a sweet and cheerful disposition as to endear her to all; Mlle. Airline, the Human Match, who contains so much vital fire that she can light a gas jet by touching it with only the tips of her fingers; Peggy, a sow imported from Ireland, who on the high seas gave birth to a litter of fourteen little pigs." Professor Hutchings garnished the introduction of each freak attraction with equal flights of oratory.

The leading freaks of the day appeared at Austin and Stone's. There was Miss Corbin, billed as the "four-legged girl born with four perfectly formed legs. Her family, being well-to-do, refused all offers to place her on exhibition, but when she reached the age of 17, she developed an inordinate desire to travel, so to humor her she was allowed to appear in several important cities." Riley, the Man-Fish, ". . . who eats, drinks, reads, and smokes under water." Alistair McWhilkie, the "Man with the 14-foot beard." Tom Thumb, the first famous midget. Madam Myers, the Bearded Lady;

Jo-Jo, the Dog-Faced Boy; J. W. Coffee, the Skeleton Dude, "who weighs 55 pounds"; Zip, the What-Is-It?; Eko and Iko, two albino Negroes who called themselves the "Men from Mars"; Howard, the Lobster Boy, "whose both hands and feet are lobster claws."

Other widely advertised features were Miss Grace Court-land, the Witch of Wall Street, ". . . who foretold coming events with startling accuracy" and "was consulted constantly by the leading financiers of the country"; Hercules, the Steam Man, ". . . a mechanical figure pronounced and indorsed by a critical press and public as the wonder of the century: seven feet ten inches in height, and containing the entire motive power within his own mechanized body"; Professor Smith and His Trained Goat, ". . . the animal who performs many unusual tricks, and who has been taught to talk and carry on an intelligent conversation with his trainer"; the Fat Ladies' Convention, ". . . an assemblage of fat ladies weighing from 432 to 806 pounds"; and the World's Champion Lady Sprinters. The Professor presented them all: he once boasted, "No subject on which I am called to speak is ever slighted, and if a moral lesson or a religious precept can be drawn from it, the opportunity is never allowed to pass unheeded. My constant aim is to elevate and instruct humanity."

Humanity kept the Professor so busy that he had no time to concern himself with the future of some of his freaks. The "Ossified Man," whose condition, according to Professor Hutchings, ". . . was caused by an overdeveloped case of arthritis and would eventually cause him one day to become his own tombstone," was found years later in the poorhouse at Calais, Maine. A promoter salvaged the solidified attraction and made a deal to send the poorhouse six dollars a week in return for permission to put the Ossified Man back on exhibition. The promoter displayed the Ossified Man in empty stores throughout New England. The Ossified Man always drove a hard bargain, but it never seemed to help him financially.

When, with his final mumblings of "Marvelous! Marvelous!" the Professor completed his freak lecture, he moved over to the wild-animal cages to extol the virtues of each individual beast or reptile on display. After this, the Professor stepped into the theater to announce the opening of "the grand variety entertainment." Many stars-to-be strutted the boards of this little vaudeville theater. Sam Bernard appeared there in "a comedy sketch." An old program lists the "Most Refined Song and Dance Team Before the Public, Weber and Fields, in their original song 'Success to the Shamrock,' Introducing Many Other Songs and Dances, Dancing a Clog, and Tearing a Tidy Out of an Ordinary Newspaper."

At the close of "the grand variety entertainment," the Austin and Stone's patron might pause to join the crowd in the Curio Hall to watch some persistent checkers addict who was trying to beat "Adjeeb," the East Indian automaton checker player who, for ten cents, met all comers. A rumor, probably started by Professor Hutchings, persisted that "Adjeeb" had been beaten only once, and then by a well-known citizen of Boston. The identity of the well-known Bostonian was never disclosed, nor was that of the expert who manipulated the checker-playing robot.

Austin and Stone's eventually succumbed to progress; indeed, the museum was *in extremis* when I started frequenting its vicinity in 1912. But Austin and Stone's had been the seed that enabled Scollay Square to flower. In passing, I want to pay my respects to the memories of Professor Hutchings, Adjeeb — and the colorful, cheerful dime museum that brought pleasure to several generations of Bostonians.

Across on Hanover Street was Walker's Nickelodeon. The Nickelodeon was more of a penny arcade and shooting gallery. One attraction always seemed to be there. He was Sam Johnson, who ate glass and poison, then drank two buckets of water which he held down for a short time and then expelled. While admission to Austin and Stone's was ten cents, with ten cents extra to see "the grand variety entertainment," the Nickelodeon charged five cents admission and ten cents extra for the Big Girl Show. The Big Girl Show consisted of six misshapen females singing off key and executing dance routines completely devoid of skill or rhythm. If sex had been known in Boston at this time, these girls would have set sex back two hundred years. Terpsichore was defiled on the hour on an upstairs stage that looked like the interior of a packing case; a roll curtain in front mercifully concealed the stage and its desecrators from view. As the Big Girl Show started and the principals romped onto the stage, the last girl on the right pulled up the roll curtain and tied it off; when the show was over the same girl lowered the curtain. For manipulating the curtain the girl received two dollars extra each week.

With the passing of Austin and Stone's the most popular amusement emporium in Scollay Square became the Old Howard. The Old Howard, first known as the Howard Athenaeum, occupied the site of the Millerite Tabernacle. In 1845, the Adventists had assembled in white ascension robes on Howard Street to be ready for the end of the world. By 1912, the Adventists in ascension robes worrying about the end of the world had given way to burlesque-show chorus girls wearing short dresses and worrying about making both ends meet.

Howard Street was the smalltime actor's Broadway. The Old Howard dominated the street and every week presented a new burlesque show. This show went on in two acts; in between the acts there was a program of three acts of vaudeville. The Old Howard's slogan was "Something doing from 1 P.M. to 11 P.M."

Between five and eight when the burlesque performers went out to dinner, the vaudeville acts and an old movie carried on. The burlesque shows of that era were clean and funny; the smut and the strip tease came later. All of the great burlesque stars appeared here, as did boxing champions, six-day bicycle riders, and other sports celebrities. The Old Howard's clientele was predominantly stag, and the theater was a popular rendezvous for sailors. The Charlestown Navy Yard was but an anchor's throw across the river from Howard Street, and sailors returning from long cruises invariably rushed to the Old Howard to check on the current models of female pulchritude and to see if any improvements had been made during their absence.

Gallery admission to the Old Howard was ten cents, and order was preserved in the gallery by a burly special policeman carrying a billy club. Before the burlesque show started, the officer appeared in the first row of the gallery and announced loudly, "Hats off! And no smoking! Keep your feet off the rails!" To convince the galleryites of his sincerity the officer smote the iron gallery rail with his billy. Metallic reverberations ensued, and for minutes no galleryite could hear a thing.

Outside the Old Howard, there were many places to eat and things to do. On one corner of the alley there was a fixture named Martin. The years and the elements had worn away his first name: he was just Martin. Martin was "the Hot Dog Man"; he stood by a small steaming copper-colored boiler on the sidewalk, dealing out succulent masterpieces to famished epicures for five cents.

Jack's Café was across the alley on Howard Street. A few

doors down was Higgins's Famous Oyster House. The Higgins enterprise consisted of five small buildings joined together, merging into a hotel, a bar, the Café Oriental Room, and the famous glassed-in Palm Garden. The oysters must have had something to do with the hotel's success. There were thirty-five rooms in the hotel, and many days five hundred were rented. Bellboys at the Higgins averaged fifty dollars a day. The Higgins slogan was "Your grandfather dined here." The slogan didn't mention what else your grandfather might have done there.

Diagonally across from Higgins's on Howard Street was the William Tell Hotel, an actors' hotel. At the William Tell, the rates were five dollars a week, room and board. A full-course dinner, for those who were not guests, was twenty-five cents. On the corner under the hotel, facing Howard Street, was Hamm's Periodical Store. Mr. Hamm was very popular with actors, and depended on them for most of his business. Mr. Hamm had one trait that endeared him to the acting fraternity: Mr. Hamm extended credit. If times were bad, any actor known to Mr. Hamm could get cigarettes — Sweet Caporals, Meccas, Piedmonts, Turkish Trophies — or anything in the periodical or candy line on the cuff. Hamm's became a hangout for actors; under the street light in front of the store singers and dancers congregated late every night, the singers to form barbershop quartets, the dancers to swap steps or to try to outdo each other dancing. At the side of Hamm's, on Somerset Street, an old colored gentleman stood every night, bending over a large basket from which he sold fried chicken, pigs' feet, and soft-shell crabs.

At the end of Howard Street, on Bulfinch Street, stood the Rexford Hotel. This was the most famous of Boston's actors' hotels. The girls with the touring burlesque shows always stopped at the Rexford. This inspired most of the single predatory male actors who were appearing in Boston for the week to make the Rexford their home. Also, many of the small-time actors playing in and around Boston for a number of weeks made the Rexford their headquarters. At night the lobby was a madhouse: comedians laughing and telling stories, dancers trying out routines, owners of animal acts with their pets with them, actors sitting in groups panning better actors, criticizing bookers and managers, or bragging about their acts and the number of bows they had taken that night at the theaters where they had worked. Upstairs in the hotel rooms the actors seemed to be awake all night. Rooms were lit at four or five o'clock in the morning. Saxophone, cornet, or xylophone solos or ensembles could be heard blocks away. If a xylophone player had a small room, he would keep his door open and leave an octave or two of his xylophone out in the hall. If you were a single man, it was not unusual to have a lady knock at your door at 4 A.M. and ask you for a needle and thread. Everything went at the Rexford. The Rexford was responsible for that much-abused hotel joke: "They ring a bell at 3 A.M., and everybody has to go back to his own room."

Actors' rooming houses were plentiful on Bulfinch Street. After midnight, if you heard a subdued whistle, you knew it wasn't a bobwhite with insomnia in the neighborhood. The whistle was the mating call of an actor. If you were nosy and peeked around the corner of Bulfinch Street, you saw the actor standing in front of a darkened rooming house. After a few muffled whistles, a room above lit up, a window opened silently, and a girl's head appeared. Following a muted exchange, the girl tossed something out the window; a metallic clink was heard as it struck the sidewalk. The girl's head disappeared, the window closed quietly, the actor picked up the key from the sidewalk, opened the door of the rooming house, looked around furtively, and stepped inside.

The firehouse on Bulfinch Street separated the Rexford from another famous establishment — the Revere House. The Revere House lowered its big wide stone steps like a great portcullis into Bowdoin Square. It was a venerable inn whose hospitality had been sampled by Boston's dignitaries for many years. As the entire neighborhood deteriorated, the Revere House kept abreast of the trend, but although the visiting dignitaries began to stop at the newer hotels uptown, the Revere House's reputation for good food kept the hotel's dining room crowded until the end.

The Grotto, too, was very popular. Boston had a law that no lady without an escort could enter a café where liquor was sold. When a girl was unescorted, but wanted to have access to the Grotto for reasons that were rather obvious, she walked around to Howard Street, stopped in front of Hamm's, and asked one of the actors on the corner to accompany her into the hotel. Once inside, the actor and the girl sat at a table and ordered two beers. When the beers had arrived and the girl had paid the waiter, she excused herself and disappeared. The actor sat at the table and finished his beer; then he left the Grotto and returned to his place in front of Hamm's. The actor construed this action as one which was done as a favor to another performer and which was also a chivalrous gesture. On nights that actors were not available, the girl stopped any single male in sight and offered to pay him to escort her into the Grotto. The escort fee, paid when the girl was safely inside and seated at a table, was fifty cents. Some of these girls took their work seriously. They often paid the office boy at the Keith booking office a few dollars to learn the names of the big-spending actors who were booked at the Keith Theatre for future weeks.

Howard Street had other attractions for the actor. The Daisy Lunch, next to the Old Howard, was popular. The Daisy diner could get up slowly off his stool after consuming beans, frankfurters, bread and butter, apple pie and ice cream, all washed down with a large mug of hot coffee, and settle his obligation for twenty-five cents. If the waitress was pretty and the diner was in a generous mood, he might throw her a nickel tip. A little alehouse, next to Hamm's, was a gathering place for some of the older performers, who liked to sip their ale, puff at their pipes, and discuss their yesterdays. The Bucket of Blood was a poolroom down in a cellar under Higgins's; it was in this sunken billiard emporium that the betting fraternity consorted.

The Howard Street habitué soon became acquainted with all the coast defenders, the smalltime actors who lived in rooming houses nearby. As they walked down Howard Street on their way to the Daisy Lunch or to the streetcar, to leave for some suburban theater, they formed a parade of unique characters. There was Dancing Bandy, who featured his famous Bandy Walks: during his final dancing number Bandy walked in step like a fat man, a minister, a Jewish pushcart salesman, an effeminate male, a Civil War veteran and so on. There were Malumby and Musette, an Englishman and his wife who impersonated costermongers, wearing suits and dresses covered with pearl buttons, and singing Cockney songs. There was Hindu Sam, the fire-eater, and his famous Hindu Basket Trick. Hindu Sam placed his small son in a small wicker basket and, after closing the top and chanting a few incantations, proceeded to thrust long swords through the basket from every possible angle without impaling the boy. Sam claimed that his Hindu powers enabled him to protect his small son from harm. Sam's Hindu powers, however, could not stop his small son from growing. When the boy became too large to fit into the basket, Hindu Sam's theatrical career came to an abrupt end.

Also in the procession would be the Minstrel Maids, featuring Cassie French. Cassie had an enormous bust. With her short neck and protruding bosom, Cassie always looked as though she were looking over somebody else's behind. When the Minstrel Maids played the Old Howard, if there were only four men in the horseshoe balcony, they would all be huddled together at the extreme ends of the horseshoe to enjoy a bird's-eye view of Cassie. There was also Major Doyle, the midget, who was an accomplished baton twirler. There was Mike Scott, the Dublin Dancer. Mike was a heel and toe artist. The Lancashire Clog, as well as other clogs and reels, confined the dancer and his jigging to one spot; he did his entire act on a marble-topped pedestal. As age robbed Mike of his agility, and he found the altitude bothering him, he took the marble top off his pedestal and placed it on the floor. Everybody knew when Mike had a date booked. He would come down Howard Street with his wooden shoes under one arm and his marble slab under the other. I have often wondered if, when Mike Scott passed on, they used the marble slab for his tombstone.

Also on regular view was Tom Heffernan, a dancer who had but one leg. To keep up appearances, and for purposes of dancing, Tom wore an old-style wooden leg. He lived in a small room on the second floor of the William Tell House, and when he was out of work, Bacchus often beckoned, and Tom would go out for a romp. Once he was under way, Tom drank through the days and nights until his blotting potential had been exceeded. At this point, friends delivered Tom, a limp tweedy bundle, back to the William Tell House, carried him up two flights to his room, and deposited him on his bed. To make sure that Tom could not rejoin his roistering friends until his stupor had run its course, the lady who ran the William Tell House would unfasten his wooden leg, walk it downstairs, and stand the leg in a corner of her office. This strategy paid off many nights. There were other nights, however, when Tom, refreshed after a few hours' sleep, would awaken after midnight and realize that he had to have a drink immediately. After a few attempts at standing, it would dawn on Tom that his wooden leg was missing. In Tom's code, thirst did not concede to gravity; he would improvise locomotion. Seconds later, the colored man selling his fried chicken on the curb and the actors gathered under the street light in front of Hamm's would see the front door of the William Tell House open and would also see something that looked like an alligator wearing a vest slither along the sidewalk close to the wall and turn the corner. It was Tom Heffernan, who had crawled down two flights of stairs on his stomach en route to the little alehouse next to Hamm's.

Toby Lyons, the comedian, was a great favorite. Toby's famous song was "Hinky Dee." During the chorus of the song Toby shouted to the audience, "What's his name?" And the audience, to a man, shouted back, "Hinky Dee!" Then there was Dainty Irene. Dainty Irene had an unusual talent. Although she was only four feet tall and weighed only eighty-five pounds, Dainty Irene did an iron-jaw act. At fairs and circuses Dainty Irene performed on a crossbar one hundred feet in the air. She finally married the man who operated the rigging for her act, and as soon as they were married, the husband decided that they could economize on travel expenses. He said that because of her small size, Dainty Irene should travel for half fare. He made her buy children's clothing and, riding on trains, she was compelled to curl up and lie in one corner of the seat. When the conductor passed through the car, the husband handed him one full fare and one half ticket. This went on for forty years. When Dainty Irene died at the age of sixty, her husband had her laid out in baby clothes and insisted on a discount by having the mortician bury her in a child's casket.

The Bostonian was a small rooming house on Howard Street, interesting chiefly because it was here that all the female impersonators lived. The other actors called the Bostonian the Y.W. Three of the coast-defender impersonators were Calvette, Jaquette, and Willie DeTello.

This was the world, then, in which the actors lived in Boston in 1912. I had eaten there, at the Daisy Lunch, and LaToy had taken me around to the Rexford, but I had no official artistic standing in the community. The other actors had never heard of Fred St. James. Frankly, I hadn't thought much about him myself until the Monday morning I arrived at the Scenic Temple and saw my picture in the lobby. Underneath the picture it said, "Fred St. James — Comedy Juggler." There were four other acts: a man and wife acrobatic and high-kicking act known as Miller and Miller; the Riley Sisters, two girl singers; Bartlett and Earle, an old couple who did a comedy talking act; and a studious-looking gentleman who operated a mechanical man. The mechanical man had no name and no talent. His act consisted of lighting up his eyes, raising his hands stiffly, bowing stiffly to the audience, and walking stiffly around the stage. The gentleman who operated the mechanical man sat stiffly at the side of the stage, lecturing on the wonders his mechanical stooge was performing; he pulled switches, pressed buttons, and lighted up bulbs as the mechanical man was cutting his dull, buzzing didoes.

The actors at the Scenic Temple did three shows daily: a matinee at two-thirty and evening shows at seven and nine. When I had appeared on Amateur Nights, there was excite-

ment backstage, and the audience exuded an air of anticipation. Both of these stimulants were lacking at the Scenic
Temple. The audience consisted of middle-class families,
mostly women and children. All of these smalltime-theater
audiences were composed of the same ingredients: the enthusiastic and not too discriminating element who enjoyed
the show and applauded everything, or the tired set who just
wanted to sit back and rest and ignore the whole thing.

I had never done my juggling act three times in one day
before. To my surprise, I found the audiences varied. At the
matinees, people would laugh and applaud. At the seven-
o'clock show, I went through my act to riotous silence. At the
nine-o'clock show, all was well again. After two days, and the
mixed reactions of the audiences, I started to worry that perhaps I had rushed my career. My act was really a crude
monologue with incidental juggling tricks. It was neither fish
nor fowl. At the National Theatre, to a metropolitan audience, my act had been accepted as a burlesque of a routine
juggling act, and it had been thought funny. The East Boston
housewives, and their young that they hadn't eaten, who came
to the Scenic Temple weren't interested in innovations. When
an act was a monologist they wanted to hear him talk. When a
juggler showed up on the stage they demanded that he
juggle. "None of that shandy-gaff," as they say in England.
The other acts obviously knew I was an amateur trespassing
in their profession and ignored me. My act was getting
worse each day, and my ego was being deflated at a rate that
would eventually reduce it to caraway-seed proportions.

On Thursday, however, the deflation was halted, and the
slow leak in my confidence was vulcanized. Coming over
from Boston on the ferry, I met Miller and Miller, the opening
act. Mr. Miller acknowledged my existence by saying "Hello."

I was so flattered that I started to talk. I confessed to Mr. Miller that this was my first professional vaudeville date, and that I was worried about my act. Mr. Miller told me that my trouble was that I didn't make up. All comedy jugglers, according to Mr. Miller, used comedy make-ups, and when they came on the stage the audience laughed at the comedy make-up and knew that the act was going to be funny. Mr. Miller assured me that if I would assume a grotesque guise the success of my act would be instantaneous. Why I listened to Mr. Miller I will never know. Mr. Miller himself was about forty years old, and his act consisted of a few tumbling tricks, after which his wife announced that Mr. Miller was the high-kicking champion of the world. To live up to this claim Mr. Miller proceeded to kick a number of cigar boxes out of his wife's hand. First, his wife stood on the stage and held out one cigar box. Mr. Miller adjusted it, placed himself under the cigar box, and executed a back somersault. When his feet were aloft he kicked the cigar box out of his wife's hand up into the air. His wife then stood on a chair and held out another cigar box, and Mr. Miller repeated his aerial prank. After the applause Mrs. Miller stood on a kitchen table and held out a cigar box. Then the chair was placed on the table, and Mrs. Miller mounted the chair with her cigar box. Here was the climax of the act: Mr. Miller first executed two somersaults and purposely missed the cigar box both times. Now that the suspense was at its peak, Mr. Miller ventured a third try. On this attempt Mr. Miller's toe made contact, the cigar box flew into space, Mrs. Miller was helped down, and Miller and Miller rushed to the footlights to bask in acclaim. Mr. Miller had been traveling around smalltime theaters kicking cigar boxes out of his wife's hand for years without ever fixing up his own act, and here he was telling me how to fix mine. I should have smelled a rat, but the wind of my enthusiasm was blowing in Mr. Miller's favor.

When I asked Mr. Miller about a specific comedy make-up for my act, it developed that this was my lucky day. Mr. Miller had a red wig at the theater that was very funny even without me. I could become the owner of the red wig by crossing Mr. Miller's palm with ten dollars. By the time the ferry had docked, and Miller and Miller and I had arrived at the Scenic Temple, the deal had been consummated. When I admitted that I didn't even know how to make myself up, Mr. Miller agreed to throw in one stick of greasepaint, one can of powder (complete with puff), and make-up instructions along with the red wig. Before the matinee, Mr. Miller made me up. Wearing the red wig that came down over my forehead and blended into my skin, with my eyelids whitened, with a clown mouth and my front teeth blacked out, I looked like a Patsy Bolivar. (Patsy Bolivar was a slang name applied to a bumpkin character; later it was shortened to Patsy, and referred to any person who was the butt of a joke.)

I didn't have any comedy wardrobe to go with my red wig and my funny head, but Mr. Miller assured me that with a juggler nobody would know the difference. At the matinee, my act seemed to go better. The audience laughed when I walked out onto the stage. The jokes didn't have anything to do with my new character, but this didn't affect my reception. The remaining shows of the week were done under Mr. Miller's guidance. He made me up for every show, and showed me how to make up my eyes and mouth, and how to black out my front teeth with a sort of wax that he had decided to throw in with the red wig. The last night at the Scenic Temple Mr. Miller predicted that, fortified with the red wig and my new make-up, my act was going to be a sensation. I was taking a short cut to success. We shook hands and parted. I haven't seen Mr. Miller since. It is fortunate that I haven't.

The next Monday I was booked to play the Superb Theatre in Roxbury. The person who named the theater the Superb was careless with his adjective. The Superb was like a hundred other small neighborhood theaters that sprang into existence with the coming of the motion picture. Architecturally they were all alike. There was no balcony; the seats were all on one floor, with aisles on either side. The white screen with a wide black border surrounding it was painted on the back wall. The so-called stage had no scenery. It was a five-foot scaffold jutting out from under the picture screen. Popping up along the outer rim of this stage there was a row of naked light bulbs which posed as footlights. Some months before, I had graced the Superb stage at an Amateur Night. Now I was back as a professional. At rehearsal, the piano player and the drummer didn't recognize me. To them I was Fred St. James, the opening act. As matinee time approached I went to my dressing room to make myself up, but without Mr. Miller I couldn't seem to do anything right. The front of the red wig wouldn't blend into my forehead, the white on my eyes looked as though somebody had hit me with two marshmallows, my clown mouth looked like an incision that hadn't healed, and the wax that blacked out my teeth kept slipping down. When I finished I looked like a nearsighted schoolboy who had dressed himself up to frighten the neighbors on Halloween.

The show finally started. I was the first act and in spite of my incongruous appearance the audience responded fairly well. My act finished with some hat tricks that could be relied upon for applause. I returned to the dressing room and started to remove my make-up. As I sat before my mirror, busily spreading cold cream over my cheeks, I heard a strange sound behind me. It was a sort of swishing that came from the general direction of the door. I turned around, looked down, and there on the floor I saw my music and my lobby photographs. They had been pushed under the door. It seemed rather strange at first. Then I thought that perhaps the piano player had memorized my music and that, since the theater had a small lobby, the manager was returning some photos that he couldn't use. After I had washed up and put on my street clothes I opened the dressing-room door. The vaudeville part of the show was over, and the piano player was coming out of the pit. I thanked him for returning my music; he said, "I'm sorry, kid." When I asked him why, he told me. The theater manager had watched my act and remembered that I had appeared at the Superb at an Amateur Night. The theater catered to a neighborhood audience with the same people coming every week. The manager knew that the audience would recognize me; he couldn't afford to have his patrons think that when he advertised professional vaudeville he was trying to put something over by booking amateur talent. When the piano player had finished I said, "And that's why my music and photos were slipped under the door?" He said, "Yes, kid. You're canned!"

It was too much for me. I knew that the manager would inform the Keith booking office that Fred St. James, the great personality out of the West, was really no more than a local amateur who had recently been working for Sam Cohen. Fred St. James, red wig and all, had come to an untimely end. I was afraid to call the booking office, and I was sure that my other contracts would be canceled. I didn't know where to find LaToy in my hour of need. Left to my own devices, I packed up my juggling equipment and went home.

I said nothing to my Aunt Lizzie. I knew she would tell me about the actor who went to school with her and later went to a drunkard's grave. The next day I went into Boston, and avoiding Howard Street and the actors' haunts, started looking for a job.

# 6

## Freddy James — The World's Worst Juggler

I KNEW that I couldn't go back to the library or the Colonial Piano Company; two weeks before, I had left both these institutions on a high note to make my name in the theater. Consulting the HELP WANTED ads in one of the newspapers, I discovered that a wholesale paper concern, the Carter, Rice Company, wanted a boy. I was the boy.

My weekly salary was back to eight dollars again. My activities were confined to the stockroom. When I learned the different types of card and paper stocks, I filled the orders and delivered the paper or cards to the cutters or to the shipping department. But my heart wasn't in the paper business. In my lunch hours I walked around Howard Street. When I came to a group of actors, I'd stand on the fringe of the crowd and just listen to them talk. When I caught up with LaToy, he told me I had made a mistake. He said that after being canned I should have rushed right back to the booking office to castigate the manager of the Superb Theatre and accuse him of a case of mistaken identity. It was too late for this strategy now. At least I was getting my eight dollars every week and LaToy was showing up at noon every day as my guest for lunch.

I continued to practice my juggling and still saw all of the new jugglers who came to Boston. I brought my hats, balls, and plates in to work and kept them hidden in the Carter, Rice stockroom. During lunch hours, and when things were slack, I regaled the other employees with my embryonic dexterity. Learning to juggle was difficult. The jugglers who were headliners performed uncanny feats and, to retain their skill, had to rehearse many hours a day. If a juggler had spent as many hours practicing a musical instrument as he had to spend mastering his tricks, he would have been a concert artist. When I saw the really great jugglers — Cinquevalli, Rastalli, Kara, Chinko, and others — I was discouraged. I could juggle four balls; Frank LeDent juggled eleven. I handled silk hats clumsily; Paul LaCroix featured his dancing hats. There was no comparison at all.

Finally, a juggler came to Boston who solved my problem. William Morris had opened theaters in many of the Eastern cities to try to break the B. F. Keith vaudeville monopoly. The William Morris theater in Boston was the Academy of Music, which later became the Orpheum. To combat the Keith combine and attract audiences, the William Morris circuit imported many headliners from Europe. One week, the headliner at the Academy of Music was a British artist named Griff. Griff was a former juggler whose act was billed as "A mono-dramo-singo-danco-ventrilo-juggo-logue." The act consisted of a long, rambling monologue during which Griff burlesqued a tightrope walker (with a rubber wire that sagged down to the floor when he stepped on it); he imitated a ventriloquist (having somebody else sing off stage while he held the dummy on his knee and drank a glass of water); and he next missed several juggling tricks, explaining that he had done them the night before and that the audience should have been there then. He also did a dramatic sketch in which he played all the parts. Griff was a star, and actually he didn't do any difficult juggling. He was a star because of his talk and his comedy. It seemed to me that if I could be as funny, I could save a lot of time practicing juggling tricks, and some day maybe I might have an act like Griff's.

Now, instead of watching jugglers, I started to study comedians. When I heard a good joke or a funny line, I wrote it down. Here are a few gems embalmed in my first notebook:

> Summer is going — Winter draw(er)s on.
> What has four legs and flies? A dead horse.
> I'd rather have two girls at 17 than one at 34.
> A sardine is a herring's pup.
> My uncle is a Southern planter. He's an undertaker in Alabama.
> He's a good boy — everything he steals he brings right home to his mother.

Some of these jokes are still seeing service today.

With new jokes and weeks of practicing during lunch hours, my act seemed to improve. This was my personal opinion, although it's possible that I was biased. As I ran through my jokes and tricks up in the loft at the paper house, I often wished that I could hear an audience react to the reconditioned Fred St. James. One day my wish was granted. The Good Fairy arrived, disguised as LaToy. Late one afternoon an urgent call was received at the Carter, Rice office; it was LaToy. He told me excitedly that he was playing out at Waltham. It was Wednesday, his last day at the theater. He was suffering from rheumatism and could hardly walk. He had worked the matinee but couldn't possibly do the night shows. He had spoken to the theater manager, and if I would come out after work and do my act for the last two shows, the manager would pay LaToy for the entire three days. This was my chance. I assured LaToy I was on the way.

When I stepped off the train at Waltham, LaToy was waiting. Too cheap to buy or rent a cane, LaToy had pried a tall picket off a neighboring fence to support him as he hobbled along. After a sandwich and coffee we adjourned to the theater. I selected the hats and props I needed from LaToy's things, and did the two shows. They came off very well. Although I had never done this version of my act before, both audiences were enthusiastic. LaToy collected his full salary, he picked up his picket, I picked up his two suitcases, and we started for the train. On the way back to Boston, LaToy commented on my great improvement and remarked that I was demented if I stayed another day with the Carter, Rice Company. Before the Waltham applause had stopped echoing in my ears, I had promised him to start visiting Mrs. Mead, Pop White, and some of the other smaller agents to try to book some dates. My ego must have been vulnerable.

The next day I made the rounds. After a month or more of these daily visits, Mrs. Mead weakened and booked me into the Dreamland on Washington Street, and Dream Theatre in Winthrop, and the Dream Theatre in Revere. Pop White had given me the Star Theatre in Scollay Square. A small club agent had booked me at four or five club affairs. When I added these future obligations together, I had more than two weeks of professional work. My career had gotten up off the ground again. I removed my juggling trinkets from the stockroom and resigned from the Carter, Rice Company.

Now that I was an actor once more, I made two changes. I started wearing patent-leather button shoes, and I removed the St. from St. James and became Freddy James. After the first show in any theater I always sat waiting in the dressing room, but my music and photos never made their sliding appearance under my door again. During the day I spent all my free time on Howard Street. Now that I had played on bills with different smalltime acts they accepted me. It is always easy to talk to actors about show business; that is almost the only business you can talk to them about. At night, after my shows, if LaToy was in town we met for a late snack and some discussion on his favorite subjects: a new "chicken" he had picked up, or the number of bows he had taken at the theater that night.

While I was playing the theaters, I made the rounds every day looking for more bookings. Nobody seemed to be interested. I didn't dare to ask for work at the Keith office after the Superb Theatre fiasco. Mrs. Mead and Pop White liked my act, but they had given me the few theaters they booked and had nothing more to offer. After I had finished playing the Dreamland, the Star, and two Dreams, and the final club date, I made the rounds of the agents every day for two more weeks. One booker named Fred Mardo sat in his little office behind a green screen. When the office door opened, Mardo wouldn't even get up to see who had come in. He'd shout, "Who's there?" The actor gave his name and if Mardo wanted to book him, he'd answer, "Come in!" This was an invitation for the actor to step behind the screen and join Mardo for a session of salary bickering. When I opened Mardo's door and heard his "Who's there?" I would answer, "Freddy James." Mardo would shout, "You're a coast defender. Go home. If there's a war I'll send for you!"

Mardo was formerly a juggler. It was said that when he first opened his booking office, a theater manager who didn't know him called in and asked him to send an act out to his theater immediately. Mardo, who could use the money, promptly booked himself. He rushed out to the theater, did his juggling act, and the manager canned him.

I finally reached my quota of rebuffs. I had to earn money to help support the house. If I couldn't be an actor I had no choice. I had to go back to work. This time, the HELP WANTED ads didn't look encouraging. I applied for a job at Raymond's, now one of Boston's leading department stores, at that time a small store on Washington Street that sold everything. There was a position open for a bright boy in Raymond's basement. I went down. The air was bad, and the salespeople who were working in the basement looked a little puffy, as though they had stopped breathing years ago. I enjoyed breathing and knew that if I was going to continue to enjoy it, I would have to stay out of Raymond's basement.

I left Raymond's and walked down Franklin Street to Federal. Turning into Federal Street, I saw a large sign in front of a hardware store that said Chandler and Farquhar. I wasn't psychic so far as I knew, but the name Chandler started to rattle around in my subconscious. The closer I came to the hardware store the more I felt convinced that if I were drowning and all the events of my life flashed through my mind, somewhere during the hurried parade of people and experiences I would see Mr. Chandler and the circumstances under which we had met. Then I remembered. At the High School of Commerce, every week one of Boston's leading businessmen had visited the school to give an informal talk to the students. Mr. Chandler had been one of those speakers; his talk came back to me now. He had said, among other things, that if any Commerce student ever wanted to learn the hardware business, Mr. Chandler would make an opening for him. I didn't hope to make any name in the hardware business, but I thought it might be an opportunity to test Mr. Chandler's sincerity.

I entered the store, asked for Mr. Chandler, and was immediately shown to his office up a short flight of stairs. When Mr. Chandler inquired about the nature of my business, I reminded him of his talk at the High School of Commerce. Mr. Chandler seemed taken aback. His talk had been given two years before, and he had obviously forgotten some of the salient details. I told him how much his talk had impressed me and that I was interested in the hardware business. Mr. Chandler seemed flattered that I had been influenced by his speech, and told me that he would give me an opportunity to learn the trade. He called a clerk who was working behind one of the counters on the main floor and told him to take me down to the shipping room. I thanked Mr. Chandler and followed the clerk out of the office, on my way to a new career.

The shipping room was a grimy corner, situated down in the cellar at the back of the store. The shipping entrance was on Devonshire Street, and it was here the express called to pick up the out-of-town hardware deliveries. The city deliveries were made by a boy motivating a hand truck. As we arrived, the shipping room was busy. Two clerks were filling orders, one nailing up a box filled with emery wheels, the other tying long saws into bundles for shipment. The boss of the shipping room was a man named Orrin: a stout, dusty-looking fellow who wore pince-nez clamped halfway down his nose; he was a chain tobacco chewer and kept a small brown-stained nail keg half filled with sawdust under his desk in which to deposit superfluous saliva. When we came in, Orrin was surrounded by expressmen; when the last receipt had been signed and the last expressman had staggered out under a heavy crate, Orrin turned to us. The clerk gave him Mr. Chandler's message, and Orrin intimated that I had just arrived in time. The hand truck outside the door was loaded; Orrin handed me a slip with an address on it. I went out the back door to start learning the hardware business.

I found the hand truck; on the hand truck I found a nice,

white, shiny toilet bowl. I looked at the slip. The address was one on Bulfinch Street. This meant that I would have to push a hand truck containing an uncovered water-closet accessory up Howard Street to Bulfinch Street, right through the heart of the theatrical district. Only yesterday I had been an actor accepted by the performers around the Rexford. Today, I was a delivery boy pushing a privy component on a hand truck through the streets. I would be laughed out of a profession I wasn't even in at the moment. I needed the job, but I needed my pride more. I had read that Benjamin Franklin had walked through the streets of Philadelphia carrying two small loaves of bread in his pockets. If I ever became famous, the history books would hesitate to record my trip through the streets of Boston accompanying a toilet bowl. I went back into the shipping room, handed Orrin the slip with the Bulfinch Street address, and started up the stairs to Mr. Chandler's office. Mr. Chandler was surprised to see me back so soon. Knowing that I was a Commerce graduate, a go-getter, he must have thought that I had returned to ask for more money, or that I had mastered the hardware business and wanted to become a member of the firm. Mr. Chandler asked me what was wrong. I told him that I didn't think I could learn much about the hardware business chaperoning a toilet bowl through the streets of Boston. Mr. Chandler agreed. He picked up his phone, called Orrin, and told him to start me to work as a packer. I am an outdoor man at heart, but I resolved that, if I was ever going to make a name for myself in the hardware world, it was going to be indoors.

The Chandler and Farquhar chores soon began to seem like those at Carter, Rice. The work was uninteresting; the people with whom I worked were dull compared to actors. In the shipping room I packed bolts, pipes, nails, screws, nuts, grindstones, machinery parts, and assorted tools. After a week or two, I brought my juggling essentials into the shipping room. Orrin told me that I might keep them in a loft up in the Chandler and Farquhar building. Again I started the same routine. I rushed my lunch every day to get up to the loft to rehearse my act, and when the fellows at the store learned that I had been an actor they started bringing their lunches up to the loft to watch me. I may have been the first floor show without even realizing it.

I had been in the hardware business for three or four months, with a diminishing desire to become a member of the firm, when one evening, as I was going home from work on the elevated train, a man introduced himself to me. He said that he was Mr. Buckley, the owner of the Roxbury Theatre, a small vaudeville and motion-picture house near Dudley Street. Mr. Buckley said that he had seen my act at an Amateur Night at his theater over a year ago. He had liked the act, and recently Sam Cohen had told him that I had turned professional. I admitted that I was still doing my act, but I didn't tell him I was doing it in the loft at Chandler and Farquhar's. As he left the train, Mr. Buckley said, "If you ever want to play my theater, let me know." I thanked him, and told him I would.

As the weeks went by, every noon, as I was practicing in the loft, I thought about Mr. Buckley. His offer bothered me. I couldn't say that I was sick and stay away from work for three days to play Mr. Buckley's theater; it didn't make sense to give up my job just to return to the acting profession for three days. During one of my pondering periods, it occurred to me that there might be other managers who, like Mr. Buckley, would book me if I went to see them personally. Every neighborhood had its own theater, and at Upham's Corner, in Dorchester, there was an upstairs movie house called Winthrop Hall, only a short walk from our house.

Everybody in the section knew that I was some sort of actor, and I thought that if the manager booked me for three days, many of the neighbors and the kids who knew me might come to the theater out of curiosity.

The manager of the Winthrop Hall was the piano player, a man named Harry Norton. Before the show, Harry sat at the top of the stairs and sold tickets. When it was time to start the picture, Harry turned his ticket job over to a girl, went into the theater, sat at the piano, and pounded out a slam-bang overture. The Winthrop Hall ran one two-reel comedy, a feature picture, and three acts of underpaid vaudeville. Harry played on through the entire evening, improvising music that he thought was appropriate to heighten the comedy and to fit the various situations in the feature picture. Harry also played for the vaudeville acts. When the first show was over, there was an intermission. All the lights would go on, and Harry would rush from the piano back out to the top of the stairs to ask the people as they were leaving how they had liked the show, and to tell them of the attractions he had booked for the coming weeks.

When the strategy of my booking offensive had been worked out, one night after dinner I donned my best suit and the patent-leather button shoes and called on Harry Norton at the Winthrop Hall. I explained my potential value as a local attraction. Harry agreed, and booked me for three days, two weeks in advance. There was another theater in Dorchester, the Hamilton Hall, located at Meeting House Hill. This was owned by Mike Lydon, who also owned several other theaters and dance halls in South Boston and Dorchester. I called on Mr. Lydon and told him that Harry Norton had booked me as a local act; Mike then said that he would book me at two of his theaters, the Hamilton Hall and the Imperial, in South Boston. I then visited Mr. Buckley, who gave me the three days he had promised me at his Roxbury Theatre. By arranging these dates consecutively, I now had two solid weeks of vaudeville booking. For a single act like mine, the standard three-day smalltime vaudeville salary was fifteen dollars. Two weeks amounted to a staggering sixty dollars. My weekly hardware wage was eight dollars. It would take me seven and a half weeks packing hardware to make sixty dollars; as an actor I could make sixty dollars in two weeks and have more fun in theaters in those two weeks than anyone had ever had in a hardware store in a lifetime. It wasn't a difficult decision to make. I notified Orrin that I was departing the Chandler and Farquhar enterprises. The following Saturday I scraped the grease off my hands, shook the sawdust out of my sleeves, picked up my salary and my juggling gear, and made a bolt for the door. (I could have walked to the door, but as a farewell gesture to the hardware business, I made the bolt.)

On Thursday, February 5, 1914, at 11 A.M., carrying my two suitcases, I struggled up the stairs of the Winthrop Hall on my way to rehearsal. Over the weeks I had changed my act considerably. The red wig had long since been abandoned; I now worked in street clothes. My monologue was much funnier and ran through the entire act. Some of the juggling had been eliminated, and the few tricks I did were for comedy effect. I burlesqued juggling, as Griff had done, and my act was billed "Freddy James — Almost a Juggler."

While I was playing those two weeks that I had booked myself, I continued to make the rounds, leaving word where I was working and when I would be available. Most of the bookers had given up trying to insult me. Some were even beginning to offer me odd jobs. I didn't work every week, but I still earned more than I had in the hardware business, and was able to give my Aunt Lizzie more to run the house.

I played one-nighters: the Town Hall in Cohasset, the Town Hall in Stoughton, the Dreamland Theatre in Beverly, and the Odd Fellows Hall in East Weymouth. In those days, promoters in small towns rented the town halls or school auditoriums to run shows on Saturday nights, and Johnny Quigley, an agent in Boston, specialized in furnishing vaudeville shows for clubs and fraternal organizations. During the rest of the winter I appeared at the Ward 18 Democratic Club, the Catholic Club at Canton, Medford Armory, Quincy House in Boston, Knights of Columbus Club, the Y.M.C.A., the Pen and Pencil Club, the Winthrop Lodge of Elks, the Boot and Shoe Workers Union, and many others.

Booking dates from different offices often complicated the actor's travel arrangements. Trying to make impossible train connections cost me many sleepless nights. Out-of-town dates paid $17.50 for three days. My route book shows that, after laying off for three days in Boston, I went to Sanford, Maine, for three days, then came back to Boston and layed off for three more days, then went to Norwich, Connecticut, for the last three days of this second week. The railroad fares and expenses ate up the $35 I received for those two weeks, not to mention the wear and tear on my two suitcases and me. Other financially disastrous bookings I accepted were from New Bedford, Massachusetts, to Rutland, Vermont, and then to Rocky Point, Rhode Island — for a one-day Sunday show to complete the week. Then I was booked for three weeks in Nova Scotia at a salary of $45 a week. The boat fare from Boston to Halifax was $8, the commission to the booking office was $2.25, my room and board for a week in Nova Scotia was $11. There wasn't much money left — and I was seasick on the boat going and coming.

When I was out of work, or playing theaters in and around Boston, I lived at home, which was a great saving. Playing the smaller towns, I lived in boardinghouses where the rates were standard: one dollar a day, room and board. Most of those boardinghouses catered to men and women who worked in the mills and factories that supported the community. These workers were early risers, and the boardinghouse day started with breakfast from six to seven-thirty each morning. To get their money's worth, the actors all got up with the workers at seven, ate a big breakfast — ham and eggs or steak and eggs, home-fried potatoes, toast, jam, coffee, and apple pie — and then went back to bed again.

Later, they arose to consume another heavy meal at noon before going off to the theater for the matinee. Eating was no problem to the actor of that era. It was impossible for him to go hungry. The danger was in the other direction: if he was working and eating three Gargantuan meals a day at board-inghouses around the country, he might contract the gout. If he wasn't working, the actor could patronize the free lunch counters in the saloons. All the actor needed was a nickel for a glass of beer; this gave him access to the assorted meats and other tasty viands heaped up on the free lunch counter. If the actor didn't have the nickel, the turn of a bartender's head was his invitation. In a saloon, food was cheaper than advice, and more people were taking the food.

The smaller the theater, in most cases, the less consideration the management had for the actor. In Gloucester, Massachusetts, there was a theater that had no plumbing or facilities. Across from the stage entrance there was a coal and lumber yard with two gates. When the new vaudeville show arrived on its opening day, and one of the performers inquired for the men's room or the ladies' room, the stagehand opened the stage door and pointed to the coal and lumber yard with the two gates. The ladies entered through the left gate; the gentle-men used the right.

ohn Florence Sullivan (age 4) with
young brother Bob

Family Portrait: James Henry Sullivan
and Sons

*J. Fisher*

*Fourth from the left:* A High School Basketeer (1910)

Fred Allen: "A Young Fellow Trying to Get Along"

Freddy James and his "Misses"

"Ben Franklin"

*Rembrandt*
Juggler in a Top Hat

*Rembrandt*

Two Studies in Elegance

Portland

Charles Justus Wick

Time Off in Florida

Bar

Another Portland — Fred Allen and Portland Mason, daughter of James Mason

At Yarmouth, Nova Scotia, the theater played but one act and had no stagehands. When the one act arrived for rehearsal, the manager showed him — or her — how to pull up the moving-picture curtain and operate the switchboard to turn on the lights. Before every show the actor (like the chorus girl at Walker's Nickelodeon) had to pull up the heavy curtain and turn on the switch for the footlights before he could go on the stage to do his own act. When he had finished his act and had taken his bows, the actor had to turn off the lights and lower the curtain so that the picture could go on.

On May 1, three months after I had cast the hardware business adrift, I was booked for a full week at the Old South Theatre in Boston. Back in the days when I had visited LaToy in his dressing room there, I had never dared to hope that some day I, too, might do my act on the stage of the Old South. A vaudeville actor who played this theater was accepted by all the Boston bookers as good enough to play in any of their theaters. Suddenly, after my week at the Old South, my act was in demand. For the first time since the catastrophe in the Superb Theatre, the Keith office booked me in some of their theaters. With the coming of summer, the amusement parks started to open. The largest parks in New England — Norumbega, Lexington, White City at Worcester, Sabbatia Park at Taunton, and many others — were owned and operated by the traction companies. The attractions at the parks were picnic grounds, a zoo housing a few monkeys and a few retired lions and tigers too old to escape, boating, cool shady dells in which to escape the summer's heat, and a rustic theater that played six or eight acts of vaudeville twice daily. The most widely advertised enjoyments of the trips to the park were the breezy trolley rides coming and going. Mothers, with their children, crowded the trolleys during the day. The romantically inclined set, headed for secluded rocks and canoe rides, and older couples out to enjoy a refreshing ride and to see the vaudeville show kept the trolleys packed at night. It was the profits from these trolley rides that had inspired the traction companies to subsidize the amusement resorts. In 1914, the Gorman Brothers, two men who booked the shows for the trolley lines, were sending tabloid companies and vaudeville acts through New England to some twenty different parks.

That summer I played at Norumbega, Lexington, and Sabbatia Parks, and at Penacook Park at Concord, New Hampshire. In the bigger theaters I met acts who had come from New York. A number of them with whom I had become friendly told me that I was wasting my time staying in Boston. They all assured me that my act was good enough to get bookings in New York. The ambition of every smalltime vaudeville actor who lived in Boston was to go to New York and try to get on the big time. Many who had risked the trip and failed returned to Boston and remained coast defenders until their dying days. One or two of the New York actors had given me the names of their agents, and advised me to write them about bookings. Also, all of the New York actors read a magazine called the *Players*. The *Players* was a weekly magazine, the official publication of the vaudeville actors' union, the White Rats. The first time I saw the magazine it intrigued me. It contained reviews of all the shows at the leading vaudeville theaters in New York: the Proctor theaters, Hammerstein's, Keith's Union Square. There were route cards of many of the vaudeville headliners, listing the towns in which they were appearing; there were ads for song-publishing firms, hotels, boardinghouses, popular restaurants, and business firms, all of which catered to actors. In one copy of the *Players*, a boardinghouse ad caught my eye. It read:

Mrs. Montfort
104 West 40th Street
New York City
Room and Board — $1 a day

I cut out Mrs. Montfort's ad and placed it in my pocketbook, just in case.

In the early days of vaudeville, before the founding of the booking offices, the vaudeville actors booked themselves by writing to the theater owners and managers. To save time explaining the nature of their acts in each individual letter — and there were many letters to be sent to cities all over the country — the acts managed to condense all of the essential information into letterheads. Letterheads of this sort covered everything:

### MOREY and MOREY

Novelty Musical Artists

Playing Intricate Arrangements of Popular and
Characteristic Music on Many Unique Instruments

From Rag-time to Grand Opera

Open with Full Stage with Bells,
Xylophone, Chimes, etc., and Close
in One with Banjos

Act Runs from 12 to 20 Minutes

### CROW and KELLY

"The Chinaman and the Rube"

Notice to all first-class Managers. This is one of
the Strongest Comedy Acts in America — bar none.
Specially arranged for Lady and Gentlemen audiences.
A Combination of Skill and Laughter from Start to Finish.
Introducing Many New and Novel Feats in Comedy.

Act runs 15 minutes

Summer Season enroute with the Great Wallace Show

THE GREAT JOHNSON

CONTORTIONIST

The Only Man in the World who can sit on a glass 2½ inches wide.

When the letterheads no longer served their original purpose, many acts kept them anyway and used them for stationery. I had some personal stationery printed that read:

FREDDY JAMES
"The World's Worst Juggler"
12 Minutes in One

An act who worked "in one" was simply an act that could work in front of the front curtain. Full-stage acts used the entire stage for scenery or acrobatic rigging; in vaudeville, a full-stage act had to be followed by an act in one in order to enable the stagehand to remove the scenery or rigging and prepare for the next full-stage act. When my "World's Worst Juggler" stationery arrived, I started to write all of the leading bookers and agents in New York City. I had no intention of going to New York at the time. I just had the stationery, and thought it would be good advertising. The bookers and agents were so accustomed to vaudeville actors bragging and lying about their acts that they probably felt that an actor who claimed to be the "World's Worst Juggler" must have something different. All of them answered my letters and invited me to see them when I arrived in New York.

The Telegraph Four, known as the "Singing Messenger Boys," and I had played on several bills together. The quartet consisted of four boys of my age who did harmony singing and comedy. The boys — Georgie Lane, Harry Dobson, Mickey Moran, and John Bowles — lived in New York, and young as they were, they were seasoned vaudeville veterans. Every time we were on the bill together, they predicted that my act would be a great success in New York. When we met in Haverhill, the boys told me that that was their last New England date; from there, they were going back to New York. On the closing night, as we said good-by, Georgie Lane and Harry Dobson begged me to go to New York. They promised me that if I would come over from Boston they would take me to their agent and make sure that I was booked. I promised the boys that some day I would accept their generous offer.

Work was plentiful in Boston. With the additional money I had been able to bring home, my Aunt Lizzie had moved us into a large and better apartment. The sisters, after a number of family battles, had moved out months before, and Aunt Lizzie, Uncle Mike, and my brother Bob and I had been living in a small duplex flat: three rooms on one floor and some stairs that led into an attic. With the dawn of my affluence, and Aunt Lizzie's improved financial status, the two sisters, Aunt Jane and Aunt Mary, returned to the fold. All this left me with a problem which I had ample time to brood over while I sat on the train alone, coming back to Boston from split weeks in New Bedford, Brockton, Newport, and other towns. I was trying to decide whether or not I should risk a trip to New York. My Aunt Lizzie needed my help to run the house. I couldn't be without work for too long. Yet, if I stayed in Boston, I knew I would never get ahead in the theater or make any big money. After many debates pro and con, I devised a plan. I would work until I saved a hundred dollars. When this sum was amassed, I would take sixty dollars and go to New York. If I failed in New York, after my sixty dollars was spent I would return to Boston and use my remaining forty dollars to start life anew. I would then withdraw from the acting profession and try to get into some business in which I might have a future.

I confided my plan to my good friend John Murphy. John

and I had worked together at the library, and he had followed my career with interest coupled with dire forebodings. It was agreed. When I was reduced to my last cent in New York, word was to be flashed to John and he would send me the fare back to Boston. I opened a savings account at the Provident Bank on Temple Place; in a few weeks the one hundred dollars had been deposited. I told my Aunt Lizzie that I had to work out of town for a week. I knew that if I explained my New York trip and the risk involved, she would again recite the true tale of the actor and the drunkard's grave.

During my last date in Boston, at the Scenic Temple on Clarendon Street, I bought a new large-sized suitcase to hold my few belongings, and a black patent-leather sample case to carry my juggling hats and props. My farewell New England appearance as a coast defender was made at the Princess Theatre, Wakefield, Massachusetts.

On Friday, September 18, 1914, carrying my suitcase and sample case, I walked into Boston's South Station and boarded a local train for Fall River. Later that afternoon, as I started up the gangplank of the boat, I had forgotten Johnny Sullivan. Freddy James, the "World's Worst Juggler," was heading for New York on the old Fall River Line.

# 7

## Mrs. Montfort's Boardinghouse

MY arrival in New York created as much commotion as the advent of another flounder at the Fulton Fish Market. As the S.S. *Priscilla* docked, and I walked down the gangplank, the man in the street was too busy reading his morning paper even to raise his head. World War I was under way; the headlines that morning were ominous:

KAISER'S STAFF CONFIDENT — SAY GERMAN ARMY GETTING STRONGER

LLOYD GEORGE: "MONEY MAY WIN THE WAR"

PRESIDENT WILSON'S ACTIVITIES TO GET WARRING POWERS TO LISTEN TO PEACE PROPOSALS HAVE COME TO STANDSTILL

I bought a *New York Times* to read on my ride uptown. Among the items of the day I found that Sir James Barrie had arrived in New York and was anxious to see Pittsburgh; that Jack Johnson was no alien: he swore he was still an American; that Bad Bad Gunda, the Bronx Zoo elephant which had shown murderous proclivities, was now quite docile. Among the ads were those for a corset hospital, a sale of 145,000 music rolls, and the Kensico Cemetery, which reminded readers that "Today, Tomorrow, Next Year — any time, and often without warning — the last call may come."

I put down the paper. I was in no mood for cemetery propaganda. I was starting a new life, and New York was the city of opportunity. I couldn't wait to get settled in my room. I was eager to see Broadway. The cab turned into West Fortieth Street and stopped at 104. I paid the driver, picked up my bags, kicked open the door, and entered Mrs. Montfort's boardinghouse. The lobby was dark, and the place seemed deserted; the only sound was coming from behind a rolltop desk in the corner. Somebody was snoring. I dropped my suitcases on the floor with a thud, the snoring stopped, a light snapped on, and a sleepy head, that of Jimsy Jordan, the clerk, appeared over the top of the rolltop desk. Jimsy said that my letter had been received, but that I was a little too early, my room would not be available for a few hours. At Jimsy's suggestion, I deposited my cases behind the rolltop desk and started out to have breakfast.

Walking up to Forty-second Street, I saw Times Square and Broadway for the first time. Eight o'clock in the morning was not an ideal hour to savor the glamour and splendor of the Great White Way, but the hour meant nothing to me. This was Broadway, the street paved with the dreams, the hopes, and the broken hearts of generations of actors. Here were the famous theaters and cafés that I had read and heard about: at Forty-second Street, Hammerstein's, the most famous vaudeville theater in the world; at Forty-third Street, Shanley's, the restaurant frequented by the stars. Walking up Broadway, I saw in rapid succession the Astor Hotel, the Astor Theatre, the Gaiety, Globe, Criterion, New York, Palace, and Winter Garden Theatres. There were Churchill's and Rector's, the society cafés; there was the Automat, the first restaurant to make it possible for the poor man to enjoy food served under glass. As I walked along Broadway with new surprises coming from every direction, I felt like Alice taking her first step through the looking glass.

After breakfast at the Automat, I walked down Broadway again and, passing the Putnam Building (which a later generation replaced with the Paramount Theatre), I remembered that some of the vaudeville agents who had answered my letters were located at this very address. I checked my list, but after trying a few locked doors, I remembered that it was Saturday, and that the agents' offices would be closed. Passing down one hall, I noticed an open door; the name on the office door was Tom Jones. I hadn't written to any Mr. Jones. As I hesitated at the door, a frail character looked up from his desk and said, "Is there anything I can do for you?" I told Mr. Jones who I was, the nature of my act, and the purpose of my visit to New York. He beamed and chuckled; it seemed that he booked the Keeney Theatre, in Brooklyn. An act had just fallen out of the bill for the coming Monday, and Mr. Jones was ready to put me on as a replacement for three days. A contract magically appeared on Mr. Jones's desk, which I signed. He gave me instructions to guide me through the wilds of Brooklyn to the Keeney Theatre and promised to see my act at the matinee on Monday and then discuss my future. But Mr. Jones neglected to give me one bit of information that I could have used: he didn't tell me that the Keeney Theatre was in opposition to a Keith theater and also to one of the Loew theaters in Brooklyn; any act that played the Keeney Theatre was automatically blacklisted by the Keith and Loew circuits. What I didn't know at the time couldn't hurt me. I thanked Mr. Jones, and, stepping out of the Putnam Building onto Broadway, I was well pleased with myself: only off the boat three hours, and I had already booked myself for three days. Things moved fast in New York. Wetting my lips to whistle on the way, I started back to see if my room was ready.

Mrs. Montfort's boardinghouse, at first sight, smacked of the drab. The lobby was a large dark room in which a circle of plain wooden chairs hugged the wall. Two large soiled windows looked out into the street. Fortieth Street, between Sixth Avenue and Broadway, was a short block. At the Broadway end, on the south side, there was the Empire Theatre; on the opposite corner, a large business building. The Sixth Avenue end had Dickinson's Saloon on the downtown corner; and on the other side, the Union Dime Bank. Dotting the middle of the block were a few shops, a fruit store, and two small red brick houses. During the day, Fortieth Street was busy with traffic. Later in the afternoon, when the shops and banks closed, the neighborhood was abandoned. To look out of Mrs. Montfort's lobby windows into the street, or to look from the street into Mrs. Montfort's lobby, was to enjoy nothing at its peak.

When I returned to Mrs. Montfort's that morning, my room was ready. The establishment boasted no bellboys. Jimsy picked up one of my suitcases and started up the stairway on the right; I followed with the other. As we struggled up the narrow stairs, Jimsy informed me that Mrs. Montfort no longer owned the boardinghouse and, furthermore, meals had been discontinued. The new owners had retained the Montfort name, but the place was now merely a rooming house. This was quite a blow to me. The advantages an actor enjoyed living in a boardinghouse were rather obvious. If he was short of money, the actor knew he could eat three meals every day until he found work or his credit succumbed.

As we continued up the stairs, Jimsy added that my room would be $4 a week. There were no telephones in the rooms. All messages would be put in my mailbox, or, if there were urgent phone calls, I would be summoned to the lobby to answer them. When we arrived at the second floor, Jimsy started down a long dark hall. I followed. I had the feeling I was walking down a giraffe's throat. One small bulb on the wall furnished the only light; the feeble ray gave the impression that a glowworm had impaled itself on the wallpaper. Stopping part way down the hall, Jimsy stopped, opened a door, stepped forward, and was enveloped in complete darkness. Following a sudden click, a tiny bulb in the ceiling went on, and the darkness brightened a shade into gloom. This was my room. After depositing the suitcase he was carrying on the bed, and showing me the general direction of the bathroom down the hall, Jimsy handed me my room key and disappeared back into the murk.

I closed the door and took inventory of my new home. When my eyes became accustomed to the gloom, I discovered that the room had no windows. The air, if any, came from the hall and entered the room through a transom over the door. The single bed looked like a frozen hammock. There was no closet; the closet problem was solved by a tilting wardrobe in one corner that leaned back and rested against the wall. The upper part of the wardrobe could be used for suits, while two long drawers at the bottom afforded space for shirts, underwear, or extra ties, if the Montfort guest owned any. One chair stood at the left of the door, and a small old-fashioned marble sink seemed to be trying to conceal itself under the head of the bed.

Years later, this room was responsible for a number of jokes, among them: "The light in this room was so bad, all I could read was Braille"; or "The room was so small that if you were lying in bed and somebody opened the door, the doorknob got into bed with you"; or "The halls were so dark the mice had a seeing-eye cat to lead them around." The only rooms in the Montfort that had windows were those in front, facing Fortieth Street, or those in back that overlooked the low roof of a movie theater on Sixth Avenue. The aroma of despair that permeated my furnished niche didn't dampen my ardor, however. I hadn't come to New York to sit in a room. I was there to do things. The room would be used for sleeping purposes only. Since I slept with my eyes closed, what difference did it make where Morpheus and I met?

The Montfort functioned as an autonomous community. The guests were all smalltime actors: a loud, brash, easy-going crowd who wallowed in success when it came, or who tightened their belts during the lean periods, accepting the good and the bad days with the same complacency. The husbands gathered in the lobby to discuss their show-business problems. The wives met in their rooms to wash clothing, prepare meals, and to discuss whatever subjects the wives of smalltime actors had in common. The children played in Bryant Park, across Sixth Avenue. At the end of the day, when the members of each family assembled in the privacy of their room and exchanged gossip, every Montfort guest knew everything there was to be known about every other Montfort guest.

When a guest was accepted, he became a member of the Montfort family. The family soon accepted me, and I was promptly introduced to some economy practices that were in vogue among the lobby set. A few oranges, a loaf of bread, and a jar of jam, hidden away in a dresser or wardrobe drawer, furnished many breakfasts at little cost. If you required liquid with your breakfast, a quart of milk could easily be concealed in the wardrobe or kept cool on the sill — if you had a room with a window. If you craved hot coffee, after finishing your orange, bread, and jam you could step around to Sixth Avenue and for five cents the caffein craving was satisfied. The Olive Lunch on Sixth Avenue featured a filling bowl of pea soup, with three thick slices of bread and a large blob of good butter, all for ten cents. Next to the Union Dime Bank, there was a sprawled-out self-service restaurant that served liver and onions, rolls, butter, and coffee for fifteen cents.

The Montfort guest who found himself temporarily with no funds depended on Mr. Dickinson. Mr. Dickinson owned the saloon at the corner of Sixth Avenue, and his son was a member of a very successful musical act in vaudeville. Mr. Dickinson genuinely liked actors. As he welcomed them to his saloon, he would ask them if they knew his son and if they had met him on the road in recent weeks. The Montfort drinking group, when prosperous, patronized Mr. Dickinson's. If money was scarce, the regular patron was still welcome, and credit was extended until work set in. Mr. Dickinson never wanted any vaudeville actor to go hungry. When the chef had prepared the free lunch, and had set it steaming hot on the bar, Mr. Dickinson dispatched his bartender to the Montfort lobby to announce that lunch was ready and everybody was welcome. If an actor was hungry, he could stand by the free lunch until his pangs had subsided. If the actor couldn't buy a beer, nobody questioned him, and as he left, he didn't have to thank anybody. Mr. Dickinson understood. New York was the same as Boston. All an actor needed was a nickel to buy a beer, and the strength to walk up to the free lunch. At Mr. Dickinson's he didn't even need the nickel.

My optimism was tempered on occasions. The periods of unemployment suffered by some of the acts at the Montfort worried me; I often imagined myself in the same predicament. The Miller Brothers, three boys who did a club juggling act, didn't work for almost a year. They had permission to rehearse in the dining room. Every day at the same hour the boys came down from their rooms, carrying Indian clubs, large straw hats, and other paraphernalia, and disappeared into the dining room to run through their act for an hour or two. They wanted to be prepared if work should unexpectedly appear. Since Mrs. Montfort had abandoned her domain, the dining room had been unused, and Jimsy permitted the Miller Brothers, acrobats, singers, and dancers to use it for rehearsal purposes.

Down in the cellar, Mr. Lamont kept his cockatoos. Lamont's Performing Cockatoos and Macaws was a standard act for many years. One season, bookings were slow, and the bird act was without work for many months. Every day Mr. Lamont went down cellar to spend some time with his cockatoos and macaws. The birds stayed down in the cellar for so many months I was sure that eventually the cockatoos would start looking like owls. Only Mr. Lamont realized that the act was out of work. The birds didn't, and continued to eat as though things were normal. One of the lobby wits launched a rumor that he had caught Mr. Lamont taking a cockatoo up to his room to consume it. I maintained this report was a fabrication. In defense of Mr. Lamont I claimed that two of his cockatoos could talk and would certainly call the police if they suspected that Mr. Lamont was eating the act piecemeal. I also added that I had never seen Mr. Lamont at lunchtime spitting out feathers, nor had I ever smelled macaw on his breath.

I met a number of interesting guests at the Montfort. There was Twisto, the contortionist. There was "Broomstick" Elliot, the rube comedian who was the first musician to convert a broomstick into an instrument. One long steel string was pulled taut against the handle and, using a bow and playing his instrument viola style, "Broomstick" coaxed beautiful music from his kitchen Stradivarius, and stopped shows from coast to coast. There were the Four Banta Brothers, a musical act that specialized in brass and wind instruments. When the Banta Brothers rehearsed, blowing their bass saxophones in their room, the vibrations put permanent ripples in the wallpaper. And when the Texas Tommy Dancers ran through their violent dancing routines, chandeliers swung like tassels, and when the plaster stopped falling, it was impossible to tell the floor from the ceiling.

John Carbrey, a neighbor of mine at the Montfort, was one of the Carbrey Brothers, the first act to have two men dance in one suit. The Carbreys did a routine dancing act until their closing number. For their finish the brothers donned one large harlequin costume and, dancing close together, executed intricate steps with such precision it appeared that only one person, with two heads, was dancing. John Carbrey and I became very friendly and later roomed together. Paying four dollars each, we were able to give up our single caves with doors on them and move into a room that had a window. This was a relief, because the inside rooms, in addition to their lack of air, posed another problem. When the Montfort guest who lived in a windowless room got up in the morning, he had no way of knowing the state of the weather. One morning, dressed in his best suit, he would descend to the lobby to find that it was pouring rain outside. The next morning, clad in light garments, he would arrive in the lobby only to find that it was freezing out. The seasoned Montfort guest took no chances. He would step out of his inside room, clad in his robe or underwear, and shout down the stairs an inquiry about the weather. Jimsy, or anybody else in the lobby, would call up a weather report. Fortified with this atmospheric data, the guest returned to his inside room and dressed accordingly.

Eventually, the Montfort closed. On the final day, as the actors were parading out of the lobby with their belongings, I saw a guest I had never seen before. This man had a room on the top floor. His rent was two dollars a week. When he left, he owed eighty dollars. Somewhere along the line, this actor had not paid his rent for forty weeks. And he wasn't the only guest who was remiss. That was why the Montfort was closing.

John Carbrey and I moved to Mrs. Lowery's boarding-house, on Forty-eighth Street. The rooms were better, and the home-cooked food was good, but the fun we had had at the Montfort was missing. The boardinghouse was run by Mrs. Lowery, a Scottish lady, but the building was owned by a professional beggar. This man had no legs and moved around the house on his two stumps, using his hands to bounce him-self along from room to room. The actors called him "the Seal." The Seal had his begging business well organized. He toured the country to attend the state fairs, the outstanding sporting events, and whatever resorts were in season. The Seal would leave New York wearing a shabby suit. His bedraggled ap-pearance augmented his physical plight and enhanced his appeal to the passer-by as he rolled himself along, sitting atop a little board supported on castors. After a few weeks of concentrated begging, the Seal would return home to the boardinghouse to relax for a few days. The Seal's homecom-ings always called for a celebration. After their shows at night, the actors would gather in the kitchen, and the Seal would be lifted up and placed next to the sink to dominate the festivities as host. Drinks were passed around, stories were in order, and the jinks were high as the Seal regaled those as-sembled with accounts of his travels and experiences on the road.

The Seal liked actors and enjoyed being in their com-pany; perhaps this was because he was an actor himself, propelling himself through life in a very lucrative role. Some of these "Welcome Home" parties lasted for days, but pleas-ure never interfered with the host's profession. When the time came to leave for the Brockton Fair or the World's Series, the Seal sobered up, donned his shabby suit, mounted his little board, and wheeled himself away to business.

These events, however, took place long after I had checked in at the Montfort for my first day. My early days in New York were discouraging. After I had made my appearance at the Keeney Theatre in Brooklyn, I couldn't seem to get another date. My act went well with the Keeney audiences, but Mr. Jones booked no other theaters. I was sure that I wasn't blacklisted for playing the Keeney, because nobody knew my name or who I was. Finally I looked up the Telegraph Four, and Georgie Lane took me to their agent, Barney Myers. Barney was an important agent, and handled big acts. This was not so good for me. If Barney could book me for sixty dollars, his ten per cent commission would be six dollars; with less effort he could book a headline act for eight hundred and get eighty dollars for himself. Day after day I sat in Barney Myers's office hoping, and talking to other acts who seemed to be sitting there because they, too, had no place else to go. After days of waiting, Lou Edelman, a young boy who worked for Barney, booked me into a Masonic Club show on Twenty-third Street. My act went well at the club, but it didn't help. None of the bookers had seen me. The next day I was back sitting in Barney's office.

At the Montfort, Jimsy tried to help me. Jimsy could be important to an actor at the Montfort. On opening days, Mondays and Thursdays, if one of the smaller agents needed an act in a hurry to fill in at a smalltime vaudeville theater, he would phone the various boardinghouses and cheap hotels and ask the clerk if there was an act out of work on the premises. If an act was available, the clerk made the booking, okayed the salary, and notified the act. On Sundays, many of the theaters in New York and New Jersey booked eight or ten vaudeville acts, billing the shows "Sunday Concerts." Many acts who hadn't worked during the week rushed around to play two or three theaters on Sunday to make enough money to pay expenses. Every Sunday morning two or three calls for acts came into the Montfort. Jimsy took these calls, and when the agent asked who was available, Jimsy would look hurriedly through his books to see which act owed the most room rent. If the agent wanted a dancing act and Jimsy had a dancing set at the Montfort but also discovered that Twisto, the contortionist, owed more back rent than the dancing act, he would quickly answer that Twisto was the only act he could find. The agent, in no position to quibble, would book the contortionist. Jimsy would note the salary and instructions, if any; then he would hang up and bound up the stairs and down the hall. If you were trying to sleep on a Sunday morning, you would hear the banging on a nearby door and Jimsy yelling at the top of his voice, "Twisto! Twisto! Get up, you bum!" When a muffled voice from within the room would remonstrate about the disturbance, Jimsy would assail the door again and shout, "Twisto, get up, you bum! You're working at East Orange! Three shows! Rehearsal's at eleven o'clock! You're getting twenty-five dollars! And bring back fifteen dollars tonight to pay on your room rent! Get up!"

With this deal consummated, Jimsy would return to the lobby and his rolltop desk to await other artistic emergencies that could have a bearing on the improved financial status of a registered Montfort guest. Jimsy tried to book me several times, but despite Jimsy's oaths that my act was good, the bookers didn't know me, and refused to take a chance.

As each monotonous day repeated itself, I finally became discouraged. I had to send money to my Aunt Lizzie every week, and I knew that she would worry if she thought I was in trouble. One night, after not having worked since the Masonic Club show, I got a chance to help Eddie Vogt. Eddie lived at the Montfort and worked steadily. He was the front legs of a prop horse, part of an act called Fields and Lewis. The act opened with the horse dragging a hansom cab on stage. The driver of the cab descended from his seat and became embroiled in an argument with the gentleman riding in the cab. The horse reacted to the insults and threats of the two men. Fields and Lewis were a headline comedy act of that era, and Eddie Vogt was the act's property man and a segment of the horse. The night he asked me to help him, I joined him in the equine pelt. I appeared as the lumbar section. There was no money involved. I received no adulation. I was in a big act, appearing in a big theater in front of a large audience, but nobody knew I was there. After the show, I decided I might just as well have stayed in the horseskin. When I stepped out of it, nobody in New York knew I was there.

One Monday morning I decided to go home. I thought it over all day. My money was almost gone. With the forty dollars I had left behind at the Provident Savings Bank I could keep going until I got a job in Boston. About five in the afternoon, I left the Montfort to send a telegram to my friend Johnny Murphy, to ask him to send me my fare. As I turned from Fortieth Street into Broadway, walking towards the Western Union office, I heard somebody call my name. When I located the voice, I found it was emanating from Lou Edelman, the boy at Barney Myers's office. Lou was excited. Grabbing my arm, he said, "How long will it take you to get your juggling stuff?"

"About two minutes," I said.

"Great!" Lou said. "Get over to the Empire Theatre in Paterson, right away!"

When Lou calmed down, I learned that an act had been canceled after the matinee, and Lou had been sent to find any act to fill in for the night show. Lou told me in confidence that Mr. Clancy, the Poli circuit booker, had an interest in the Empire Theatre, and if everything went well, Lou was sure he could book me on the Poli time. Lou wished me luck, and went off. I flew back to the Montfort, packed my juggling equipment, and started for Paterson. For the time being, Western Union could wait.

# 8

# Mark Leddy, Agent

THE Empire Theatre in Paterson had a resident stock company which presented a new play each week; between the acts of the drama, there was vaudeville. The audience got its money's worth, but the innovation didn't make much sense. When I arrived on the first night, as I stood in the entrance I saw that the play was a tear jerker. The act I followed ended with a very emotional scene in which a daughter denounced her mother and left home. The mother slumped over and started sobbing. The curtain came down. I walked on the stage to start my comedy monologue and juggling. The audience was ready to laugh at anything, and I was a big success.

Mr. Clancy, the booker, saw my act under these favorable circumstances, and the result was that the following Monday I opened at the Palace Theatre in Hartford. The Palace was one of the theaters on the Poli circuit. Mr. Sylvester Z. Poli lived in New Haven and owned, operated, and booked vaudeville theaters in Bridgeport, Hartford, New Haven, Waterbury, Springfield, Worcester, Scranton, and Wilkes-Barre. In most of the New England cities, Mr. Poli operated two theaters: one big-time theater, and a smaller house playing family-time vaudeville. The big-time theaters played the highest salaried stars and gave two performances daily, at two-fifteen and eight-fifteen. The family-time theaters booked cheaper acts, showing them in conjunction with a feature picture and running a continuous policy. The family-time acts did three and four shows daily. The big-time audience was sophisticated and appreciated artistry and subtle types of entertainment. The family-time audience had a somewhat lower level of enjoyment and was impervious to subtlety. The family-time audience wanted its comedy rough and ready.

My salary on the Poli circuit was sixty dollars. As my agent's commission was ten per cent, this left me with a net weekly income of fifty-four dollars. Fares were small, living was cheap, and I was still able to send a few dollars home to my Aunt Lizzie. After playing three weeks on the Poli time I returned to New York with my optimism rejuvenated. Back in the Montfort, now living with John Carbrey and a window in the room, things appeared to be a lot brighter. One afternoon on Broadway I met Georgie Lane, who told me that the Telegraph Four had left Barney Myers and had acquired a new agent. This new agent had recently been working in the Loew office. Marcus Loew had built up a circuit operating more than twenty theaters, most of which were in New York City and Brooklyn. The theaters were all alike, playing a continuous policy of a feature picture and five acts of vaudeville. Hundreds of smalltime acts were required to supply the Loew theaters year in and year out. Now, since most of the Loew acts were represented by two agents, Frank Boehm and Irving Cooper, this left these agents with a monopoly on supply, and they were able to make heavy salary and other demands for their acts. To break up this control of the act market, Jack Goldberg, the Loew circuit booking manager, took five bright boys from his office and made them Loew agents. They were to go out and find new talent and develop acts for the Loew circuit. The Telegraph Four's new agent was one of these boys. His name was Mark Leddy, and Georgie Lane took me to meet him.

This meeting I have always felt was the turning point of my career. Mark Leddy, at the start, represented only five acts; he had ample time to concentrate on each act and keep it working. At the outset Mark told me that he liked my type of comedy, and he raised my salary from sixty dollars to seventy-five dollars in conversation. Then he booked me at two Fox theaters in Brooklyn to prove that he meant what he said. After two additional weeks in independent theaters, Mark booked me into the Academy of Music on Fourteenth Street.

The original Academy, long since demolished, was an enormous barn of a theater used for opera and concerts; in 1914 it was playing three-a-day vaudeville shows booked by the Fox office. The Academy stage was so large that, in order to adapt it to vaudeville, the musicians had to be taken out of the pit and placed on the stage. Another stage was built atop the original boards, and on this top layer the acts appeared. My first show there was a matinee, and I was second on the bill; the headliner, Maude Earle, was in the next-to-closing spot, trying out a new act. Miss Earle had new songs, new patter, new wardrobe, and new scenery. She was an important act, and the Loew and Keith bookers had promised her agent to come to the theater that night and appraise her new vehicle. After she had finished her second show, however, Miss Earle decided that her new act was not satisfactory, and informed the theater manager that she would not appear and face the bookers at the last show. It was too late to get another headline act. The manager called the Fox office, and finally obtained a sister act. At the night show, the sisters were put on second, in my spot, and the manager had no choice but to move me down the bill to Maude Earle's place. The

Keith and Loew bookers, who were aware that Miss Earle had canceled, still stayed through the entire show, and my act, appearing in the next-to-closing position, went unusually well. Mark came backstage to tell me that all of the bookers had liked the act, and the following week he booked me to start on the Loew circuit.

When an act was approved by the Loew bookers, it played the entire circuit, and when, on the following Monday, I rode out in the subway to the Fulton Theatre in Brooklyn, I knew that I would be working for many months to come.

I played three weeks in New York City itself, appearing in a number of different theaters, one memorable one being the Greeley. The Greeley Theatre was located in the garment district; its manager, wishing to stimulate business for the early show on opening day, advertised that the audience was welcome to come in at 9 A.M. and see the acts rehearse. The audience consisted of floaters and salesmen who wanted to rest for a couple of hours and who came into the theater and tucked their sample cases under their seats. As the audience sat in the theater watching, the actors arrived in the theater and walked out on the bare stage in their street clothes to rehearse music, songs, and dances with the orchestra leader, or to discuss the hanging of their scenery with the stage manager, or the handling of their props with the property man, or their spotlight cues with the motion-picture operator. When the acts had finished rehearsing, the motion-picture screen was lowered, and the feature picture started the show. If an actor spent too much time rehearsing his music, some of the impatient members of the audience responded audibly, and if an actor was foolish enough to answer the heckler, he had to accept the consequences: the moment he stepped onto the stage in the regular vaudeville show, he was greeted with the bird. The heckler didn't care whether the act was good or bad. He was mad at the actor because he had taken too much time at rehearsal.

Late in December, I returned to Boston to play the St. James and the Orpheum Theatres. I had left, three months before, a coast defender, and now I was coming home a New York actor. My Aunt Lizzie was surprised to see me looking so well; she had been sure that, having been an actor for three months, I was well on my way to that drunkard's grave. The Boston actors gave me a royal welcome back to Howard Street. LaToy borrowed some money from me, and told me secretly that he was about to abandon Boston and take New York by storm. My three aunts came to see my act at the Orpheum. When they saw me missing the juggling tricks and heard the people laughing at me, I'm sure they felt sorry for me. My act was never mentioned during the remainder of my stay at home. (I'm sure, too, that my Aunt Lizzie never did understand how I was able to make a living in the theater. Years later, when I was a big success at the Keith Theatre in Boston, I took her to the show one evening. Later I asked her how she liked it. She made no mention of my comedy. She said she did like Galetti's Baboons, and asked me how long I thought it had taken Mr. Galetti to train his monkeys. I know that she was convinced that one of my uncles, who worked in Cambridge, was funnier than I would ever be.)

My smalltime acquaintances treated me as a big shot while I was in Boston. But I didn't experience any feeling of accomplishment. I was still an unimportant act and my salary was small. I have always felt that success is a status a person enjoys only in the estimation of another. To me, progress meant steady work, the chance to give my Aunt Lizzie more money, and to appear in better theaters before smarter audiences, and the opportunity to learn and improve my act.

Under Mark Leddy's management I worked hard. Thus

far, my appearances had been confined to cities and towns in New York State and New England. I had never been west of Philadelphia. In September, 1915, Mark asked me if I would like to go to Australia. He said that he had been talking to a man who represented an Australian circuit. Some days later, at the Eighty-sixth Street Theatre — which, strangely enough, was situated on Eighty-sixth Street — a gentleman looking at me through bloodshot eyes stepped into my dressing room before a matinee. He introduced himself as Roy Murphy, representing the Fuller circuit, whose headquarters were in Sydney, Australia. He explained that he was booking talent for his circuit, that he was there to see my act, and that after the show he would return and tell me if I had any Australian potential. Mr. Murphy departed, and I finished putting on my make-up. The show started; I was fourth on an eight-act bill. At that particular matinee the audience outdid itself, and my act was a laughing success. Back in my dressing room I started to remove my make-up and await Mr. Murphy's return. The way my act had gone I knew he had to be impressed. I started to wonder if I should buy a cane to beat the kangaroos off the sidewalk as I walked down the Australian streets.

As I dressed, it seemed to me that Mr. Murphy was taking considerable time. I comforted myself by telling myself that he was sitting through the entire show to see the other acts. When the show was over and the audience had left the theater, however, there was still no Mr. Murphy. Just as I had given up and was ready to leave, Mr. Murphy appeared at my dressing-room door. He didn't seem too enthusiastic. I confronted him with the fact that my act had been a big hit. He said he really didn't know; when he had gone out into the theater it was dark, and the picture was on; he had dozed off, and had slept through the entire vaudeville show.

Three months later, long after I had forgotten Mr. Murphy and Australia, Mark booked me for a full week at McVicker's Theatre in Chicago. Here there were two headline acts. The first was Onaip, a man with a flying piano. Onaip was piano spelled backwards. The other headliner was Battling Nelson, the famous fighter. Nelson did an informal act, talking about his training methods, his fights, and his experiences. To finish his act the Battler punched the bag and boxed two rounds with a sparring partner. For some reason, Battling Nelson liked my act, and watched it every show. One night he called me into his dressing room and said that he was going to give me a big laugh for my act. He explained that he had trained many times in Chicago, and did his roadwork running through the streets wearing an old gray felt hat. A number of holes had been cut in this hat, and as the Battler jogged along, his blond hair stuck out through the holes. According to Nelson, everybody in Chicago knew this hat and his protruding hair. The big laugh, also according to Nelson, was going to materialize when I ran on the stage wearing Battling Nelson's old gray hat with my hair sticking through the holes. Brother Nelson promised to bring the hat to the theater the following day. I didn't know what to do. I was afraid to refuse his magnanimous gesture; to anger Battling Nelson could be fatal. I did the only thing a sane person could do under the circumstances: I kept my mouth shut. Battling Nelson was as good as his word. He produced the hat and for three days, before every show, he put his gray hat on me and pulled my hair through the holes. Four shows a day I ran on the stage without getting one solitary laugh. Battling Nelson may have heard laughter. They say some boxers who have had one fight too many sometimes hear strange things.

Battling Nelson had me so confused I paid no attention to a

note I received during the McVicker's week. The note came
from Mr. Benjamin Fuller, owner of the Fuller circuit in
Australia and Mr. Murphy's employer. Mr. Fuller — who was
later to be knighted and become Sir Benjamin Fuller — had
recently been married and had taken his bride on a honeymoon trip to America. Mr. Fuller was middle-aged, which
enabled him to make his honeymoon sort of a sideline; he
had ample time, during the day, to visit vaudeville theaters
and look for acts to book in Australia. Mr. Murphy must have
listed me as the "World's Worst Juggler" in one of his earlier
reports to the Sydney office; in any event, the note said that
Mr. Fuller had heard about me and was intrigued with the
"World's Worst Juggler" billing. Seeing me billed in Chicago,
he had come to see my act, which, he added, he had enjoyed.
I didn't meet Mr. Fuller personally, but late in the week a
telegram arrived from Mark, saying that he could book me
for sixteen weeks in the Fuller circuit. I would sail from San
Francisco in February. It was now December, and I was in
Chicago. I wired Mark that if he could book me in some
towns on the way to California, it was a deal. Mark had been
born in New York City and had never been west of Grant's
Tomb. Either he had no sense of direction or he had flunked
geography in school. After Chicago, Mark booked me in
Cleveland — as my first stop on the way to California. After
Cleveland, he arranged a week off — for me to travel to St. Joe,
Missouri. Following St. Joe, I was booked in Topeka, Wichita,
Tulsa, Oklahoma City, Dallas, and Shreveport, in that order.
Mark was getting me to California the hard way.

During my three days in Shreveport some friend of Mark's
who had been out of New York must have told him that I was
going in the wrong direction. A wire suddenly arrived advis-
ing me that Mark had booked me for the last half of the following week at the Victory Theatre, San Jose. At least San Jose

and San Francisco were in the same state. The wire also said that my boat tickets would be waiting at the Oceanic Steamship Company's office in San Francisco, and that if I brought my birth certificate the Oceanic office would arrange for my passport. I wired to my brother Bob in Boston asking him to obtain my birth certificate and mail it to the steamship office.

Up to now, I had been touring the country with two suitcases. A child could lift my entire worldly possessions, and I was now twenty-one years of age. All of the acts I had met on the road since leaving New York owned trunks. Instead of being burdened with bulky suitcases, they packed their clothes and other belongings in trunks which they checked on trains and shipped from town to town. Now that I was going to San Francisco, and then to Australia, it seemed to me that I would gain a measure of artistic stature if I was accompanied by a trunk. I discussed this move with a gentleman on the bill who owned a big musical act. The gentleman told me that he had an extra trunk that he would be glad to sell me; I crossed his palm with folding money and became the owner of a small Taylor trunk. The Taylor Company specialized in indestructible trunks for a circus and vaudeville clientele. Now that I had the trunk, it dawned on me there was just one thing wrong: I had nothing to pack in it. All I owned was contained in two suitcases. There was only one solution to my problem: I packed the two suitcases in the trunk.

The next morning the train left Shreveport. The trunk and I were on our way. It was a four-day trip to San Jose. As the train rattled along, it began to occur to me that I had all the ingredients available for a first-class predicament. Shreveport to Australia was a long trip. (As it turned out, eventually I went from Shreveport to Brisbane — a two-day train ride from Sydney. W. C. Fields always claimed that he held the record for making the longest jump known to show business: from Capetown, South Africa, to Syracuse, New York. I never pinned W.C. down, but my trip from Shreveport to Brisbane was no hop, skip, and a jump.) I knew that my Aunt Lizzie would worry while I was out of the country. I knew nothing about the audiences in Australia. After going that distance, supposing they didn't like my act? What would I do?

To make matters worse, as the train went west, the weather became hotter, and the Pullman car was stifling. One night, as I was lying nude in the lower berth to get some relief, I started to think about what I would do if I was lying in a sleeper and there was a train wreck. I decided that if I was in a lower berth I would roll out into the aisle and grasp anything solid that I could get my hands on. I had scarcely completed this plan in my mind when I felt the Pullman car bumping along as if it was off the track; I rolled out into the aisle and held on to the arm of the seat. The car careened along crazily, the lights went out, women started to scream, men began to shout, and then the car stopped abruptly, teetered, and tipped over on its side. The windows of my berth were resting on the ground. The glass had broken and the jagged edges had scooped up a mound of dirt that covered my bed. It was pitch dark, and I was standing nude in the berth with my head sticking up in the aisle. Women were calling for help which I, in my present unclad state, was in no condition to render. Two men were trapped in upper berths which had snapped partly closed when the car tipped over. When the shrieking died down, we heard voices outside the car, and a light appeared at the door: it was the engineer and some trainmen, wanting to know if anyone was hurt. In this flickering light I crouched down in the berth and managed to get some clothes on. After they had inspected the rest of the train, the trainmen returned with lanterns and helped the passengers out of our car; when I finally crawled out, I saw that the engine and the baggage car were still on the track, but that five of the Pullman cars were strewn along the roadbed on their sides.

Fortunately, the desert land was flat, the cars had fallen no great distance, and nobody was killed or seriously injured. The only passenger hurt was a man who had a broken leg in a cast. He was in one of the upper berths that had snapped shut; his cast had been cracked, and his leg had been broken again. It turned out that we were just a few miles outside of El Paso; we had nothing to do but sit around and wait for help to arrive. While we were waiting I took inventory of my wardrobe. My coat, shirt, underwear, stockings, and shoes were intact, but my trousers had been hanging over the little hammock at the window: the broken glass had sliced the seat in three different places. I now had a herringbone portcullis permanently lowered in the back. I confided my plight to one of the trainmen, who miraculously produced two safety pins. Hours later, the relief train arrived and we were all taken to El Paso; on the way, hot coffee was served and a railroad doctor prodded each passenger and, finding no bones broken, assured each person that he or she was "all right." Another train was assembled and shortly after noon, with two safety pins bringing up my rear, I left El Paso for California.

I arrived in San Jose Thursday morning, a day late. I was booked to play the last half of the week, however, and I was still on time. But when I located the Victory Theatre, I saw that my name was not billed with the acts currently playing. When the stage manager made his appearance, he told me that they had been looking for me on Wednesday, and when I hadn't reported, the manager had called the booker and gotten another act. In the East, the split weeks, as they were called, were split so that Monday, Tuesday, and Wednesday made the first half; the last half started on Thursday and the acts played through to Sunday night. But in California, I now learned, the "last half" shows started at the matinee on Wednesday. I was in the right town and at the right theater, but it was the wrong day. I explained to the theater manager that I had been in a train wreck. He said that he was sorry that I had lost the three days' work after my long trip and suggested that I stay over in San Jose, and he would let me work Sunday to make one day's salary to help pay part of my train fare. I accepted his offer, visited a tailor to have my trousers' incisions healed, did three shows on Sunday, and left San Jose for San Francisco on Monday morning.

San Francisco was a revelation to me. I had thought that every city west of Chicago was a Hackensack. San Francisco convinced me that I would have to revise my concept of Western metropolises. San Francisco looked to me like New York with a hill in the middle of it. The Barbary Coast was in full swing. Market Street was teeming with populace. The night clubs, cafés, saloons, theaters — all the happy havens — were thriving. After checking in at the Continental Hotel, a caravansary that catered to vaudeville actors, I visited the Oceanic Steamship Company's office. My boat ticket was ready, but my birth certificate had not arrived from Boston. It didn't seem important, and the clerk didn't mention it; he promised to forward all my mail to the Fuller circuit offices in Sydney. The steamship company supplied the transportation for all of the actors going to Australia, and it was a routine matter. The clerk informed me that the boat, the S.S. *Sierra*, sailed on Wednesday at noon.

The next day, Tuesday, I spent preparing for my trip. I bought two fifteen-dollar suits, an extra pair of shoes, some shirts, socks, ties, and underwear. I didn't know anything about Australia, and I wasn't taking any chances. Seeing a ventriloquial dummy in a window, I bought it. I had no use for it; a psychiatrist would probably have said I was lonesome. Back at the hotel I arranged to have my trunk picked up at the depot and delivered to the boat. As I was talking to one of the bellboys about directions to the pier, he volunteered the information that he was off duty the following day, and for five dollars he would help me carry my bundles and accompany me to the boat. The deal was made on the spot; I went to bed feeling that I was fully protected. I not only had a guide to lead me to the boat; I had a friend to see me off.

The next morning, as I paid my hotel bill, the bellboy was waiting for me in the lobby. Dividing the suit boxes and the packages, we left the hotel. When we arrived at the pier, we found the S.S. *Sierra* being stormed by a gay throng. A band was playing on deck. Passengers on board were holding animated conversations with friends who were on the dock. Stewards were rushing on and off the boat with wraps and luggage as new passengers appeared. Young girls on the pier were throwing streamers at other young girls who were aboard. Confetti suddenly filled the air. The bellboy put his packages down, and I paid him his five dollars. There were still fifteen minutes before sailing time. The tumult was accelerating. Last-minute flowers and packages were being delivered by frantic tradesmen and perspiring messengers, final words of advice and shouts of *"Bon voyage"* filled the air, and tears were shed. A puff of steam appeared from behind one of the funnels, quickly followed by a sharp blast; the time had come to go on board. I turned to say good-by to the bellboy. He had gone. Gathering up all my bundles and packages, I walked up the gangplank. Inquiring at the purser's desk, I found that my stateroom was in the second class. As I started down the stairs, the foghorn emitted a succession of throaty blasts, and by the time I found my stateroom the boat had started to move. The band was playing "Auld Lang Syne"; the air echoed with hysterical laughter as the final streamers and handfuls of confetti were tossed. If the bellboy had waited to shout "*Bon voyage*," all he would have seen of me would have been one frightened eye, gazing out of a small porthole in second class.

# 9

## The S.S. *Sierra*

THE S.S. *Sierra* was a ten-thousand-ton vessel. Today, lifeboats bigger than the *Sierra* are found on the *Queen Mary* and other luxury liners. In rough weather the *Sierra* was tossed up and down in a blanket of spray as though she were being hazed as part of her initiation into some briny sorority. In an angry sea the *Sierra* resembled a female housefly caught in a fizzing Alka Seltzer. She was in the middle of everything, but had no control over the situation.

My stateroom was a form-fitting gullhole (on a ship, a pigeonhole is a gullhole). As you squeezed into the room, on the right against the wall were two bunks, upper and lower. Jutting out between the bunks and the door there was a small sink, above which hung a tiny mirror and a rack that held a carafe of fresh water and two glasses. At the opposite end of the stateroom, for purposes of ventilation and lighting, there was a porthole. My ticket called for the lower bunk, but when the passenger who was to share the stateroom with me turned out to be an elderly gentleman, I insisted that he take my lower space. The old man remonstrated feebly, but I argued that I, being younger, was more agile and better equipped to bound up into the upper bunk. He consented.

I demonstrated my superior bounding ability on only one occasion. The first night out of San Francisco I bounded up into my upper quarters; for the next four days I just lay there, an inanimate lump — seasick. I not only couldn't keep any food down; my digestive apparatus got ahead of me: my stomach was rejecting meals I had hoped to eat the following week. My *mal de mer* didn't seem to bother my roommate. Oblivious to my moaning and retching, he slept soundly through the nights, left early every morning for breakfast, and spent his entire days on deck. When he returned late in the evenings, he washed, quaffed a final drink of water from one glass, and filled the second glass with water into which he submerged his false teeth. The second glass was my glass. After the old man had gone to bed, if my throat was parched and I was dying for a glass of water, I could look down and see my glass laughing up at me. To quench my thirst I had to upend the carafe. Later, the old man told me that he raised sheep in New Zealand and had made more than forty crossings to the States.

The day before we arrived in Honolulu, I was able to crawl out of the bunk and creep up on deck. The second-class passengers were confined to a small area amidships. A few deck chairs were placed around the boat's two funnels. There was no room to play deck games of any sort, although this didn't matter, since there were no games available to play. One small group of passengers, huddled together near the rail, I took to be actors. I didn't know any of them. But, since I hadn't eaten anything solid for four days, I must have had that half-starved look that people used to associate with the smalltime actor, for one of the huddled actors unhuddled himself, came over to me, and invited me to join the others.

I was instantly brought up to date with the ship's scuttle-butt. There were six acts going to Australia to play the Fuller circuit. There was Madge Maitland, the Megaphone Lady; Madge was an abbreviated woman who sang in a booming

voice through a large megaphone. There was Estelle Wor-
dette and Company, presenting their own original playlet,
*When the Cat's Away.* The Company consisted of a middle-
aged gentleman who smoked a potent pipe incessantly. There
were the Flemings, two muscular young men who did an
acrobatic act that consisted of Grecian posing and hand
balancing. Also present were the Littlejohns, the Diamond
Jugglers, a man and wife who wore costumes studded with
rhinestones, appeared before a black velvet curtain covered
with rhinestones, and juggled Indian clubs which were bedecked with rhinestones. And then there was Doranto, a
rather serious-looking elderly man who made up as a Chinese
and provoked discordant melodies from strange-looking Oriental instruments. Doranto billed himself the "Human Xylophone." At the finish of his act he made good his billing by
causing alleged melodies to emerge from his mouth as the result of spanking his false teeth with two short sticks while
manipulating his orifice. I was the sixth on the program.

There were five or six other acts on the boat going to
Australia, but they were booked to play the Tivoli circuit.
The Tivoli theaters were considered big time and imported
stars from England and America. The Tivoli paid much
higher salaries, but the acts only played three cities — Sydney, Melbourne, and Adelaide — and were guaranteed only
twelve weeks' work. The Fuller circuit, on the other hand,
booked vaudeville shows into every city of importance in
Australia, New Zealand, and Tasmania. Our salaries were
small, but we had sixteen or twenty weeks guaranteed, and
if an act did exceptionally well, it could work steadily on the
Fuller circuit for a year or more.

All of the American acts booked for Australia were furnished second-class transportation. In vaudeville, class distinction was invariably observed. The headliner on the bill

ignored the lesser acts, and the lesser acts in turn snubbed the acrobats or the people with animal acts. The Fuller acts on the *Sierra* were victims of this class distinction. After the boat had left San Francisco, the Tivoli acts discovered that they had to associate with the Fuller acts, who were also traveling second class. The Tivoli group promptly moved into first-class accommodations, paying the difference out of their own pockets. To get their money's worth during the trip, the Tivoli actors came to the rail at the rear of the first-class deck every day to look down at the Fuller acts in their restricted quarters. The Fuller acts were not above practicing a bit of snobbery themselves. They walked to the back of their second-class deck to look down on a few sorry-looking individuals who were traveling steerage. Who knows: the steerage passengers were probably sitting on their bare deck practicing class distinction by looking down at the porpoises because they weren't even on the boat.

Another band of scarred citizens going to Australia second class represented the boxing profession. It was headed by Jimmy Dine, a boxing manager from Newcastle, Pennsylvania, who was taking George Chip, a famous heavyweight of the day, and a stable of fighters to appear in Sydney. Chip was to fight Les Darcy, the Australian favorite.

Honolulu, as the *Sierra's* captain had hoped and the travel folder had promised, was there awaiting our arrival on the fifth day. As the boat crept into the harbor, a noisy school of natives swam out to greet us. After a hasty welcome in their native tongue, the natives got down to business in broken English, and demanded that the passengers throw money into the water. If the natives had known there were so many actors on board, they would have postponed their swim schedule for that day. A few first-class passengers tossed coins to watch the natives dive for them. The instant a coin struck the surface, the nearest native followed it down into the water, bobbing up a second later, laughing and showing the coin in his outstretched hand. During their diving exhibition the natives kept the coins they had salvaged in their mouths. As I watched this demonstration of aquatic panhandling for the first time, it seemed to me that a Hawaiian native with a big mouth and a little luck could make more money in a few days than any actor going to Australia to play the entire Fuller circuit.

In 1914, Honolulu's meager attractions were Waikiki Beach and a small colony of artists and writers. The only celebrity whose name was dropped during our six-hour stay there was Jack London. Today, the tourist is welcomed by the Honolulu Ukelele Philharmonic; he is entertained at gustatory rites known as *luaus;* and as he departs, the tourist's Adam's apple is nestled in a *lei* furnished by the Honolulu Chamber of Commerce and buxom native girls gather at the plane or boat to dance and sing "Aloha." In 1914, nobody in Honolulu knew what a tourist was. Walking down the main street, if you had clothes on, you knew you belonged on the boat that was in the harbor; if you had no clothes on, you were a native. Today, the natives who swim out to meet the boats are the unemployed and the riffraff. In 1914 when the natives swam out, among them you saw some of the best people in town. When our boat, the *Sierra,* left Honolulu, the natives swam out again to see us off and dive for a few final coins. Today, they do not bother to swim along with the departing boats. The natives know that by the time the tourist leaves Honolulu he has no money left to throw.

Pago Pago was a six-day trip from Honolulu. The seasick interlude had left me weak. I was better, but my stomach still felt as though it had slipped its mooring. One morning I fell asleep in a deck chair, and one side of my face was terribly sunburned. After it had blistered and peeled I looked like a portrait of myself done by a colorblind artist. The peeled side of my face had a covering of new rosy skin; the epidermis on the other side looked dirty. Traveling with us second class was a missionary, an exponent of some vague denomination, and with him was his daughter. The missionary was on his way to the Samoan Islands, where he planned to teach the natives what they were doing wrong. Meantime, he was not averse to having an impromptu tussle with Satan on the way. His daughter was quite pleasant, but the missionary shunned his fellow passengers as if he had caught them throwing stones at a belfry. The first time the missionary saw my face with the two-tone effect he went into action. I was summoned to the captain's quarters, and when I arrived the ship's doctor was present. The captain told me that the missionary had reported that a leper, or a man with a serious social disease, was rampant in the second class. I explained my semiraw appearance. The doctor examined my face and corroborated my story. The captain apologized. There was nothing I could do to the missionary. I knew his daughter was sleeping with one of the acrobats, and I thought about suggesting a title for a future sermon: "Look Around, Brother: Sin as well as Charity Often Begins at Home." I didn't, though. I merely turned the other cheek — the one that hadn't been sunburned.

On a long boat trip, the days seem like the waves, each one alike. The *Sierra* turned into the S.S. *Monotony*, doing the same number of knots per hour, hour after hour. At first, the boxers with their training routines, bag punching, rope skipping, and boxing provided some diversion, but this soon lost its novelty. Traveling second class, it was impossible to enjoy any privacy. Our deck space was small. Lying on a deck chair you heard everyone's conversation. This was no relief. At meals there were two sittings, with the diners squeezed together at one long table, passing the meat, bread, butter, and side dishes along to each other. Below deck there was a small lounge in which an eternal card game was in progress. If you went to your stateroom, you had either to stand up by your bunk or lie down in it. There was no room to accommodate any other plan you had in mind that involved movement. Any diversion to relieve the irksome redundancy of existence was welcome. On the day that word swept the *Sierra* that we would pass another boat at two in the morning, every passenger stayed up to enjoy the sight. The boat passed us miles away. The night was dark, we saw no people, we couldn't see the name of the boat. All we saw were the lights gliding by in the distance and finally disappearing into the blackness of the night. Our passengers felt well repaid for the hours they had spent sitting and silently staring at the horizon. They retired happily, chattering about the experience, guessing the type of boat whose lights they had seen, the sort of passengers on it, and the boat's eventual destination. The important thing was that the monotony had been broken. The night before we arrived in Pago Pago many of the passengers stayed up all night. They couldn't wait to see land again.

Pago Pago, an island in the Samoan group, was then an American coaling station. The arrival of the *Sierra* was an island event. The natives lined the dock, exhibiting their handicraft to the passengers as they left the boat. Tropical fruits, trinkets for souvenirs, crude plaited straw hats, toy birchbark canoes, and miniatures carved from island woods were lying along the dock to tempt the tourist. Native men and women hawked their wares in broken English and in their tribal tongue. As Max Fleming, one of the acrobats, and I came down the gangplank, a kindly-looking old native, wearing a loincloth and a tattered white shirt that some tourist must have given him months before, rushed up to us muttering one word over and over again and pointing to the hills. The native walked along the dock with us, still repeating the same word. Finally, Max said, "I think the old guy is trying to say 'girls.'" At the word "girls" the native smiled and pointed to the hills. Max and I nodded, and answered, "Girls," together. The old man nodded back and said, "Flends?" Max decided that this meant friends, and the native wanted us to augment our party. We rounded up three of the boxers and two of the other fellows from the ship. The old man looked us over approvingly, muttered his version of "girls" again, pointed to the hills, and started off down a dirt road.

After we had gone about a half mile, the old man stopped before a path that led up a hill. When we had all caught up to him, the old man started up the path with the seven of us tagging along, single file. We zigzagged up through the thick foliage for fifteen or twenty minutes until we came to a clearing in which we saw a cluster of crude huts. It was obviously a small village, but its inhabitants were not in sight. The old man led us to what appeared to be a meeting hut. A wooden floor covered the ground. A thatched roof shaded the floor from the sun, but the hut had no walls. Anyone in the hut could be seen by any native in the vicinity. The old man motioned us to sit down. After he had arranged us all in a large circle, the old man beamed knowingly, muttered "Girls" again, and added four more words to what had been, up to now, his one-word vocabulary. The new words were "flifty cents" and "half clown." His "half-clown" rate was for patrons coming back from Australia with English money. We all handed over fifty cents apiece; the old man clinked the silver in his hands, smiled, muttered "Girls," and trotted out of the hut. In no time at all he was back again, followed by five big-breasted and Percheron-buttocked native women. The old man smiled all around, muttered "Girls" again, and then sat on the floor, joining us. The "girls" lumbered into place. The old man started to pound the floor with both hands and to chant an eerie refrain; the "girls" began some primitive form of mambo. The elephantine gyrations of these village housewives, the slapping of their massive feet on the wooden floor, the perspiration cascading down their fatty parts, and their droning *a cappella* to amplify the old man's bleating could arouse only one desire in a male: the desire to flee. But there was no escape. The provocative cavorting had to run its course. We were sitting there, cross-legged, watching these Swamp Rockettes for nearly an hour before the old man stopped bongoing the floor and dismissed the thundering ensemble. The "girls" giggled as they rumbled by us on their way out of the hut. The old man, still smiling, beckoned us to follow him as he started back down the path to the boat. On the way we were caught in a tropical rainstorm and got soaked to our collective skin. I am sure that if the missionary later ran afoul of the old man and his sinful racket, the old man's hut was closed, the native women were saved, and tourists walking down the gangplank at Pago Pago in later years were never accosted by the smiling jungle Minsky muttering "Girls."

Fortunately, this escapade consumed most of our time in Pago Pago.

When the distant Australian coast line came into view, it was a welcome sight. After spending twenty-one days cooped up with the same people in the confining second-class space, I understood how one Siamese twin often had a desire to get away some place by himself. The boat was all abustle as the passengers collected their baggage and assembled on the main deck, eager to land and explore the new country. I had donned one of my new fifteen-dollar suits, a three-piece gray shepherd-plaid ensemble. According to San Francisco dictates, I was dressed in the height of style: narrow trousers, double-breasted vest, and a coat pinched in at the waist that gave the lower part a skirted effect; my shoes were patent leather with gray cloth tops and white pearl buttons. To crown this I wore a large leghorn hat with the brim turned down in front and in back. Max Fleming and I stood by the rail watching the passengers crowd down the gangplank. Max was also an example of what the well-dressed American vaudeville actor was wearing. As we stood contemplating the exodus, we heard someone laughing. Looking down, we saw three Australian stevedores on the dock looking up, and discovered that they were laughing at us. Our clothes seemed funny to them. Their clothes, with the sloppy-looking suits and the pen-wiper caps they had on, seemed funny to us. Max and I started laughing at them. Their clothes must have been funnier than ours; Max and I were so busy laughing that we walked down the gangplank right past the official who was checking the passengers' credentials. It wasn't intentional, but it was perhaps fortunate, for I had neither birth certificate nor passport. It didn't seem too important at the time, since the steamship-company agent in San Francisco had promised to forward them to me in the mail, so I knew that eventually they would arrive. Meantime, Max and I, still laughing, were met by the representative of the Fuller circuit, who rounded up all the Fuller acts and took us and our baggage into Sydney.

# 10

## Australian Comedy

AFTER we had gone through customs, the Fuller man told us all to report at the office in the National Theatre Building for our assignments. Comedy talking acts posed an immediate problem. An audience in any country will laugh at the things it understands. But when American comedians first went to England, some of our biggest vaudeville stars were dismal failures, and many English stars were poorly received on their first appearance in America. The subject matter for songs, the implements with which the people are familiar, the sports they enjoy, the local celebrities, the current slang, all can be burlesqued or treated in many hilarious ways by the comedian. But woe betide the English monologist who attempts a comedy cricket-match routine before a New York audience, or the American monologist who essays a humorous baseball routine in London. When American acts arrived in Australia, they made their first appearance at the National Theatre in Sydney, where Mr. Fuller and his booker, Mr. Douglas, reviewed them and made any suggestions which they felt would help the acts during their Australian stay. After this, they then planned the future bookings.

When our contingent arrived at the Fuller office, all the other acts were immediately booked into the National Theatre to open the following Saturday. Mr. Douglas told me, however, that since Mr. Fuller had seen me in Chicago and had booked me personally, I would not have to show my act. I was to open on Saturday in Brisbane. My trunk was now being sent to the depot, he said, and the following morning I was to report at the office to pick up my tickets and to meet an Australian actor who was also booked in Brisbane and would accompany me on the trip.

The next morning I was introduced to my companion on the trip: Frank Herberte, billed as the "Descriptive Vocalist." In America he would have been called a singer of illustrated songs. Frank's act consisted of singing three songs. During his rendition, colored slides were thrown on a white sheet depicting the song's locale (Normandy, Erin Isle, sunny Italy) or the people involved in the lyrics (Mary, Sweetheart, Dear Old Mother of Mine), and the words of the chorus were also shown to enable the audience to sing and drown out the voice of the artist they had paid to hear. There were many Australian singers of Frank's type. Men and women roamed the Fuller circuit being paid weekly salaries that ran the gamut from three to four pounds (roughly fifteen to twenty dollars). These small acts eked out a meager living, staying in each city two or three months, changing their acts every two weeks, living in cheap boardinghouses or with friends, and economizing in every possible way. They survived only because Fuller required so many acts to service his theaters that he booked the inexpensive acts steadily, fifty-two weeks a year. The smalltime actor whose talent was limited or nonexistent had no future in Australia. The act might spend a few months in an alleged musical revue or a pantomime, playing the same Fuller theaters in the same cities and towns in Australia and New Zealand, but eventually the actor returned to his unimportant act and made the rounds again. In Australia, a Fuller act rarely rose to the rarefied heights of the Tivoli circuit.

Frank was given our two tickets to Brisbane and his instructions, and we left for the depot. I was carrying one suitcase; Frank had a large woolen blanket, rolled up and carried by a strap, and two cardboard boxes. At the baggage counter Frank checked my trunk and his hamper. Most Australian acts carried wicker hampers instead of trunks. The trunks were more expensive, and the theatrical baggage was not exposed to the abuse it received in the States. The Australian trains, like those in Europe, came in level with the station platforms. Unlike our baggagemen who, if a truck was not handy, dumped the actor's trunk out of the baggage car to bounce on the cement platform, the Australian baggagemen slid the actor's hamper gently out onto the platform.

The trip to Brisbane was to take two days and one night. I asked Frank about sleepers; he said it was a waste of money. In Australia, he said, the vaudeville actors never traveled in sleepers. Also, according to Frank, they never patronized the dining cars. The Australian actors had a system. I was not to worry. Frank was going to take care of everything. I would be all right. As the train sped along I asked Frank about the Fuller circuit, what the cities and theaters were like, and how the Australian actors liked the Americans. Frank wanted to know about America, the vaudeville actors' salaries, and their opportunities. Later, in the afternoon, Frank told me that we were going to have tea. The train slowed down and stopped at a small station. Frank flew out the door with me in tow and headed for a tiny refreshment counter. Everybody in the train had the same idea: car doors banged open, and passengers came running from all directions. In no time we were surrounded. Frank knew the routine. The counter was lined with steaming hot cups of tea and plates which were piled high with scones and frosted cakes. With Frank running the offense, we emerged from the surging swarm each carrying one cup of tea, one scone, and one set of cakes. The train stopped for ten minutes to observe the traditional tea ritual. At the precise moment the commotion had reached its peak, the engine whistle blew abruptly, cups and plates were noisily returned to the counter, the rabble siphoned itself from the platform back into the train, car doors were slammed, the train started, and Frank and I were once more on our way.

A few hours later, Frank said he thought he would have dinner. He opened the two cardboard boxes he had been carrying and started wolfing some sandwiches. I thought he was eating fast because he was afraid that I was going to ask him for some food, so I suggested that I have dinner in the dining car. Frank wouldn't hear of it. He was bolting his food, it appeared, only to accommodate me. At the next stop, while I enjoyed my dinner, Frank was going to join me in a cup of tea. When the train stopped, Frank dropped his boxes and darted out the door. I was on his heels. Again the car doors burst open, and by the time we had reached the counter, it looked as though a posse had overtaken us. Frank came through again and we each escaped, Frank with one cup of tea, I with one cup of tea, two pork pies, and a sweet. The pork pies were ninety per cent pie, nine per cent potato, and one per cent pork. When the pork pies arrived in my stomach, they felt like book ends. The engine whistle blew again, the passengers stampeded back into their cars, and the train started off into the night.

Frank and I eventually exhausted our conversational subject matter. We were strangers, and had been talking for seven or eight hours. Only two actors or two politicians could talk that long without having too much in common. Frank announced that he was going to sleep. He took off his coat and shoes, unrolled his blanket, wrapped himself up until he looked like a woolen King Tut, said good night, and slid down in his seat and closed his eyes. I had no blanket. It was too late to try to get a sleeper. It was dark and it was getting cold. I did the only two things I could do: I cursed Frank and sat shivering all through the night. When the sun came up, Frank awakened and got busy. He rolled up his blanket, put his shoes back on, and told me to prepare for breakfast. A few minutes later the train stopped, and Frank and I emerged from the scramble with two cups of tea and a brace of scones. As the day wore on, every time the train slowed up I made ready to follow Frank. I was so full of tea the letter "S" and I had something in common: every time we turned around, there was tea. Late in the afternoon Frank told me to get my things together; in a few minutes our journey would be ended.

Brisbane was the capital of Queensland. The population was three hundred thousand. The climate was hot and the city had no sewerage. Frank took me to the Menzies Hotel, an old wooden building that looked as if it had been defying time and the elements for eons. Inside, the hotel seemed bare, as if an auction had been held and the only pieces of furniture left were those that had been ignored in the bidding. The Menzies also had outdoor rest-room facilities. As the guest checked in, he was taken to the rear of the hotel, and there he had the privy pointed out to him. As the Menzies guest entered his room, he was given instructions that explained the presence of a candle which, with a few matches, he found on his dresser. This was his emergency kit. If, in the middle of the night, the guest was summoned by a call from nature, he arose from his bed and felt around until he had located the matches. Lighting the candle, he hurried through the hall and down the stairs, holding the candle in one hand and shielding the flickering flame with the other. When he reached the back door and stepped nimbly out into the night, a playful gust of wind sometimes snuffed out his candle; when this happened, the guest found himself standing in a strange yard in total darkness.

The Empire Theatre in Brisbane was a large garish-looking wooden edifice whose architectural design had been considered impressive in another era. It could have been any one of a hundred opera houses that posed as cultural traps in the small American towns. The Empire played a ten-act bill of smalltime vaudeville. The reserved seats were three shillings (seventy cents). The other seats ranged from one shilling to two shillings sixpence. The imported acts, whose salaries were higher, played two weeks at the Empire. The Australian acts, and some of the smaller acts from England, occasionally played two or three months.

As an American act, I was automaticaly a headliner; my salary was nineteen pounds ($92.34). Since the different acts varied in the length of their stay in Brisbane, the Empire never had a completely new show. Three or four acts came in every other week as three or four acts finished their engagement; the other acts remained the same. The audiences apparently enjoyed seeing some of the same acts they had seen the previous week. If a theatergoer was impressed by one particular act, he would come to the theater, buy a ticket, ascertain the exact time the act went on, go into the theater as his favorite walked on the stage, sit through the act, and the minute the actor finished taking his bows, the theatergoer reached for his hat, left the theater, and went home. Like most of the Australian theaters, the Empire gave eight shows weekly: one show at night, matinees on Wednesday and Saturday. The Empire's new acts opened at the Saturday matinee. Prostitution must have been legal in Australia at that time; in any case, at every opening matinee the girls from the brothel were permitted to occupy a box. If the girls were impressed by a male actor, he received a fan letter inviting him to visit the girls during his stay in Brisbane. I received no letter.

Saturday, before the opening show, my nerves started to heckle me. Outside the theater, I had seen my billing:

> Personally Booked in U.S.A. by Ben Fuller
> Special Starring Engagement and
> First Appearance of
> FREDDY JAMES
> The World's Worst Juggler

At this matinee, five new attractions were opening: two Australian acts and three American. Besides myself, the Americans were Billinger and Reynolds, a husband and wife wire-walking specialty, and Alf Holt, billed as the "Amazing Animal Mimic and Imitator." I had never heard of either of these acts, and they had never heard of me. Frank Herberte was on the bill, but Frank had delivered me to the Menzies Hotel and shown me the location of the theater: his responsibility had ended there. I had nobody to turn to as a wailing wall. I worried through the Saturday matinee and night shows. I am sure my billing as the "World's Worst Juggler" confused some of the people. If they were regular Empire patrons, they had seen plenty of bad acts, but they had never before seen an act being bad on purpose. Some of my jokes didn't make much sense to the Australian audience, but I did some fairly good ball-juggling routines, and at the finish of my act I had a variety of hat tricks that evoked applause. Monday, when the newspaper reviews came out, one paper said:

> Freddy James, billed as the "World's Worst Juggler," was the laughing hit of the Empire program on Saturday. James is a bright humorist, who juggles joyfully, if not skilfully.

His drolleries tickled everyone who saw him. The possessor
of a quaint and original style, James knows just what to say
in the right place and, what is more, when to stop talking.
Give us more front cloth acts of the same calibre, please, Mr.
Fuller.

Another paper said:

Freddy James presented a turn as funny as it was clever.
All the time he is revealing the art of how not to do juggling
tricks, he keeps up a flow of lively patter, embracing pointed
and humorous remarks which never fail to catch on. Freddy
is evidently in a class of his own.

The reviews and the audiences' reactions were an antidote
for my fears. I felt that with a few more shows, and by replacing the jokes that weren't understood, I would have no
artistic worries for the balance of my Australian tour. There
were other hazards, however, that I hadn't anticipated. The
food at the hotel was heavy. For breakfast, the guest had the
choice of mutton, steak, or kidneys, each meat dish with or
without fried eggs; there was also toast, marmalade, and tea.
At lunch and dinner there was always mutton or steak, together with potatoes and vegetables that invariably looked
as though they had resented being cooked, and hadn't
cooperated in the process.

Perhaps it was the heat, the food, or the drinking water, but
whatever it was, one morning I awakened terribly ill. I had
chills, every bone in my body ached, and for good measure
I had a fever and dysentery. The hotel manager summoned a
doctor. The doctor diagnosed my multiple symptoms as
dengue fever. Dengue is a form of malaria multiplied by
seven. The doctor gave me some medicine and predicted that
the dengue would run its course. When the dysentery was
running its course, I was running with it. For the next few
days I spent most of my time, with and without my candle,

in the yard back of the hotel. At night I dragged myself over to the theater, did my act as best I could, and dragged myself back to the hotel and my bed.

There is no living creature more forlorn, more desolate, and more pitiful than a vaudeville actor who is sick in a strange city. The actor is an alien in the community. He knows the theater, the boardinghouse or hotel at which he lives, and the restaurants where he eats. The actor does his act at the theater. When the show is over, the people in the audience leave the theater in a happy mood to rejoin their families at home or their friends elsewhere. When the show that he has helped to make is over, the actor goes alone to a restaurant for a midnight snack, or else to his hotel room. He gets to know only the other actors who, like himself, are playing the same city for three days, or a week at most. The actor when well, has little opportunity to know the city or participate in its civic or social life. When sick, he jousts with his germs in a lonely hotel room, ministered to by two strangers, the local doctor and a hotel bellboy. I was in Brisbane, and the hotel had no bellboy.

After a week of torture and agony, I stopped shaking and aching, and became a reasonable facsimile of myself. Since I was doing only one show a day, I had a great deal of time to myself. Back home, playing the smalltime and doing three or four shows daily, there was never time to do anything. In Brisbane, now that I was better, there was time to do everything, but there was nothing to do. After a short walk one morning I exhausted Brisbane's points of interest. With ample time at my disposal, I took up the hobby I had put down when I left the Boston Public Library: I started to read. I realized that I had a lot to learn about comedy. To study the methods two famous authors had used in developing characters and comedy situations, I started reading Dickens and Mark Twain. During the eleven months I worked in Australia and New Zealand, I spent all my spare time reading. I went through Shakespeare, Artemus Ward, Bill Nye, Eli Perkins, Josh Billings, and the works of all the current British and American humorists. All the English humor magazines were new to me. I discovered *Punch, Tit-bits, London Opinion, Answers, Pearson's Weekly*, and the others. I bought every joke book I could find in the different cities and started a collection of jokes and stories that I thought were funny. When I had an original idea I wrote it down and filed it away.

As my collection grew, and as I knew more jokes, I was able to write new versions of old jokes to use in my act. I learned that any joke or story can be told in many forms. There is the old joke about the policeman who found the dead horse on Kosciusko Street. He took out a notebook to write his report. The policeman couldn't spell Kosciusko Street. He had to drag the horse over to Third Avenue. This same story is told about the businessman in the Western Union office about to send his partner a telegram to meet him in Schenectady. The businessman can't spell Schenectady. He sends his partner a wire to meet him in Troy. Or the mother who sends her little boy to school with a note saying that the boy has been absent because his sister has smallpox. The teacher is horrified. She calls up the mother and berates her for sending the little boy to school to contaminate the other pupils. The mother explains that the sister really has pneumonia. She couldn't spell pneumonia, so she wrote smallpox. A final version deals with the boy who is sent to the store to charge a pound of tapioca. The grocer couldn't spell tapioca. He sent the boy home with a pound of rice.

This interest in jokes and comedy led to my first desire to write. My early efforts were crude. My High School of Commerce education hadn't prepared me to weld nouns and verbs together in acceptable literary patterns. I have always had a great respect for writers, and even today I stand in awe of the person who can clothe his thoughts in words. Before I left Brisbane I resolved that, with the time I had to study as I played the Fuller circuit, I would try to improve my act, my jokes, and my writing.

From Brisbane I returned to Sydney to open at the National Theatre. Frank Herberte stayed on at the Empire, and I made the trip back alone. I didn't have to worry about sleeping with no blanket and devouring pork pies, for the return trip was made by boat. Boat travel was cheaper than train, and Mr. Fuller's booker didn't care how he spent an actor's time. Many of the theaters on his circuit were not owned by Mr. Fuller. These theaters he supplied with vaudeville shows under some arrangement which, among other things, obligated the theaters to pay the transportation of the acts booked into their cities. If an act closed in Sydney and played the following week in Brisbane, the Brisbane manager had to pay the act's fare from Sydney. Single acts invariably had to make the longest jumps, for one act on a vaudeville bill took up approximately the same amount of time as any other act. Therefore a manager would turn down a quartet, which meant four fares for him to pay, and book a single, which meant only the cost of one ticket.

Because of this arrangement, when I finished my engagement in Sydney I made a tour that no Rand, McNally field man ever made. My first stop was Newcastle. Following Newcastle, I played at Ballarat, Melbourne, Footscray, Geelong, Adelaide, Perth, Freemantle, and then over to New Zealand for appearances at Auckland, Wellington, Christchurch, and Dunedin.

At this time Australia was in the war and the government had taken all the larger coastal boats to transport troops.

The remaining boats in service were floating relics that were buffeted from port to port. One famous tub was the S.S. *Dimboola*. Actors had made the *Dimboola* a target of ridicule, and the mere mention of its name in any theater sent audiences into gales of laughter. The *Dimboola* in its normal position seemed to be lying on its side. When passengers and cargo were loaded, it tipped over on the other side. There were two sides to the *Dimboola*, but they were never in the water at the same time. The S.S. *Dimboola* sailed from Albany, the port nearest to Adelaide, to Perth, West Australia, across the great Australian "Bight." The "Bight" was reputed to be one of the roughest bodies of water in the world, and as the *Dimboola's* unsavory reputation grew, many actors became seasick if they heard the boat's name in conversation. I made one trip in the *Dimboola* with three other actors. We had one stateroom containing four bunks. Before the *Dimboola* could even unfasten itself from the dock, we had scrambled into our bunks, and the four of us stayed in bed for the five days it took the boat to get us back from Perth to Albany. We ate three meals a day, played cards, told stories, and slept to kill the time. The boat rolled and tossed through the "Bight," pitching in the water day and night like a mammoth whale with insomnia. The *Dimboola's* captain and crew walked at a permanent slant. Even when in port the captain looked as though he were leaning against something that one could not see.

The *Dimboola* started me on the longest jaunt I was to make on my Fuller circuit tour. I finished playing at Freemantle, West Australia; my next date was Auckland, New Zealand. It took the *Dimboola* five days to roll from Perth to Adelaide. From Adelaide to Sydney was a three-day train trip. Train travel in Australia in those days was annoying. Australia was divided into five states: New South Wales,

Victoria, South Australia, Queensland, and West Australia. The railroad in each state had a different track gauge. Going from one state to another, the passengers had to change trains at the state line. After two changes of train from Adelaide I arrived in Sydney, took the boat, and sailed five more days to Wellington; from Wellington to Auckland was overnight by train. I had traveled two weeks to play two weeks at Auckland. It wasn't very profitable. My fares and meals were paid, but I got no salary while in transit; I was just an unemployed actor going from billow to billow. After I had made another two-week trip from Dunedin, New Zealand, back to Adelaide, I bought a sailor's hat. The next time I passed through Sydney I reported to Mr. Fuller's office and asked him if he had brought me over from America to be an actor or a sailor.

On the road, playing the different towns and cities in Australia, I lived at the pubs and digs patronized by the Australian acts. I enjoyed living where the Australian acts lived. After my candle experience during my dengue period in the Menzies Hotel back yard, I could step out into any strange yard at midnight with confidence, my candle aglow, face into a forty-mile gale and arrive at the privy as cool as an altar boy, my flame intact. After making successful appearances in back yards from Geelong to Dunedin, I did come a nocturnal cropper in Melbourne. During the Melbourne Cup season, I arrived to play a return engagement at the Bijou Theatre. The hotels and rooming houses were jammed. An Australian friend of mine took me to a house in one of the suburbs where the lady of the house had a room to rent in the attic. The room had no window; a glass skylight supplied both light and air. After the rent had been paid in advance, the lady gave me a key to the front door, and then took me through several rooms and down two flights of stairs to acquaint me with the topography of her back yard. My friend was waiting, and I guess I didn't pay too much attention. I rushed away and spent the entire day in Melbourne. When I came back at midnight, I located the house all right, and when I got inside I found my room in the attic. As I started to undress, nature nudged me. I lit my candle and started for the yard. I didn't remember anything about the interior of the house. Every room I opened possessed an occupant who was busy snoring. Everybody in the house was asleep. After I had tried every door without finding a room that led to the yard, I gave up and returned to the attic. Nature, however, had not given up hope; there was only one solution. Opening up the skylight, I placed a chair on a table and stepped out onto the roof. A short time later, I re-entered the skylight, returned the chair and table to their original positions, and went to bed. Down through the years I have carried a picture in my mind of some nameless Melbourne roofer sitting in a pub, repeating the story of the unusual bird that stopped one night on a roof in that suburb and was never heard of again.

My favorite hotel was Jock Richardson's Prince of Wales, in Adelaide. The single rate was one guinea (five dollars) a week for room and board. The rooms were comfortable, the food was excellent, and Jock was the perfect Boniface. In Auckland, there was a boardinghouse that catered to actors and was owned by a Mr. McIntosh. The food was sent up from the kitchen to the dining room on a dumb-waiter. When Mr. McIntosh came in to dinner and ordered, the waitress put her head into the dumb-waiter shaft and shouted, "One mutton! It's for Mr. McIntosh!" An order of mutton came up twice the size of the orders the actors were getting. At Newcastle, a Mr. Dougherty turned his home into a boardinghouse for actors. Mr. Dougherty owned and drove a lorry. In America his lorry would have been called a dump cart. An act booked at Newcastle wrote Mr. Dougherty for accommodations. Mr. Dougherty met the act at the train with his dump cart, loaded the actor's hamper and the actor into the cart, and drove them to the Dougherty home. My entrance into Newcastle was made riding up the main street sitting behind Mr. Dougherty in his dump vehicle with my trunk sliding from side to side in the back.

On my first night at Dougherty's I went to bed early, right after the show; the other actors stayed up to play cards. I had been asleep for some time when I suddenly awoke with a start. I was being raised up in bed, along with the mattress. Somebody was under my bed. I yelled through the bedclothes, demanding the identity of the intruder. A muffled voice replied; I recognized it as belonging to one of the actors on the bill. He explained that he and the others had been playing poker, and that at a crucial moment the lights had gone out. Somebody discovered that the gas meter was under my bed. The meter accepted only one shilling at a time. The gas had no consideration for the guests; like an old alley cat, it went out at all hours. During my two weeks at Dougherty's the interruption became a nightly routine. In the middle of a sound sleep the mattress and I would be jacked up. Replying to my mumbled inquiry, a voice would answer, "Sorry, mate!" A shilling would clink in the meter, a body would pry itself out from under the bed, the mattress and I would plop down abruptly, and I would return to sleep.

In the course of time, I got to know many of the smalltime Australian acts quite well. At first, they didn't look like actors to me. In America, you could tell a smalltimer and his wife two blocks away. The wife would be wearing too much makeup; she would be slinking along in some flashy ensemble, a ratty fur piece dripping off one shoulder; and she would be carrying a cheap oversized pocketbook of gaudy hue. The male smalltimer usually wore a derby hat cocked on one side of his head, a checkered suit, white socks, and low-cut black patent-leather shoes. If he was doing well, the male sported a cane and wore a dirty-colored diamond horseshoe pin in his red tie. The Australian smalltime actor and his wife dressed like the average middle-class couple. They looked like any two people on their way to work, and the theater was work to most of them. To be assured of steady work, the Australian smalltime comedian had to have four or five different acts, the dancers had to have a variety of routines, and a singer — like Frank Herberte — had to have a repertoire that would enable him to change his act for many weeks. With his small salary, the little actor playing the Fuller circuit could not afford to lose time in travel for which he was not paid. When he opened at a theater, the little actor had to make good because he had to stay there for many weeks. On his small salary, the Australian actor could not afford to have original material written, and if he did have money, there were no local writers who could create songs, jokes, or scenes for him. To survive in their profession, most Australian performers had to resort to plagiarism.

The imported acts were their objectives. If an English or an American comedy team played the Tivoli theaters in Sydney, Melbourne, or Adelaide, the instant that act had left for home — and sometimes even before that — an Australian act would be doing its jokes and routines on the Fuller circuit in other cities. Before I left for America, two Australian actors named Ship and Gaffney presented me with a cane. When I asked them why, Gaffney said, "It's a present. We like you. When you go back to America we're going to pinch your patter."

The boys happened to like me, and I received a cane. Most acts not only received nothing; they went back to England or America without even knowing that their acts had been stolen. English comedy songs in particular were popular in Australia. Many of the Australian comedians bought the records made by English comedians to learn their songs. The cost of three or four records was the only cost involved in the assembling of an Australian comedian's new act. One comedian I knew in Sydney didn't even buy the records. He used to sit in the music shop with an arranger and play a record over and over until the arranger had copied the music and the comedian had written down the lyrics. There were several instances when the Tivoli circuit had booked a great English star in London for an Australian tour; by the time the star arrived in Sydney, he found that his songs and comedy material had been stolen and used in every city in the country.

There were a number of excellent comedians in Australia. These men created characters and wrote their own material. On the Fuller circuit I played with several Australian comedians who could have become great stars in England or America if they had not been afraid to leave home. Roy Rene and Jake Mack were two Jewish comedians who were very popular with their tabloid revues. Con Moreni was a clever monologist who wrote his own acts. Leonard Nelson did original songs and sophisticated comedy. Vaude and Verne were sidewalk comedians who specialized in topical patter; Charlie Verne wrote all of the act's material and was Australia's most quoted wit.

To augment their incomes, many of the smaller Australian acts had sidelines. One act I knew carried a line of fountain pens and cheap jewelry. Another act, a musical one, gave violin and cornet lessons in the towns around the circuit. A woman singer sold cosmetics and beauty preparations. As they gave only one show a night, the actors had time to engage in another business or profession, and a few of the American acts wooed the elusive pound with extracurricular projects. One magician handled a line of Hamilton watches. The Littlejohns, the Diamond Jugglers who had come over with me on the boat, opened a shop in Sydney and sold rhinestones. Littlejohn and his wife carried a supply of rhinestones on the road to sell in various cities. An American musical act called Alsace and Lorraine carried an electrolysis machine. In every town they rented an empty store and advertised in the newspapers that they were accessible during certain hours to banish milady's superfluous hairs.

One English dancer named Eddie Burns specialized in photography and hauled his camera from town to town. Eddie had to fatten his income. He had come from England to play the Fuller circuit at five pounds ($24.30) weekly. To make the round trip from London to Sydney, Eddie spent eighteen weeks on the water receiving no salary. He was guaranteed sixteen weeks' work; fortunately his contract was extended or Eddie would have traveled eighteen weeks to work sixteen. To further complicate Eddie's financial plight, the war had affected the Australian pound. Many of the imported acts were constantly trying to change their paper money into gold to protect themselves from inflation. In each city, an alien actor could demand ten pounds of his salary in gold. The imported acts filled their grouch bags with sovereigns. (The grouch bag was a small cloth or chamois bag vaudeville actors wore around their necks or pinned to their underwear in which they carried their money or valuables. Traveling around the country, sleeping on trains and in strange hotels, if an actor was robbed or had to flee during a fire he knew that the savings in his grouch bag would be intact.) As the acts went from week to week, collecting their gold coins and stuffing them into their grouch bags, large lumps started to protrude from their breastbone that gave the impression they were goiters that clinked.

Eddie Burns had no grouch-bag problems. Eddie Burns had no grouch bag. His great concern was his dancing mat. Eddie posed as an American, and opened his act singing a popular song called "Michigan." As Eddie walked on the stage in a full-dress suit snapping his fingers and singing, "I was born in Michigan — and I wish and wish again — that I was back on the farm where I was born . . ." in ripe English accent, the jig was up. As Eddie completed the song with the redundant desire to "wish again that I was back home in Michigan, back on the farm," he thumped into a wooden-shoe dance. Eddie's clog routines sounded like two demented woodpeckers going mad in a lumberyard. His dance made enough noise to frighten the termites out of every wooden building in the neighborhood. To multiply his din, Eddie carried his own dancing mat. The mat consisted of a number of wooden slats fastened on a long strip of heavy canvas. (The canvas made it possible to roll the dancing mat for traveling purposes.) Following ten minutes of Terpsichorean pandemonium, Eddie concluded his act with a topical touch. Since war news dominated the headlines, for his final number Eddie stepped down to the footlights, winded, and between gasps announced, "My next dance! An impression of the German army entering Warsaw!" As he stepped back onto the dancing mat, the orchestra played a martial air, and Eddie executed a goose-step dance the length of the dancing mat and exited off stage. Coming back, he announced, "And now the German Army leaving Warsaw!" The orchestra now played a succession of discordant strains, the drummer simulated the sound of gunfire, and Eddie, wearing a bloody bandage on his head and carrying a tattered banner, danced backwards across the stage in great disorder.

This finish always stopped the show. I played on the bill with Eddie when he first arrived from England. His dancing mat was new and was long enough to cover the stage from one entrance to the other. As he toured the Fuller circuit, the dancing mat was rolled out of baggage cars onto platforms, thrown into lorries to be taken to the theaters, and toppled off lorries at stage doors. As the canvas base weakened, the slats became loose and dropped off, one by one, like a daisy's petals in a high wind. Eddie finally returned to Sydney and I went to see his act at the National. During Eddie's six months' tour the dancing mat had strewn slats all over the country and was now about three feet long. Eddie's big finish had of necessity been condensed. The German army now entered Warsaw in two or three shrunken goose steps. The army left Warsaw on what was left of the dancing mat, standing in one spot and appearing to be in the throes of constipation.

The war was not going well for the British army at this time. The colonies were under pressure to train more troops to strengthen the British forces. More and more Australian boys were enlisting. Uniforms were everywhere. The first reports of the new German menace, the U-boats, were received in Sydney; a boat named the *Arabic* was attacked and sunk. The sailings of many boats plying between England and Australia were canceled. Without the steady stream of imported acts, which were predominantly British, the Australian theaters would have had a difficult time remaining open. The Tivoli and Fuller offices solved their joint problem by extending the contracts of all the imported acts then in the country, and sending them out again over their circuits.

One personal result of this was that, seven months after I

had played in Adelaide, I found myself back there again. I was concerned about returning to Adelaide with the same act. There were no transient audiences in most of the Australian cities (Sydney and Melbourne, the bigger seaports were the exceptions), and once an audience knows all his jokes, the comedian is in jeopardy. To add some new elements to my act I thought of the ventriloquial dummy I had bought in San Francisco. This dummy had been floundering around in the bottom of my trunk all over the Fuller circuit. I used to practice ventriloquism and try to manipulate the dummy in the dressing room; I couldn't throw my voice far enough to get it past my lips. But the months of reading comedy had fortified me with a bulky collection of material. Selecting some sure-fire items from my file, I pieced together a burlesque ventriloquial routine. Now, instead of juggling, I opened my new act as a ventriloquist. My first line to the audience was, "If you are wondering which one is the dummy, this is the dummy on your left." After a few jokes with the dummy, which I christened Jake, I gave a voice-throwing demonstration. As I threw my voice, asking Jake questions, the ushers answered me from all parts of the theater. Even done crudely, this burlesque ventriloquism was funny. When, back home, I later developed it with John McCormack's voice singing on a concealed phonograph while I was drinking wine, and with Jake coming apart limb by limb as the song finished, audiences thought the bit was hilarious.

In Auckland, at an auction, I had opened my mouth once too often and had become the owner of an old-style banjo; this too now went into the act. I bought an instruction book and learned a number of chords. I also invented three imitations to be done with the banjo: a man with a wooden leg going upstairs; the Trinity chimes before they were fixed; a musician looking over a precipice. This last imitation consisted of holding the banjo, lying flat on the stage, and looking over the footlights into the orchestra pit.

In vaudeville, there was an audience psychology that never failed. If a comedian walked onto the stage holding a violin, a saxophone, or a banjo, the audience assumed he was a musician. The comedian could tell jokes for ten minutes, occasionally tuning his violin, blowing a note on the sax, or strumming his banjo. The audience reacted to the comedy and waited patiently to hear the instrument played. I used my banjo as a device. Instead of juggling, I now told many of the same jokes strumming the banjo. The jokes went better, and my act looked different. Playing return engagements, I was still the "World's Worst Juggler," but I was now a full-fledged monologist, burlesquing ventriloquism, juggling, and playing the banjo. Many American jugglers had been booked in Australia, but few monologists. I came to Australia a juggler, and was to return to America a monologist.

In the early days of the war, the Australian troops were trained at home. When the troops embarked, the bands played, great crowds assembled, and impressive patriotic demonstrations were held. There was a war, but the shooting and horrors were far away from home. Women were almost gay as they waved farewell to their sons, brothers, and sweethearts. The men staying behind exchanged jokes with those who were leaving; both knew that the war couldn't last much longer and that they would soon be back together again. It wasn't until the casualties started to return that the country realized the grim reality. After the battle of Gallipoli, at which the Australian forces suffered staggering losses, the country was aroused. Germans were put under surveillance. Men with handlebar mustaches and pompadour haircuts — the crew cuts of that day — were suspected of being Germans.

I had a short pompadour; I had to part my hair in the middle and plaster it down with Vaseline to avoid suspicion.

Two Bulgarian gentlemen who did an act called the Musical Balkans were really in trouble. They not only spoke with heavy accents; they both wore bushy Kaiser Bill mustaches. The Musical Balkans had to shave off their lip chinchilla and add a song to their act; the minute they walked on the stage the Balkans now sang, in their thick dialect, "America, Ve Loff You!"

When the Australian government passed a law that any alien traveling in the country could be called upon to present credentials in the form of birth certificate or passport, it dawned on me that I had neither. I went to see the American consul at Sydney. He couldn't understand how I had ever gotten into the country without a passport. He couldn't understand why I had ever wanted to leave America. He looked as though he couldn't understand why he had ever wanted to leave America, either. He advised me to go back home. I was willing to go, but I couldn't even go home without a birth certificate. I cabled my brother Bob. Months before, when Mr. Fuller had booked me in Chicago, I had written Bob and asked him to send my birth certificate to the steamship company's office in San Francisco. None of his letters or those from my Aunt Lizzie since that time had mentioned the birth certificate. When Bob's answer to my cable arrived, I knew why. I was born on Union Street, which was the dividing line between Cambridge and Somerville. The house in which I was born was, according to family lore, on the Somerville side of the street. When Bob went to inquire at the Somerville City Hall, there was no record of my birth. He cabled me this news, which I relayed to the consul in Sydney. The consul gloated. He was sure that he had another "Man Without a Country" on his hands. I cabled Bob that since I had worked in the Boston Public Library, somebody in that city could at least attest that I existed. Bob answered that Mayor Curley's office in Boston had given my Aunt Lizzie a birth certificate that was being sent on to me. (Many years later, a record of my birth was found at the city hall in Cambridge. My father must have overdone his liquid rejoicing at my birth. On the way to record the event he ended up in the wrong city.) Meanwhile, it would take five or six weeks for my birth certificate to arrive in Australia; I told the consul I would continue on the Fuller circuit until I could leave.

Khaki was the vogue. Soldiers crowded the streets of every city — soldiers convalescing; soldiers on leave; soldiers off to the front; soldiers who had been discharged, hobbling along on crutches or canes, with empty coat sleeves or trouser legs, reminders to carry through life of the debt their country owed them that it could never repay. There were a few able-bodied men in civilian clothes walking the streets. Men not in khaki were stopped by girls who stuck white feathers in their lapels: these were the insignia of the coward. Entertainment for the soldiers was not organized. Actors banded together on Sundays and made trips to hospitals and camps to present shows. Soldiers crowded the theaters. Many of them, back from the front and bitter, amused themselves by throwing pennies at the acts or counting out men who were performing on the stage.

President Wilson was keeping America out of the war, but Australia wasn't applauding him. The theaters were packed at every show. When the war news was depressing, the theater was a haven to which people turned to escape the ugly realities of the somber times. Usually, in the theater it wasn't so bad for an American, but away from the theater you were always subjected to the taunts about President Wilson's actions and the country's cowardice. Many times, as I would pass a group of larrikans on the street corner, they would whistle. A larrikan, in Australia, was a tough character, and his derogatory whistle was called the "Pretty Joey." The "Pretty Joey," whistled in unison by the larrikans, implied that the passer-by was either effeminate or a poltroon. This whistle was an invitation to a fracas. That I have my nose, eyes, and a few teeth intact today I credit to the fact that I never attempted to unpucker a larrikan during his rendition of a "Pretty Joey."

The only unpleasant memory I have of my entire tour of Australia and New Zealand is the week I spent in Toowoomba. Toowoomba is a small town in Queensland, about ninety miles, as the kangaroo hops, from Brisbane. The town had one theater, the Elite. The show changed every week, and consisted of one vaudeville act, one feature picture, and one short subject. To economize on travel fare, the manager always booked a single, and that act came to Toowoomba following its Brisbane engagement. I must have been the only single act available that week. Upon my arrival in Toowoomba, I found a large card leaning against the front of the Elite Theatre. On the card, to catch the eye of the Toowoomba theater lover, this message had been daubed:

VAUDEVILLE
By Special Arrangement with the Empire Theatre, Brisbane
FREDDY JAMES
The World's Worst Juggler
His Patter Whilst Juggling Is Very Humorous

Pictorial Attraction
HENRIETTA CROSSMAN
in
"THE SUPREME TEST"

The Elite had no stagehands. It was like some of the little theaters I had played in the early days around Boston. When the vaudeville was to appear, I had to switch on the footlights, then pull up the roll curtain and tie it off. After my act was finished, I had to switch off the footlights and lower the curtain to enable the operator out front to start the motion picture. I was the only American in the town of Toowoomba, and everybody knew it. Nobody mentioned the war to me, because nobody talked to me. The waitress at the pub where I stopped brought my food silently three times each day. She resented the Yank. The other people around the pub ignored me. The audiences at the theater tolerated my act. They neither laughed nor applauded. Every show to me was a soliloquy. When I walked down the main street, I might as well have been invisible. People passed me by as though repudiating my existence. Throughout the six days I spent in Toowoomba I was ostracized completely. Every day I went through the same routine. A silent breakfast, a long walk alone out into the country with my books, a reading session, a long walk back to sit through a silent lunch, another walk, another reading session, a silent dinner, and then to the theater to revel in the concerted silence that prevailed during my act. After the show, a deathlike walk back to the pub. Another week suspended in this social vacuum and I might have started talking to myself. At the end of the week I was happy to bid a silent adieu to the citizens of Toowoomba, and I am sure that the feeling was reciprocated.

Back in Sydney, the letter from my brother Bob, with the enclosed birth certificate, awaited me. I paid a final visit to the consul, who again advised me to leave Australia. He hinted that America would soon enter the war and that all Americans would be safer at home. I assured him that I would go back to San Francisco on the next boat. At the

Fuller office they offered me return dates in New Zealand and extra weeks in Tasmania. I also had offers to play in Africa, in India, and four weeks in London. It was an opportunity to make a complete tour of the world, but the nearer America came to getting into the war, the nearer I wanted to be getting to America.

The next week I sailed from Sydney on the S.S. *Sierra*. The second-class staterooms and seasickness held no terrors for me now. After eleven months of steady travel on the assorted-gauge railroads and the tossing *Dimboola*, I had developed into a seasoned traveler. I had enjoyed my stay in Australia. The people, even under the stress of war, were friendly and hospitable. The theater audiences were wonderful. Those are the only two things that matter to a smalltime vaudeville actor plying his profession in a strange land. As the *Sierra* bobbed its way out of Sydney Harbor, I forgave Toowoomba and thought of Frank Herberte, going through life with his song slides and eating hundreds of pork pies on the crowded platforms to come. I thought of the many friends I was leaving that I would never see again. As night came and darkness settled silently over the water, I walked back to the rail for my last look at Australia. Off in the distance a bright glare burnished the horizon. I heard one passenger say it was the setting sun. But I knew the cause of the glare. It came from thousands of Australians who were making their nightly trips through back yards with candles flaming, on their way to the john.

# 11

## Playing the Smalltime

THE *Sierra's* return trip was uneventful. Like the red red robin, it kept bob bob bobbin' along for twenty-one days and nights. The Musical Balkans were on board, happy to be out of Australia. They were busy growing back their Kaiser Bill mustaches. Stanley and Birnes, two boys who did a dancing act, were coming back from a very successful Tivoli tour. They asked me to hold their money for them until they got to San Francisco. Both boys liked to gamble and would rather trust me than their will power. Every time a card game started on the boat, the boys came over to me and pleaded, cried, and abused me to try to obtain some of their savings. I refused to weaken, and when the *Sierra* docked, I presented Stanley and Birnes with their pokes intact.

I checked in at the Continental Hotel, whose slogan was, "We get the stars on the way up and on the way down." I realized that I had to take inventory. The Australian audiences felt about jokes the way they did about friends: the old ones were the best. My monologue had changed and deteriorated, and I realized that my act had to be rejuvenated before I could hope to appear in any decent theaters.

After seeing the shows at the Orpheum, Empress, and Pantages Theatres, and paying particular attention to the material used by the monologists and the comedy acts, I returned to the hotel to hibernate. Three days later, after poring over current newspapers to select topical subjects and spending countless hours making selections from my new joke collection, I felt ready to unfurl my new version of me to American theater audiences. To remove the juggling stigma, I had adopted a new billing: "Freddy James and His Misses." (A juggling act was classified as a novelty act that normally opened or closed a vaudeville show; with my new props, my juggling had become merely the by-product of a monologue.) The "Misses" explained the tricks I couldn't complete, and concealed the juggling content of my act when people saw it billed. I wired Mark Leddy to break my jump back to New York. Mark sent word that he had booked me for several weeks on the "Western Vaudeville Time."

The Western Vaudeville Managers Association maintained headquarters in Chicago. Through their offices, and in association with the B. F. Keith and the Orpheum circuits, they booked forty or fifty smalltime vaudeville theaters in Illinois, Michigan, Ohio, Indiana, Wisconsin, Iowa, Missouri, and Minnesota. These theaters split the week three ways. If a monkey act played Springfield, Illinois, the first half—from Monday through Wednesday — and Champaign, Illinois, the last half — from Thursday through Saturday — on Saturday night the owner of the act had to pack up his monkeys and the act's paraphernalia and travel to Ottawa, Illinois, to do three shows on Sunday. The salaries were paid pro rata: to receive his salary for the seventh day the actor had to go to the extra town. The Bible tells us that on the seventh day God rested, but the Bible had never been the Book-of-the-Month with the Western Vaudeville managers. Around the circuit on the seventh day, nobody was resting. Acrobats, dancers, and assorted actors were running for trains, unpacking and doing shows, then packing and running for more trains.

The cities and towns in the network of the eight states could seldom be reached by any one railroad. To go from Chicago to the various theaters where he had been booked, the actor traveled on the New York Central, Chicago and Alton, Santa Fe, Wabash, Union Pacific, Big Four, Chicago and Burlington, Chicago, Milwaukee and St. Paul, and perhaps one or two other railroads. There never seemed to be a direct way the actor could go from one date to another without changing trains once or twice during the night and spending endless hours at abandoned junctions waiting for connecting trains. One trip always annoyed me. Terre Haute and Evansville, both in Indiana, were a split week. The acts playing the Hippodrome Theatre in Terre Haute for the first three days went to the Grand Theatre in Evansville for the last three. If it had been possible to go directly from one town to the other, the trip could have been made in three hours. It took the acts eight hours. Finishing at Terre Haute, they would leave there on a midnight train. After riding for an hour, they had to get off at some small town and wait four hours for a train to pick them up to ride the remaining two hours to Evansville. Most of the railroad stations were deserted at night. When the actor's trunk was thrown off the train, he had to put it on a truck, pull the truck to the baggage car on the next train, and help the baggageman load it if he wanted to assure the arrival of his wardrobe and his props at the theater the next day. In the Middle West during the winter months the snowstorms were frequent and severe, trains were late, and baggage was lost, but neither rain, sleet, hail, snow, lack of sleep, nor empty stomachs kept the Western Vaudeville acts from making contractual rounds. The show must go on. Through the years I have spent a hundred nights curled up in dark, freezing railroad stations in the Kokomos, the Kenoshas, and the Kankakees, waiting for the Big Four,

the Wabash, or C. & A. trains to pick me up and whisk me to
the Danvilles, the Davenports, and the Decaturs. Most of the
actors playing the Western Vaudeville theaters looked as
though they hadn't been to sleep for many months. They
looked that way because they hadn't.

Cedar Rapids was the first of my Western Vaudeville
dates. The Majestic Theatre played seven acts and was one
of the better houses on the circuit. The manager, a Mr.
William J. Slattery, was an old showman who stood in the
lobby before the show and called his patrons by name as
they walked into the theater. If Brother Slattery thought the
show was bad, he warned the people as they bought their
weekly ticket. The vaudeville shows were reviewed by the
newspaper critics. In Cedar Rapids, Mr. Slattery also bought
space in the papers to print his personal opinion of each
act. Mr. Slattery's columns were headed:

MAJESTIC
VAUDEVILLE
Makes Millions Merry

The Manager's Comment on
Current Program

WILLIAMS AND WOLFUS — the advance notices of
this team had them the funniest pair in vaudeville. They are
the funniest pair on any stage. Williams had the house in a
continual uproar with his clowning and piano tricks. Aside
from his funmaking he is a dandy pianist.

DUNBARS SALON SINGERS — an organization of vocalists featuring popular and classical numbers. An offering
of the better kind. A very refined and pleasing specialty.

FREDDY JAMES — this boy is billed as a juggler but
fortunately does very little juggling. Possibly he learned that
the public likes jokes more, as he spends most of his time
pulling puns with good results. They ducked some of his
surefire stuff but he got on nicely in the main. Pretty good.

SULLIVAN AND MASON — a blackface team with comedy talk and popular songs. Their talk was mildly received but the songs and the wench finish put the act over.

And so on. The ad was signed "William J. Slattery." The act that did not make good in Cedar Rapids was out of luck. It not only had to read the adverse reviews written by the local newspaper critics, the act also saw the theater manager's personal opinion in his semiweekly column. Mr. Slattery, like most of the old-time vaudeville theater managers, was a member of the community, and felt that he had an obligation to the community. When his merchandise was shoddy, Mr. Slattery warned his customers.

The actor on the Western Vaudeville was always on the defensive. If he missed an opening show because trains were late or because he couldn't make connections through no fault of his, the money was deducted from the actor's salary. The average smalltime manager looked down on the actor. The manager sent in his weekly report to the office in Chicago, commenting on the act's wardrobe, general appearance, condition of scenery, the audience reaction, the attitude of the performer while he was working at the theater, and any untoward incidents that involved the actor: drinking, gambling, fighting with his wife. If a manager took a dislike to an actor on general principles, it colored his report. At Centralia, Illinois, the manager had a report blank tacked up over the mailbox backstage. When the incoming actor went to pick up his mail, he saw the manager's unfilled report with a finger pointing to it. Under the finger, it said, "What will it be? It's up to you!"

This particular manager had a theater that looked like a freight car minus the wheels. He played three acts of vaudeville for three days and changed the feature picture every day. The opening day he started the show with the vaudeville and followed with the feature picture; the remaining two days he played the new feature pictures before the vaudeville. If you were in the audience and had seen the vaudeville, you could walk out as soon as the picture finished. In Centralia I was on the bill with Walter Huston's brother Arthur, who did a pantomime act; also on the bill was a sister team. There was a terrific snowstorm, and during the night the snow had drifted into the alley back of the theater and covered the stage door completely. The next matinee, when I tried to come in through the front of the theater, the ticket taker advised me that the manager had sent out an order: the sister team could use the front door, but snow or no snow, Arthur Huston and I had to use the stage door. The manager didn't like our acts and this was his way of getting even.

At Logansport, Indiana, the manager of the theater was also the drummer in the orchestra. He had his drums raised up, and he sat so high in the pit that people in the audience could see him from any part of the theater. The Logansport populace felt that since the manager made frequent trips up to Chicago — the big city — to book his vaudeville acts, he was the smartest man in town. The comedians soon discovered that the Logansport audiences laughed only when the drummer laughed. At opening shows every comedian worked to the drummer. As soon as the drummer started laughing the comedian turned his attention to the audience.

It was during these Western Vaudeville weeks that I started to advertise. I had been away from New York for over a year, and had only played one week in Chicago. I hoped that by using a personal approach I could make every theater booker and manager acquainted with my act and aware of my whereabouts and activities. LaToy had stolen my "World's Worst Juggler" billing and I had mailed out several hundred cards to actors, managers, and bookers accusing him of plagiarism. Since several of the trade papers had reprinted the cards, it was a form of advertising for me. I now began to do more in this direction. My first attempt at a comedy letter was sent out on mourning stationery, and read:

> DEAR SIR:
>
> It is with intense grief that I inform you of the death of my act at the Parthenon Theatre, Hammond, Indiana. The mortality occurred three times daily, between January 15th and 17th. Services at the Simon Agency, held by Mark Leddy, each morning at 11 A.M. until I start to work again.
>
> FREDDY JAMES

Playing in St. Louis, I mailed out hundreds of two-ounce bottles filled with dirty water. Each bottle carried a printed label: PERSPIRATION TAKEN FROM THE BODY OF FREDDY JAMES AFTER DOING FOUR SHOWS TODAY AT THE GRAND THEATRE, ST. LOUIS. The Grand was one of the few smalltime theaters in the country at that time doing four shows daily; this made the perspiration semirelevant. For a few weeks I sent out a report on the theaters I was playing. One of my reports was called to the attention of Mr. Albee, the head of the great Keith circuit, who advised my agent to ". . . have that young man discontinue making fun of our theaters." My cards were in rebuttal to the manager's reports. Here is one of them:

ACTOR'S REPORT

Orpheum Theatre, South Bend, Indiana

Theatre — Good

Audience — Fair

Dressing rooms — Clean

Manager — Doesn't talk to the actors

Orchestra — In tune

My position — Next to closing

My 1st show — Didn't kill anybody

Bows — Three
Excuses — Up all night to make jump
Other acts — Sociable

FREDDY JAMES

At Christmas, I mailed out a twelve-page pamphlet entitled *What I Know About Show Business,* by Freddy James. When the pamphlet was opened, it was found to contain twelve blank pages. Whenever I had a comedy idea I had cards or photos made and bombarded the agents, managers, and bookers. My personal cards read:

Freddy James
Acting Done Reasonable
12 minutes in One — Benefits a Specialty

Chicago was second only to New York in importance as a vaudeville center, with the Orpheum, Sullivan and Considine, and Pantages circuits all booking their talent in Chicago. In addition, the Gus Sun time and other smaller circuits bought most of their attractions in Chicago. The city itself had two big-time vaudeville theaters: the Majestic and the Palace. Smalltime was on display at McVickers and at a number of small, untidy-looking haunts on State Street. Away from the Loop, on the north and south sides, every neighborhood had its own theater playing a split-week policy. A good act could obtain routes for two years or more from Chicago bookers, and hundreds of smalltime acts were always playing, passing through, or laying off in Chicago.

The three hotels in Chicago which were the most popular with the smalltime acts were the Grant, at the corner of Clark and Madison Streets; the Revere House, across the bridge on State Street; and the Saratoga, on Dearborn Street. Leonard Hicks, the manager of the Grant Hotel, was one of the most popular hotel men in the profession. Leonard helped actors for many years. He knew the vicissitudes that plagued the smalltimer, and he had a warm spot in his heart for his vagabond guests and did everything he could to help them enjoy their stay at the Grant. The Revere House was a super-annuated hotel whose guest list contained the names of characters ranging from the nefarious to the negligible. At one time there was a rumor that so many guests at the Revere House were smoking opium that a stranger, checking into the hotel, would fall asleep before he could cross the lobby. The Saratoga, popular with vaudeville actors, also housed the grifters and pitchmen who worked through the Midwestern states and came up to Chicago to buy their cheap fountain pens, Little Dandy Potato Peelers, Magic Cement, and guaranteed remedies they hawked to the gullible many in the smaller towns.

When I arrived back in Chicago to play the Academy and Kedzie Theatres, I stopped at the Grant. The acts met in the tiny lobby after their shows at night, and swapped gossip and experiences, or went out to Henrici's, the famous restaurant that advertised "No Orchestral Din," or to one of the cheaper places on Dearborn or Randolph Streets for a midnight snack. The single men, or the loose, usually adjourned to the Grant basement bar to knock off a few beers and a basket of shrimp. A single man might also give Cupid a test run with a single girl playing on the bill whose mother didn't travel with her, or with some succulent charmer he had run across in the lobby.

One night, Eddie Rowley and I were discussing comedy and jokes over a basket of shrimp. Eddie was a dancer who had a fine sense of humor, and he told me that he had recently, and on several occasions, visited a political club where the bartender was very funny. The saloons in Chicago closed at 1 A.M., but certain important politicians operated alleged clubs that were actually camouflaged saloons to accommodate their thirsty constituents all through the night. These political clubs were scattered all through the city. The club members paid no dues; any parched citizen who carried a free membership card, or who was known to the bartender, was admitted. Eddie Rowley raved about this bartender he had met. He marveled at the tapster's natural wit and his ability to coin original jokes without provocation, and he insisted that I visit the club with him to get some new material for my act.

At 1 A.M. we took a cab to an address on Wabash Avenue. The cab stopped in front of a gloomy-looking building. The street was dark and deserted. I paid the driver and followed Eddie into the building and up the stairs. On the first floor we walked down a dingy hall and Eddie stopped at a door. At Eddie's knock the door opened a crack, Eddie greeted an eye that squinted through the aperture, the opening widened, and we entered. The club was an unfinished loft that contained a small bar and ten or twelve tables. Through the haze of smoke I could see that the club was about half filled. Small groups of men were talking and drinking, other solitary members sat smoking and contemplating their libations. Nobody was laughing. I glued my eyes on the bartender and alerted my ears. I didn't want to miss any of his natural wit. Eddie stepped up to the bar and ordered two beers. When he brought the beers back to the table, Eddie said that we had picked a bad night. The bartender had a toothache. Eddie didn't see how he was going to be funny tonight. I suggested that we return to the hotel and try another night, but Eddie thought we should finish our beers slowly and then leave. He said that it would look better, and then too, perhaps the bartender's toothache might improve and he would start getting funny again. We raised our beers and hoped for the best. A loud knock sounded and the bartender went to the door. As he opened it slowly, loud voices could be heard in the hall, an arm was thrust in and pushed the bartender aside, the door flew wide open, and six burly policemen charged into the club. All the members and their guests — about fourteen of us in all — along with the bartender were herded down the stairs and into a waiting municipal vehicle.

On the way to the station house, the bartender, who now had a headache to go with his toothache, told us that some rival politician was responsible for the raid. He advised us not to give our right names; the minute we were booked he could call the politician who owned the club. I told Eddie that the bartender sure was doing a lot of talking, but it wasn't funny to me. It was after 2:30 A.M. before we were all searched, questioned, and led to the detention room. The bartender called the politician. Shortly after five o'clock, the politician, a small, sleepy-looking character, arrived with a bail commissioner. Bail was arranged and we were all told to be back in court at 8 A.M. Eddie and I adjourned to an all-night restaurant to mull over our plight. I had a matinee to play; if we were incarcerated, I would have some explaining to do at the box office.

At eight o'clock, Eddie and I were back in court with the others. The politician arrived promptly, with his bail friend and a lawyer. The lawyer instructed us individually to ask for a trial by jury. We did, and the judge granted our requests. When we got outside, the politician told us to forget the trial, which I promptly did. Since this experience with Eddie Rowley, nobody has ever mentioned a funny bartender to me.

# 12

## A Monologue with Turnips

AFTER a few more weeks of Western Vaudeville, Mark booked me on the Pantages Time. The "Pan Time," as it was called, was owned by Alexander Pantages. Fable had it that some years previous, Alexander had come down from the Klondike with a duffel full of gold dust and had opened a small theater in Seattle. He had prospered, and by 1917 he owned and controlled theaters all through the West.

Playing the Pan Time was a step up the ladder for me. My salary was $150, and it was the first time I had ever had a contract that guaranteed me twenty weeks' work. I wrote the good news home to my Aunt Lizzie, and went around to the Pantages office, in Chicago, to pick up my tickets. The acts were advanced tickets to cover the entire tour; weekly deductions were made from the actors' salaries until the total amount was paid off. The train tickets, including side trips, were seven or eight feet long. Two dancers, the Williams Brothers, were so afraid they would lose their tickets that they carried them in their shoes. Walking around and dancing three or four shows a day on the tickets, by the time the "Boys with the Musical Feet" arrived in Seattle their tickets were reduced to pungent shreds.

I arrived in Minneapolis to join the road show. The three

sheet in front of the Pantages Theatre listed the attractions on the inside:

CAPTAIN SORCHO
And His
MONSTER SUBMARINE SHOW
Spectacular Exhibition Showing In A Huge Glass Tank A Submarine At Her Deadly Work. Also A Startling And Intensely Vivid Demonstration Of Deep-Sea Diving And A Submarine Telephone In Operation.
(NOT A MOVING PICTURE)

ANDERSON'S SONG AND DANCE REVUE

ED AND JACK SMITH

FREDDY JAMES
And
"HIS MISSES"

STODDARD AND HYNES
"The Absent-Minded Professor"

JEROME AND CARSON
In A
"Vaudeville Breeze"

PHOTOPLAY
ROSCOE ARBUCKLE
"FATTY AND THE BOWERY STARS"

Captain Sorcho, the feature act, was a great attraction. The U-boat was now playing a vital part in the war. The *Lusitania* had been sunk. People knew very little about this new menace. Captain Sorcho's lecture explained the tactics employed by the submarine, the firing of the torpedoes, the explosion of a mine, and the eventual salvage work. During the Captain's talk the various actions were demonstrated by a diver submerged in the tank.

Anderson's Revue was a mediocre all-girl act. For some reason known only to Mr. Pantages, every Pantages show had to have a girl act. Ours consisted of two principal girls who sang and did specialty dances and six forlorn-looking chorus girls who did every ensemble number as though they had become panic-stricken in the entrance and had stampeded onto the stage. For the act's big finish, the girls were dressed in red, white, and blue costumes and a large American flag descended from the flies. Ed and Jack Smith were brothers who essayed some sophomoric comedy that proved their specialty was dancing. Stoddard and Hynes, a middle-aged couple, had a musical act. The man wore a white wig to disguise his age, and told some jokes that didn't have to wear white wigs to disguise theirs. As the act finished, the wife at the piano and the husband at the viola played "The Rosary." Jerome and Carson, a man and his wife, did a fast acrobatic number.

All vaudeville road shows start friendly. As the weeks wear on, however, familiarity breeds a variety of contempt. Incidents arise in theaters, hotels, restaurants, trains; the women develop likes and dislikes; the men argue about gambling; one act stops the show dead in some town and high-hats the rest of the bill: a thousand things can happen when six acts of vaudeville are compelled to stay together for five or six months.

I was the only single man present; all the others were married. Captain Sorcho didn't speak to the other acts. Mrs. Sorcho, a Christian Science practitioner, beamed on humanity, but kept aloof. Ed and Jack Smith brought their wives along; Jack was on his honeymoon. Stoddard and Hynes likewise kept to themselves. Anderson's wife was along, starring in his Girl Revue; she and her husband kept their eyes peeled on their chorus girls, to prevent poaching. I became friendly with Jerome and Carson, and then, as the tour progressed, I made another friend in Percy Franks, Captain

Sorcho's calliope player. Percy had a good sense of humor. His job was to start out at nine every morning with his steam calliope and go through the streets of the town, playing as loudly as possible to call the attention of all citizens who were not deaf to the fact that Captain Sorcho and his submarine tableau were at the local Pantages theater. Percy liked one of the principals in the girl act, and for weeks, if I was trying to sleep late in the morning and was awakened by the shrieking melody of "Oh, You Beautiful Doll," I knew that Percy was passing the hotel, mounted on his calliope, and was serenading his girl friend.

Things went along peacefully at first. There were a few complaints about Jack Smith's wife and her behavior at breakfast. Many mornings when the show was traveling, the entire company checked out of the hotel at five-thirty to catch a six o'clock train. With only one lunchroom open on the main street, twenty people would crowd in to get their breakfast. Jack Smith's wife would always manage to be there first, giving the counterman instructions. She wanted her orange juice "not too cold," her eggs "fried in butter" and "fried not too hard," or "she wouldn't eat them." Her toast had to be "trimmed," and her coffee was "black, with cream on the side." By the time she had finished, there was no time to order anything you had in mind; the rest of us would settle for a set of greasy doughnuts and a flagon of scalding coffee.

One night, in Butte, Montana, Frank Jerome and I heard a tumult in the Smith dressing room. We rushed in and found the brothers battering each other for keeps. Frank and I separated the boys and held them until they cooled off. When the fisticuffs had been replaced by invective, the brothers announced that the act was splitting up for good. Jack went out to the orchestra leader and demanded the act's music, which he immediately started tearing into pieces. Ed opened his trunk and began tearing the act's lobby photos to bits. During the night, however, sanity set in. It dawned on the Smith Brothers that they were not in the cough-drop business. They were actors who lived in New York, they were now in Montana, they would have to pay their own fares home, and they would lose seventeen weeks' work. Next morning, when Frank and I arrived at the theater to pick up our mail, we found the Smith Brothers busy on the floor of their dressing room, pasting their music together to be ready to go on at the matinee.

We found that the reactions of the audiences differed widely. In the Canadian cities, the acrobatic, dancing, and novelty acts were better received. Back in the States, the talking comedy acts were the favorites. The newspaper critics, reviewing a smalltime vaudeville show playing for ten or twenty cents admission, went into detail in airing their assorted opinions. I was either a riot or a stage wait. At Tacoma, Washington, one critic wrote:

> Freddy James is easily as good a single as ever appeared in Tacoma, having an original line of witty sayings and new jokes that have never been heard here. His comedy had the audience in an uproar.

I did the same act, word for word, at Regina, Saskatchewan; here the review was somewhat different:

> PANTAGES BILL IS GOOD EXCEPT FOR
> THE SO-CALLED NUT.
> ONE WEAK ACT DOES NOT, HOWEVER,
> SPOIL A GOOD SHOW.
>
> Freddy James, who has a single, takes up a lot of time with his mouth. He springs a number of gags, most of which, were they omitted, wouldn't be missed.

Playing one- and two-night stands, Captain Sorcho and his marine exhibit were always in trouble. The fifteen-thousand-gallon glass tank had to be hurriedly assembled on arrival and fifteen thousand gallons of city water filtered and run into the tank. At Anaconda, Montana, one section of the tank cracked, and half the audience on the lower floor was drenched. The most unusual review the Captain's act received on the trip resulted from the act's nonappearance. At Great Falls, Montana, the critic wrote:

WITH HEADLINE ACT LEFT OUT ON ACCOUNT OF FILTHY CITY WATER, OTHER ACTS MAKE PAN SHOW GOOD.
The act that did not appear was the submarine show, and the reason that it was not presented is that the divers refused to risk their lives entering Missouri River water in the condition that it now comes from the hydrants.

When I finished the Pantages Time at Denver, Mark booked me in Chicago, Cleveland, Detroit, and Toronto to bring me back to New York. I had been away for two years. My act by now was completely different. Most of my jokes were sure-fire:

"Condensed milk is wonderful. I don't see how they can get a cow to sit down on those little cans."

"Was she old? When they lit all of the candles on her birthday cake, six people were overcome with the heat."

"I dreamed I was eating Shredded Wheat. When I woke up, the mattress was half gone."

"My father never raised his hand to any one of his children except in self-defense."

To go with several verses I sang with the banjo, I had written some new song titles:

"She used to be a schoolteacher, but she has no class now."

"I don't have to look up my family tree, because I know that I'm the sap."

"You can lead a horse to water, but an architect makes his own plans."

I wore a funny whiteface make-up, with a small derby, big shoes, and a comedy suit. To save wear and tear on the audience, I carried my own applause. I had four pairs of wooden hands made. After certain jokes, four stagehands thrust the wooden hands in front of the curtain on both sides of the stage and slapped them together. When the clatter of my homemade applause died down, I explained to the audience that some of my jokes and tricks merited applause, but I didn't want to bother the paying customers.

A monologist had a great problem to finish his act in a manner that would provoke applause. He could convulse the audience with hilarious verbal comedy for fifteen minutes, then walk off the stage and receive one bow. A two-man comedy team could bore the audience to death for fifteen minutes, but by singing a parody of a popular song as the finish of their act, they would stop the show. The memory, or the appreciation, of an audience was as short-lived as the life span of a butterfly who had died prematurely. Smalltime acts had many devices to build up the applause at the finish of their show. There were those who sang parodies: when they had finished one parody on "Irish Eyes Are Smiling," they would have the orchestra play the introduction to another song, "By the Beautiful Sea," as they were taking their bows. The audience, hearing this new music, assumed that the act had another parody and raised the roof to bring the act back for an encore. Singers of popular songs employed the same chicanery. As they took their bows, having sung "Dinah," the orchestra would begin "Waitin' for the Robert E. Lee"; the audience, wanting its money's worth, applauded until it had heard this additional song. When the encore was completed, the trick was repeated. Lou Holtz with his "O Sole

Mio," Gallagher and Shean with their song, and Lewis and Dody with "Hello, Hello, Hello" had audience-proof finishes. The audiences knew that these comedy songs had many choruses and they applauded until they had heard them all.

Musical acts who played banjos took their bows holding saxophones; the audience would bring them back. After the saxophone number, they would bow holding clarinets, and so on. Comedy acts put on funny hats for each bow, to stimulate the applause. Some two-man acts never completely left the stage during their bows; they alternated running off and bowing individually. Other acts, after they had finished, stood in the entrance with their rumps visible to most of the people in the audience, to show that they were still available if the audience wanted them back. Some acts brazenly ran down to the footlights and shouted, "More?" All of these contrived devices were called "stealing bows," or "milking the audience."

The finish of my act had never been too strong. Originally, with the juggling act, the concluding hat tricks had helped, but my present banjo and singing finish stood in need of improvement. Trying to find something that would make people applaud, I went back to the standard commodities: the American flag and pictures of deceased Presidents. The minute I completed my banjo finale and exited, the stage went dark and a picture of Abraham Lincoln appeared on the screen. The audience, seeing Lincoln, started to applaud. The lights flashed on and I appeared, as though I had heard the applause backstage and had returned to take a bow. After my bow, the lights went out and a picture of George Washington appeared on the curtain. The audience applauded, the lights flashed on, I was back for a second bow. Lights out, the American flag was on the screen. By now the people had gotten the idea. The audience was laughing and applauding.

I was a riot. As I left the stage, the lights went off for the last time, and a sign flashed on that said "Thank You."

Mark Leddy decided that with this new material I now had a big-time act. He had a two-part plan for me. First, I would have to change my name. As Freddy James, I had played the smalltime theaters in the East two years previously at a salary of $75. If Freddy James was submitted to the bookers, they would look up my old salary and offer me the same money. With a new name I could demand a new salary. Second, since Mark had a Loew franchise and couldn't book with the Keith office, he was turning me over to Claude and Gordon Bostock, who were big-time agents. He wanted the Bostock brothers to see my act, and he arranged three days for me at the City Theatre.

The City was booked by the Fox office and was situated on Fourteenth Street near Third Avenue. The Keith office booked the Jefferson Theatre, also on Fourteenth Street but across Third Avenue; this, according to the unbiased Keith powers, made the City Theatre an opposition house, and any act playing the opposition was blacklisted by the Keith office. To conceal their identities, most of the acts that played the City changed their names. Twice each week an usher from the Jefferson was sent up the block to list the acts playing at the City. The usher didn't go into the theater to see the show. He simply stood outside the City and copied the acts' names down from the sign in the lobby. When the usher turned in his list of aliases, the Keith office promptly blacklisted these nonexistent acts. When I reported to the City Theatre for rehearsal, I looked on the dressing-room list and found that my new name was Fred Allen. Edgar Allen, the Fox booker, had generously given me half of his name. I have been Fred Allen ever since. Only one person has ever been upset by this change of names. A Boston politician named Francis X. Coyne at one time tried to pass a bill to compel actors playing in Massachusetts to bill themselves under their true names. Fred Astaire would appear in Massachusetts as Fred Osterlitz, Jack Benny as Benny Kubelsky, and so on. Brother Coyne said that all Sullivans near and wide were outraged when my name was changed to Fred Allen. Coyne declared, "Captain John Sullivan, Bunker Hill hero, and John L. Sullivan, the famous fighter, must have turned over in their graves!"

After both Bostocks had seen my act they agreed I should be on the big time. "Class" was rearing its glossy head in vaudeville at this time. Claude felt that I had been playing the smalltime for so long that the act was funny, but it had no "class." With "class" he could double  my salary. To acquire "class" I would have to abandon the funny make-up, the little derby, and the big shoes. I would also have to visit Claude's tailor and get fitted for a custom-made suit. Claude had some other suggestions about my jokes and comedy bits. Meanwhile, to give the tailor time to rush my suit and myself time to make the suggested changes, Mark and the Bostocks booked me on the Fox and Poli Times.

Six weeks later, Claude saw the act again and agreed that I now had "class." My suit was immaculate, my new derby was snappy, my shoes were the latest style. With my redcheeked make-up I looked more like a young member on his way to the Harvard Club than I did a comedian who was going to try to convince an audience he was funny. Claude also changed my billing. I was no longer "Freddy James and His Misses" or "The World's Worst Juggler." I was now "Fred Allen, a Young Fellow Trying to Get Along." I had so much class I trespassed on the pretty. In my whole life I never looked as well on the street as I now did on the stage. I still had the dummy, but the banjo had been changed for a guitar; the guitar had more "class." I couldn't play the guitar. I had to have the neck taken off the banjo and grafted onto the guitar; this enabled me to play the guitar using banjo tuning and banjo chords. A few juggling tricks survived. One involved a turnip: I threw a large rutabaga up into the air and tried to catch it on a fork held in my mouth. After a number of tries and jokes, the turnip would miss the fork, hit me flush on the head, and split into pieces. Audiences screamed at the rutabaga's disintegration, and they screamed again later when I stepped behind a screen and, after throwing the turnip up in the air twice so that the audience could see me trying the trick, stepped out from behind the screen with the turnip on the fork as though I had done it out of sight. This bit had survived Claude's editing. Claude took a final look at his handiwork and announced that I was ready.

The Alhambra Theatre, at One hundred twenty-fifth Street and Seventh Avenue, was to be my first big-time date. After all the three, four, and five shows daily, I was now going to do "two-a-day." Monday morning, at rehearsal, I decided that instead of staying uptown all day, I would go back to the hotel on Forty-seventh Street between shows. To prepare for the week, I bought fourteen turnips, one to be broken at each show. I pared and washed every turnip so that it would have "class," too. The fourteen turnips were placed in single file on the dressing-room shelf. My music was rehearsed, my new suit sent out to be pressed, my make-up, grease paint, powder, and powder puff placed before the mirror: I was ready. It was agreed that Claude, who was very busy, would see my act at the night show when the audience would be better. Gordon planned to see the matinee to report to Claude how I had opened. I was fourth on the bill, which was a good spot. The matinee started. I was a little nervous; after all, it was the big time. My act went rather well, I thought. I sat in my dressing room to wait for Gordon; finally he arrived. It developed that he had taken a taxi uptown from his office. Going through the park, the taxi had a flat tire, and Gordon was delayed. He arrived at the theater just as I was taking my bow with the patriotic slides. The applause was big. Gordon asked an usher how the act had gone, and the usher reported favorably. Gordon was very happy, and we rode back downtown together.

When I came back for the evening show, the doorman told me I was no longer on the bill. I had been canned. No photographs had been slipped under the door. This was the big time: the bad news was delivered in person. I packed my trunk and went home. At night, when Claude came to the theater, the manager, Mr. Harry Bailey (I have never forgotten him), told him that he hadn't closed me because my act was bad; it was simply that the first four acts were all working "in one" — that is, before the front curtain, and with no special scenery. This made for monotony; the start of the show lacked variety. And, as the other three acts were established big-timers, he couldn't can them. That was the manager's story. As far as I know, there are thirteen unpared turnips still lying in that Alhambra Theatre dressing room today.

The Bostocks were undaunted. Canned on the big time Monday, on Thursday I was back on the smalltime at Auburn, New York. After three more weeks out of town I was brought back into New York to play Proctor's Fifth Avenue Theatre. The Fifth Avenue Theatre was on Broadway at Twenty-eighth Street. Why a theater on Broadway should be called the Fifth Avenue was one of the myriad things that didn't make sense in show business. The Fifth Avenue played split weeks and was a "show house." New acts and other acts attempting to get better booking or more money "showed" their acts there at cut salaries. The Keith bookers attended the shows and, at weekly meetings, graded the acts, determining their future salaries and what dates could be arranged for them. The trade magazines — *Variety, New York Clipper, Zit's Weekly,* and the *Billboard* — had representatives at the theater who, on opening days, slyly hinted to the performers that taking an ad in their respective sheets would assure the act a good notice. The magazines didn't call it blackmail. Their selling point was that an ad called the attention of the bookers and theater managers to the act, and a good review created a demand for the act's services.

On my opening day, the *Variety* representative attempted to sell me space that cost $125. My salary for the three days was $62.50. The *Variety* man couldn't understand my untutored reasoning: I said that by giving him $125, I would not only work the entire three days for nothing, but would lose $62.50 as well. When I was obdurate, he played his trump card: he told me that Sime, the editor of *Variety*, was going to review the show that night, and that he, the representative, would like to go back to the office and tell Sime that I had taken an ad. I told him what he could tell Sime. I don't know what, if anything, he did tell Sime, but I do know that Sime appeared at the theater that night, reviewed the show, and panned the life out of me and my act. If *Variety's* pronunciamentos had the power to wither an actor's future, today I would be gainfully employed as a pretzel salter.

After reading Sime's diatribe, I winced, picked up my $62.50 (minus commission), and went on my smalltime way, thinking that the actor and the lobster had a lot in common. The lobster, during its shedding season, lives in fear. After nature has divested it of its old shell, the lobster sits around in its bare meat waiting to grow a new husk. Crabs and starfish crawling by nip little chunks out of the lobster's jowl, and barnacles attach themselves to his exposed rump. The smalltime actor, like the lobster, lived in fear eternally. The manager's report, the booker's opinion, the trade papers' reviews, the local newspaper critics, and scores of other people and forces conspired to disturb the small-timer's peace of mind.

The Palace Theatre was the goal of every act in America. The Palace was the towering symbol of vaudeville. An act that had played the Palace was booked by any theater manager in the country, sight unseen. A Palace program, with an act's name on it, was a diploma of merit. Opportunity didn't knock to summon me to the Palace — it rang. One Saturday night, as I was preparing for my last show at Proctor's Theatre in Yonkers, the manager sent for me to come to his office immediately. I rushed out front to learn that Mr. Albee was calling me from New York. Mr. Albee, the head of the Keith circuit, the sachem of the great vaudeville tribe, was calling me: it was like God bending from His empyrean throne and summoning an ant into His presence. Suppressing my aspen tendencies, I picked up the phone. Mr. Albee, it seemed, was in great trouble. The City of New York had passed a law prohibiting acrobats from appearing in vaudeville theaters on the Sabbath Day. Dancers could dance, singers could sing, comedians could tell jokes on Sunday, but acrobats were forbidden to don their silken tights or leotards with intent to commit somersault. Mr. Albee had the Four Boises, a flying act, opening the Palace bill on Sunday, and they couldn't appear. Mr. Albee wanted me to save his life and substitute for the Boises. He would have my trunk brought down from Yonkers, and he would be eternally indebted to me. I had no choice. If I turned Mr. Albee down, I might as well have started pricing brine and gone into the pickle business. Scarcely a minute after I had agreed and said good-by to

Mr. Albee (if he was still listening), Gordon Bostock phoned. He had been alerted by Mr. Albee's office. Gordon thought I had done a smart thing. Even though I was the opening act of the show, I was finally in the Palace; if things went well, this would counteract the Alhambra disaster. According to Gordon, after the Palace manager had seen my act he would be sure to bring me back later in the season for a full week.

The next day came on schedule, as next days always do. I opened the Palace show. The theater was almost empty. As I carried on, telling my jokes and doing my tricks, the audience dribbled in. By the time I had come to the finish of my act, with Washington, Lincoln, and the flag flashing on the screen, the theater was half filled. The applause was surprisingly good. I had barely arrived back in my dressing room when Gordon rushed in, puffing and exuding enthusiasm. He had seen my act. The audience had been trickling in throughout, but it hadn't been bad — at night it was going to be great. Gordon left, promising to return for the evening show.

Promptly at eight-fifteen, Gordon took his seat in the orchestra. During the overture he looked around and smiled to himself. The theater was filling up. There were many more people seated than at the matinee. All was going to be well. The show started and the act which had originally been billed second now opened the show. Gordon smiled again. It was obvious that the manager had seen my act at the matinee and had moved me into second position. When the second act came on, it proved to be the two girls who had originally been billed third. Gordon sat back in his chair to relish the moment. The manager thought I was good enough to take over the third spot. This was going to affect my future salary: Gordon decided to ask for $175. Holding the third spot at the Palace, I would be the talk of the booking office in the morning. Gordon would ask, not for $175, but for $250. The two girls finished, and now the third act came on — it was a sketch. Gordon chuckled. The manager knew something, changing the bill around. The house was filled: when I came on *fourth*, I would be a riot. Instead of asking for $250, Gordon would demand $400. He was holding the trump card. But when the fourth act turned out to be Duffy and Inglis, a standard big-time comedy act, an aroma of rodent tinged the air and made itself known to Gordon's nostrils. He bounded out of his seat and started for the stage door. Coming around the corner of Forty-seventh Street, he saw me standing on the sidewalk with my trunk. I had been canned again. My big-time career had ended abruptly a second time. The next day I was back on the smalltime, opening at Proctor's Theatre in Troy, New York.

Two weeks later, on February 25, 1918, I arrived at the Poli Theatre in New Haven to find, in with my mail, what the boys called a German Hunting License. It was a notice from the draft board.

# 13

## Pantages and the Shuberts

THE draft board in Dorchester graciously arranged to interview me without an appointment. After answering the routine questions, I was given a physical. The draft board's medical staff was probing the male specimens of the neighborhood on the second floor of an abandoned factory near Edward Everett Square. I joined about eighty nude characters standing in a line that zigzagged around the loft. It was February, it was early in the morning, it was cold, and there was no heat. Standing around in my pelt, with the frigid drafts caressing my nates and adjacent areas, I felt like an Eskimo awaiting his turn at a public shower bath. Late in the afternoon, when I could have modeled for Gainsborough if he were contemplating another *Blue Boy*, the line moved up to where I was confronting a doctor. Actually, he wasn't a doctor: he was a computer. He counted my eyes, ears, fingers, toes, and anything I had more than one of. He told me to get dressed. The following day I was lucky enough to see the draft board again without waiting. I explained my predicament. With several weeks of vaudeville booked, I would need a few days to cancel the contracts if the draft board had plans for me. The head of the board told me that since my brother Bob had enlisted, and since I was the sole support of my Aunt Lizzie and her crippled husband, I would be deferred temporarily. If my status changed, I would be notified.

The next week I started at Norfolk, Virginia, on the Delmar Time. This circuit took its name from Jules Delmar, who booked some twenty theaters which ranged through the Southern states from Norfolk down to New Orleans and Hattiesburg, Mississippi. A number of army camps were situated in the South, but, just as it had been in Australia, entertainment for these army camps was unorganized. Groups of entertainers were assembled to do occasional shows at camps: the Knights of Columbus and the Y.M.C.A. arranged shows that were special events. I did many camp shows in this Southern area, and in the early days, shortly after this country's entrance into the war, it all reminded me of Australia: the enthusiasm, the boys eager to enlist, the girls seeing them off, the gaiety, the thought that it was all happening so far away from us and would soon be over. I hoped that I would not live to see the disillusionment and casualties I had seen in Australia. I did, unfortunately, live to see them both.

The Delmar Time terminated in New Orleans. It was May, and the summer parks were opening all around the country. To break my jump East, the Bostocks booked me into Forest Park, St. Louis, and Fontaine Ferry Park in Louisville. The Bostocks' faith in me had never been shaken; they were convinced that I had a big-time act. They had hopes. And, in Louisville, they wired me that an act had fallen out at the Hippodrome in Cleveland. They had booked me to open there Monday as a replacement. The Hippodrome was a big-time theater. My previous big-time appearances, at the Alhambra and the Palace, had been artistic debacles. I approached the Hippodrome with trepidation. All the others on the bill were big-time acts. Blanche Ring was the star of the show. and there were such acts as Helen Ware in a dramatic sketch called *The Eternal Barrier;* Ben Deeley, the "New Bellboy"; Paul Decker in *The Ruby Ray;* and the Olga and Mishka Company, presenting a miniature classic Russian ballet. In this big-time company my act went exceptionally well. The critics' reports were good, and the manager's report was so good that the Bostocks were able to book me on the Interstate Time. The Interstate was a big-time circuit that operated theaters in Fort Worth, Dallas, Houston, and San Antonio. The reports on my act continued good, and in August I was booked into the Palace Theatre in Chicago. The Chicago Palace was second in importance to the New York Palace. I was second on the bill there, but I was finally on the big time. Reviewing the show, one of the critics wrote:

> Fred Allen has an original idea of entertaining, and gets laughs every minute. His act is wholly his own, and is full of the best kind of fun. When Allen trotted out the pictures of George Washington, Woodrow Wilson, and the American Flag, the audience fell in with the spirit of this far from subtle dig at the proclivities of some artists to exploit patriotism, and cheered Allen lustily. He was one of the big hits of the bill.

Following this minor triumph, I was booked into all the out-of-town Keith theaters during the following season, playing Toledo, Cincinnati, Canton, Dayton, Erie, Buffalo, Toronto, Boston, Providence, Portland, and Lowell. Back in New York, I played the Royal, the Colonial, and the Bushwick. Everything, in short, but the Palace.

In June of 1919, I went back to Boston to spend the summer with my Aunt Lizzie. Many of the vaudeville theaters closed or cut salaries during the summer months. After forty weeks of full and split weeks, of losing sleep on prehistoric trains, of eating at lunch wagons, coffee pots, and one-arm restaurants, the busy vaudevillian needed the summer months to recharge his organic and mental (if any) equipment to be strong enough to cope with the hazards the coming season would present. For me, summers at home in Dorchester were relaxing. Acquaintances were renewed, we had a baseball team representing St. Margaret's Church, Carson Beach was a short walk from my aunt's house, and as "The Actor" I was a big shot with the gang that congregated in front of Hodge White's store every night. During the spring of 1919 I had played the Keith Theatre in Boston, which established my status as a celebrity with "Inky" Sheehan, "Flatfoot" Mc-Gilvrey, "Finky" Mallard, and the other patriarchs of the adolescent herd.

In 1919, the Keith and Orpheum circuits were signing vaudeville acts to three- and five-year pay-or-play contracts that guaranteed the acts forty or more weeks each year. These contracts could be used as collateral. When the actors' colony at Freeport, Long Island, started, a vaudeville performer could present his five-year Keith contract at any local bank and borrow enough money to buy or build a home. For the previous season I had been playing the Keith theaters, both smalltime and big. My reports had been good, my salary of $225 was reasonable. From the $225 I paid fifteen per cent commission. The United Booking Office, owned by the Keith interests, had set up what it laughingly called an employment office. The U.B.O. employment office collected ten per cent of the actor's salary at the source, five per cent of which it retained as a service for employing the actor, and the remaining five per cent it designated — in theory — as belonging to the actor's agent. But from this five per cent which belonged to the agent, the U.B.O. deducted two and one half per cent as a service for collecting the five per cent! The agent's residue, when crystallized, came out to a pure two and one half per cent. Most of the vaudeville acts who worked the Keith Time sent an additional five or ten per cent to their agents. Added to my fifteen per cent commission, I had travel and living expenses, cut weeks were frequent, and I had to send money home regularly. By working all season, I could amass about enough money to enable me to spend the summer months at home with my Aunt Lizzie. As a rule, late in August my savings had vanished, and I had to seek employment. After my success in the out-of-town Keith theaters, I felt sure that I would get a route for the coming season. But back in New York, the Bostocks advised me that while the Keith bookers liked my act and would book me from week to week at the same salary, they would not give me a long-term contract.

This was disappointing; I relayed my disappointment to Mark Leddy. Mark said that he was sure he could book me for the entire Loew circuit and a return trip over the Pantages Time. A few days later he reported that he could get me $275 — which represented a fifty-dollar raise — and guarantee me a solid year's work. The steady work, and the additional fifty-dollars, scuttled my big-time ambitions. I went back with Mark. The first time I had gone around the Loew theaters, I had opened the show, and my salary had been $75; now I returned, a feature act, next to closing, and getting $275. I was back on the smalltime, but I was a whale in a goldfish bowl. Being on the smalltime again didn't upset me. It had always been my contention that the only thing important to an actor is the money he has in the bank. Money talks, and it is the only conversation worth hearing when times are bad. An actor's popularity is fleeting. His success has the life expectancy of a small boy who is about to look into a gas tank with a lighted match. There is no nourishment to be derived from an actor's yesterdays. The applause he received, the bows he took, and the faded press notices he saved are but dusty ingredients that make up an old actor's memories. Nobody is interested in the actor's past.

The Loew tour assured me of many weeks in New York. I moved into the Stanley Hotel on Forty-seventh Street. The Stanley solicited the actor's patronage. Some of the Stanley's lady guests weren't so particular. On Forty-seventh Street, between Sixth and Seventh Avenues, there were eight hotels that housed actors and actresses of every description. The Somerset, adjoining the Palace Theatre entrance, had the high-class clientele; many of the big-time vaudeville acts lived there. The America, across the street, was the favorite of the burlesque chorus girls: it was a sort of roughhouse Y.W.C.A. The other hotels advertised reasonable rates, and their registers listed smalltime actors, bootleggers, pimps, bookmakers, and an assortment of nefarious characters who frequented actors' hotels for a reason. With the actors coming and going at unseemly hours, the bootlegger or the gangster could ply his trade at will and go completely unnoticed.

The Stanley Hotel had seen its best days. The lights were always going out, and the old-fashioned tank water closets refused to function at crucial moments. A call to the clerk brought the colored bellboy to the door with a ball of string. It was the management's belief that there was nothing that happened to the Stanley's lighting fixtures or its plumbing that could not be fixed with a piece of string. After a few months at the Stanley I could cope with any electrical or flushing dilemma that arose. You could always tell an old Stanley guest. To avoid tipping the bellboy, he kept a ball of string in the bureau drawer.

The Loew circuit had theaters in every neighborhood in New York City and Brooklyn. The acts moved from neighborhood to neighborhood. At the Delancey Theatre, on the lower East Side, Mae West was the star of the bill. At the National Theatre, in the Bronx, there was Harry Jolson, Al's brother; at the Columbia Theatre in Brooklyn, there were Burns and Lorraine. The Burns was George, later to acquire fame and fortune through marriage — his marriage to Gracie Allen. George's talents in those days were confined to dancing. He had ambitions to become a talking comedian, but his initial attempt at verbal fun was restricted to one joke. Burns and Lorraine opened their act with a song and double dance routine. After the dance, apropos of nothing at all, the following dialogue ensued:

> BURNS: I had a fight with my wife last night.
> LORRAINE: What happened?
> BURNS: She chased me around the house with a red-hot poker.
> I finally ran into a closet and shut the door.
> LORRAINE: And then?
> BURNS: My wife started knocking on the closet door and yelling, "Come out of that closet, you coward! Come out of that closet, you coward!"
> LORRAINE: Did you come out of the closet?
> BURNS: Not me. In my house, I'm boss.

After consummating this joke, Burns and Lorraine finished their act by dancing for ten minutes.

I met many good acts on the Loew Time. Most of them worked steadily through the years, but few of them became famous. Have you ever heard of Niblo's Birds, the Bootblack Four, Melodious Monarchs, Wormwood's Animals, Deltorelli and Glissando, Hoyt's Minstrels, and Harry Slatko's Rollickers? These and hundreds of other smalltime vaudeville acts entertained the audiences of their generation.

The Loew tour completed, I started back West, playing Cleveland, Detroit, and Chicago again, on my way to Minneapolis to join the Pantages road show. The bill this time promised more fun. The headline act was Asahi and Company. Asahi was a Japanese illusionist who featured routine magic tricks, and finished his act by causing water to spout from lighted candles, his assistants' heads, a steel rapier, and anything else his magic wand touched. The inevitable Pantages girl act was on the bill. This one was called "Girls Will Be Girls." In it, a Miss Florence Lorraine was starred. Florence essayed a Swedish domestic character, and was assisted by a straight man, Johnny Sullivan, and four singing and dancing girls. Also on hand were McGrath and Deeds, two boys who sang popular songs and indulged in comedy for good measure; Lucie Bruch, a petite Viennese violinist, who played classical selections; the Haas Brothers, two acrobats who offered "something new" on the horizontal bars. I completed the bill.

Trouble started early on this tour. Following the Minneapolis week, the show went into Canada for four weeks. As I said earlier, the Canadian audiences enthused over the novelty acts which were apt to be received mildly in the States, and ignored the comedy acts which were popular at home. Many times the acrobats let this transient success go to their heads, where there was plenty of room to accommodate it: acrobats' heads, in most cases, are not cluttered with the by-product of thought. The Haas Brothers, opening the show, found themselves a big hit in Winnipeg and started venturing *sotto-voce* opinions that involved the dubious skill, inflated salaries, and lack of audience appeal of the headliners. The Haas Brothers were muscular and powerful, and any comments they cared to make would never be challenged by me. In the process of upstaging the other acts, one of the brothers took to carrying a cane. The night we left Winnipeg it was thirty below zero; as the acrobat walked up the steps to enter the sleeper, the cane hit the car door and snapped in two. Three weeks later, when we left Canada and the show reverted to its normal pattern, the acrobat's ego dwindled until it matched the length of his cane.

As the weeks and the towns rolled by, minor squabbles broke the show up into factions. McGrath and I were inseparable; the acrobats never fully recovered from their Canadian success; the violinist was in love with her violin and practiced all day; and Florence Lorraine, a self-appointed prima donna, stopped talking to McGrath, Deeds, and me. This was because Master McGrath had caught the fancy of one of the girls in her act. And in the small towns, where we stayed in boardinghouses, Asahi and his five Japanese were always up, dressed, and off the train first. This meant that by the time the rest of us arrived at the boardinghouse, the Asahi troupe had taken the best rooms.

At Bozeman, Montana, the Asahis came a cropper. At the various one-night stands on the tour, the through train would drop our Pantages Pullman car off at a siding. After the show, we would return to the sleeper and go to bed; during the night, the next through train would pick up our car from the siding and take us to the next town on the tour. After the last show at Bozeman, we all returned to the car and retired as usual. At 6:30 A.M. I awakened in my lower berth and heard whispering in the aisle. The train had stopped and the Asahis were up, ready to leave to rush for the boardinghouse. Everybody else in the car was still sound asleep. The Asahis gathered up their baggage and tiptoed off the Pullman. Ten minutes later, I heard Asahi and his countrymen filing back into the car. I peeked out and saw them talking excitedly and preparing to go back to bed. I said, "What's the trouble, Asahi?" He said, "Holy smloke, Boosman!" There had been a snowstorm. The through train hadn't picked us up. Our

Pullman had stayed on the track all night at Bozeman and we were still there.

On a Pantages trip, there were certain cities in which each show caught up with the show ahead of it. If you knew an act with the preceding unit, that act would leave a note at the theater, telling you the best hotel, the better eating places, and any other information that might be helpful in a strange town. If the act ahead was a single man, and he met any girls in the town, he would leave the girls' names and phone numbers, and any suggestions that he felt were vital to further his successor's conquests. In most of the towns there were girls who made it their business to meet vaudeville actors. If they bestowed their favors on the town boys, they risked gossip. The girls felt secure with the actors, who were gone at the end of three days or a week. Like dead men, actors told no tales.

Many good-looking vaudeville actors, after each matinee, dressed hurriedly and rushed out to stand in front as the audience left the theater. As the girls came out, the male peacock preened himself, hoping to catch the attention of one of the corn-fed belles. This practice was called "three-sheeting." (A three sheet is a large sheet of paper used on billboards to advertise an attraction or a show.) Many male concubines on the prowl used devices to lure their prey. One male chaser carried a jeweler's assortment of rings in a plush sample case. The rings had small price tags attached and these were marked in code, supposedly for the jewelry trade. If a chambermaid entered his hotel room, or a single girl on the bill strayed into his theater dressing room, the procedure was the same. The plush case was open on the room dresser or on the make-up shelf at the theater; the rings sparkled in the light. If the chambermaid or girl was attracted to the case, the actor started his routine. He said that his sideline was jewelry, that these were sample rings he was to show to local jewelers. He carelessly looked at the tags and quoted some of the prices. Then he invited the victim to select any ring she liked. It was a present. The rest was generally easy. When his supply of rings ran low, the actor filled his plush case at the nearest ten-cent store. For many years this actor posed as a jeweler and left a trail of gullible girls with green fingers from coast to coast.

Prohibition posed great problems for the drinking vaudeville actor. He had to find a bootlegger in a strange city and take the word of some newly made acquaintance as to the quality of the hootch available. Usually, the stagehands could be depended upon for this information. Some of the stagehands were themselves bootleggers, and others knew some reliable party who could accommodate the actor. On the Pantages Time, the shows made two different trips into Canada, and coming back to the States, many acts packed cases of whiskey in with their wardrobes and scenery. At Seattle, thanks to this habit, the Pantages theater manager and the customs men were drinking the actors' whiskey for months. It happened this way: following the Seattle engagement, the road shows played one week in Vancouver and one week in Victoria, British Columbia. When the show finished at Victoria, it came back by boat to Seattle, and then went immediately by train to Tacoma. The first show to smuggle liquor successfully through the customs at Seattle wrote back to the next show, and from then on every show leaving Victoria brought back all the whiskey the actors could conceal. It was routine. The trunks and scenery baggage with the concealed whiskey passed through customs with only a perfunctory examination. This smuggling went on smoothly for weeks, and then suddenly, with no advance warning, one show's baggage was stopped at customs and examined mi-

nutely. The cases of whiskey were found and confiscated. The
actors were threatened with arrest but were finally let off
with a warning. The actors had lost their whiskey but felt
they were fortunate in escaping a fine or a jail sentence.

As a result of this, the acts quickly wrote back to Victoria,
warning the next show, and for a few weeks the show baggage was passed through customs with no examination. The
word went back, and the shows started coming through with
cases and bottles once more. Then, another inspection: the
trunks were combed and every last bottle was seized by the
customs officers. No one knew why the shows would go
through customs unmolested for weeks, and then, suddenly,
one show would have its entire baggage combed. It was all
very simple. It was the stage manager in Victoria who sold
the whiskey to the actors and helped them to pack it safely.
When the theater manager at Seattle needed a fresh supply,
he called the stage manager in Victoria, who would tell him
which acts had bought the whiskey and where they had put it.
The manager reported to the customs officials, and they
did the rest. The actors left Seattle quaking, and the theater
manager and the customs gentlemen divided the loot.

Our show arrived in Victoria at a bad time. The previous
show had been pillaged at Seattle, and the word was flashed
back to us. McGrath, Deeds, and I decided to outwit the customs. We bought twelve cheap rubber hot-water bottles and
filled them with Scotch. Each hot-water bottle held two
quarts, which meant that we had two cases. The four girls in
the act agreed to take three hot-water bottles each and conceal them under their dresses. The girls all looked pregnant,
and gurgled en route, but with the three of us helping them
they passed through customs without incident. We arrived in
Tacoma with four tired girls and our fluid contraband intact. We bought twenty-four quart glass bottles and one fun-

nel. The minute we all checked in at the hotel, the girls reported and divested themselves of their hot-water containers. McGrath, Deeds, and I manned the funnel and filled the bottles. The job finished, it called for a drink to celebrate. The instant the Scotch touched our lips we knew we had made one fatal mistake. We had bought cheap hot-water bottles; the body heat of the girls had cooked the liquor. The delicate taste of Scotch had vanished, and we were drinking liquid rubber. The venture wasn't a total loss. The Scotch was consumed but not enjoyed. We had the constant fear that our insides would eventually be vulcanized.

My friends McGrath and Deeds were later responsible for an episode that entangled me with Texas jurisprudence. When we arrived at El Paso, our road show had been together for twenty-four weeks. Miss Lorraine now no longer talked to anyone. The rest of us were sick of looking at each other and were eagerly awaiting the end of the tour. At El Paso, the district attorney was a friend of Miss Lorraine's. She must have told him of the aggravation she had suffered on the trip because of the constant desire of McGrath and Deeds to amplify the love life of the girls in her act. The district attorney, to prove his friendship, assured Miss Lorraine that he had some influence in El Paso, and while the troublesome cads were in town he would teach them a lesson, as a favor to Miss Lorraine.

The lesson took this form: one morning, as I was seated in my dressing room repairing my ventriloquial dummy, a stranger appeared at the door. He showed me a badge, explained that he was a detective, and asked me to come with him. When we arrived at the police station, it developed that the detective had arrested the wrong man. The district attorney wanted either McGrath or Deeds, in order to avenge Miss Lorraine's grievance. However, it appeared that I couldn't be released gracefully, and so I was charged with using indecent language in Miss Lorraine's presence. I didn't talk to the woman and hadn't used any language in her presence for many weeks. The theater manager arranged for my release, and the next morning my case came up in court. Miss Lorraine testified that McGrath, Deeds, and I were disreputable characters, and that she had heard vile language in El Paso, and the language could have come from any one of us. My character witnesses were the Asahi Company, none of whom understood English too well; the Viennese violinist, who spoke with an accent; and McGrath and Deeds. They were all to testify to my exemplary behavior on the entire tour.

The district attorney compelled my witnesses to stay outside the courthouse on the street; he didn't want them to hear each other's testimony. The district attorney had only one full arm; on his left side he ran out of arm just a few short inches below his elbow. He could close this stump and hold a pencil or papers in the crease made in his sleeve. To impress Miss Lorraine with his forensic dexterity during my trial, the district attorney kept rolling cigarettes with one hand. I must say he was very deft. He proceeded by kinking his short arm and placing a cigarette paper in his sleeve, then shaking the opened Bull Durham bag across the paper. After closing the top of the bag by tugging at the string with his teeth, the district attorney lifted the laden paper from his stump, rolled the paper adroitly with one hand, wet the edge with his lips, and placed the finished cigarette in his mouth. The district attorney was a chain smoker. By the time he had completed six or seven cigarettes, his sleeve was well sprinkled with Bull Durham flakes, the floor had enough tobacco on it to contract the habit, and my trial was over. The trial was a farce. The district attorney had nothing to sum up. To rescue him from his predicament the judge fined me ten dollars and costs. The theater manager insisted on paying everything; he also sent a telegram to Mr. Pantages explaining the circumstances. Mr. Pantages removed Miss Lorraine, her dialect, and her attraction from the circuit.

At Detroit our road show disbanded, and I bade good-by to McGrath and Deeds. A few weeks later I learned that they had stolen some of my song titles: "After the Ball Is Over, by Babe Ruth" and "I Had to Step off the Sidewalk, so the Local Board Could Pass Me By." They also stole a few of my other jokes. But that was the smalltime. You didn't expect strangers to steal your material; you depended on your friends. I went back to Chicago to play eight months on the Western Vaudeville Time. Sammy Tishman, one of the Western Vaudeville bookers, was a good friend of mine. He enjoyed booking me in towns where he was sure that the audience wouldn't understand my act. Having booked me, he would sit in Chicago and wait until he received the theater manager's report, or a personal letter from the manager about my act, as well as a letter from me. Eons later, when Sammy had moved to New York, he showed me copies of some of my letters he had kept.

From Mason City, Iowa, I had reported: "These jumps will help me rise in show business. I had to rise at 3:45 to leave Cedar Rapids. I have to rise again at 6:45 to leave here for Clinton. Rip Van Winkle must have played a season out here, and took the twenty years' rest to get acquainted with a mattress."

Centralia, Illinois: "This theatre is so far back in the woods the manager is a bear. There is no running water. You have to wash up with one of those crockery battery sets, pitcher and catcher."

Granite City, Illinois: "The audience is so low the ticket-taker is a dwarf to make the people feel at home. They have barbed wire under the door to keep people from crawling into the theatre. Also, the audience laughs in the wrong places — at the drug store and the pool room. People in this town are laughing everywhere except at the theatre."

Sammy had a collection of these comments, and another assortment of reprisal complaints sent in to him by managers from these same towns.

On the Western Vaudeville Time I had played several dates with Harry Langdon. Harry was a very talented pantomimist who did an act called "Johnny's New Car." Charlie Chaplin was enjoying great success in silent pictures at the time, and Hollywood was looking for other comedians suitable for the medium. The comedy character Harry played was a shy, bashful, quaint little fellow. Theater audiences loved Harry, and I knew that, properly presented in motion pictures, he would be a great success. When Harry received his first offer to go to Hollywood, he wanted me to go with him. He thought that I had a future as a comedy writer. The silent comedies of the day all used comedy titles; Harry wanted me to write titles and to work with him on his stories. The night before Harry and his wife Rose left for Hollywood, we stayed up all night discussing his future and mine. I decided to stay in vaudeville. I had my aunt to support and had to keep working. I couldn't afford to take the risk. My motto has always been "A bird in the hand may soil your sleeve, but as long as you've got the bird in there, you don't have to worry about where your next meal is coming from." Harry Langdon became a great success in Hollywood. But success in Hollywood is as fleeting as any fragment of a second.

I had another reason for not going to Hollywood. I had been working smalltime theaters for eighteen months. Down in Texas I had bought a mock ballad called "The Fatal Wedding" from a blackface comedian named Culpepper. After I had put it into my act, some months later I found that "The Fatal Wedding" had been stolen. I deleted the song, and wrote another mock ballad called "The Electric Chair." My act now opened with the singing of this ballad. During the song the music stopped every few bars as I explained the story, the characters in the song, and the musical accompaniment. I had gone back to the comedy make-up, my face was pallid, I wore a tall black derby hat and a skimpy Inverness cape that pinched me around the shoulders. I carried an umbrella that had no ribs. When it hung down straight, it looked like an umbrella; when I raised it up to point at something, it simply slumped down limply. I had big shoes and wore white gloves to accentuate my gestures during the song. Most vaudeville theaters were small, and mugging was a great asset to the comedians; from any part of the theater audiences could see an eyebrow lifted, and the comedian heightened his laughs with facial expressions. I sang "The Electric Chair" standing in a spotlight, plying my limp umbrella, explaining the story, and mugging. If the audience was good, the song took five minutes to render; after the song, the ventriloquial burlesque followed, and this took another five or six minutes. The banjo imitations were now accompanied with some sure-fire jokes, and by the time I had added a series of comedy verses to sing with the banjo, my act had become so long that I had to eliminate the juggling entirely.

I was now working three, four, and even five shows daily. (Pantages started five shows on Sunday in Seattle. The acts went on so often they had no time to leave the theater to eat. When it became obvious that with no food to eat, the tapeworms would quit the actors and crawl over the footlights to attack the audience, Mr. Pantages gave every actor fifty cents to pay for a dinner to be sent to his dressing room. Mr. Pantages, demonstrating his loyalty to his Athenian heritage, decreed that the only person to be permitted backstage to take these dinner orders was a man who owned a restaurant near the theater. He was a Greek friend of Mr. Pantages.)

In working so many shows, I had had ample opportunity to experiment with jokes, and I had appeared before audiences of every conceivable mental level. My act had been reduced to its essentials. On the smalltime it was a solid comedy hit. If the act could get the same results on the big time, I was confident that I could increase my salary and obtain a long-term Keith contract. That is why I didn't want to chance the uncertainty of Hollywood. I thought that my future would be brighter in New York.

Mark Leddy was sure that at last I was ready for the big time. I had explained the new version of the act to him, and he had booked me at Union Hill, New Jersey, and brought Leo Fitzgerald, a Keith agent, to see the new juggleless presentation. Leo was enthusiastic and booked me, through the Keith office, at the Colonial and Alhambra. At my last Alhambra appearance I had been canned. This time I was a great success. Even *Variety* wrote:

> Fred Allen scored the laughing hit of the bill, with one of the most original monologues seen in vaudeville. He proved himself to be a thorough showman all through his offering.

It was late in May and the season was closing, but Leo booked me in Keith theaters until the first of July. My act was a big laughing hit every place. I was sure that the Keith office would be anxious to offer me a contract. But before Leo Fitzgerald had a chance to ascertain my Keith prospects, I had a call from Frank Fay. Frank was a very clever monologist and light comedian who was popular with New York audiences, and he was about to produce his own revue, called *Frank Fay's Fables*. He had seen my act at the Colonial and wanted me to work with Jimmy Duffy in his show. Duffy was an original comedian who wrote his own material. His weakness was alcohol. When we started rehearsing together, Prohibition and liquor costs had reduced Duffy to drinking Ed Pinaud's Hair Tonic. He used to say he had consumed so much hair tonic that his appendix had a goatee on it.

Fay had a fresh idea for his *Fables*. The revue opened with Fay in the audience explaining his new show. After the chorus had started the opening number, a dapper-looking elderly gentleman and a beautiful girl would arrive late and settle themselves conspicuously in an upper box. Fay would stop the opening chorus and explain to the elderly man that he had missed the start of the show. The elderly gentleman would reply that he hadn't missed anything, that he had been going to Broadway revues for fifty years and that they were all alike. He would then tell Fay that he would give fifty thousand dollars if he could come to the theater just one night and see something different, the sort of thing that he would like to see. Fay would reply that the man was obviously joking. The elderly gentleman would say that he was perfectly sincere; he would identify himself as a wealthy stockbroker. At this point Fay would bring the theater manager down the aisle to corroborate this identification. The stockbroker would then repeat his offer, and say that if Fay could give him the kind of entertainment he had wanted to see for years, he would give Fay his certified check for fifty thousand dollars as soon as the revue was finished. The revue would start again, and during the evening Fay and the elderly gentleman would exchange comedy talk about the scenes and numbers and the old man's likes and dislikes. At the revue's finale, the cast would appear in street clothes. After the elderly gentleman had presented the check to Fay, the cast would sing the finale, cross over the footlights, and walk out of the theater with the audience.

In rehearsal, the show looked wonderful. Everybody who saw a run-through said that Fay had a hit. Duffy and I had collaborated on several comedy scenes and songs. I had never been in a Broadway show, but now, listening to Fay and his friends, I thought I had one foot on the first greasy step to the threshold of success. The step proved to be greasier than I thought. When the show was finally assembled, it developed that Fay had no money. His credit was nonexistent. The scenery, props, costumes, wardrobe, and orchestrations were all held up awaiting advance deposits. When Duffy's mother had no food in her apartment, and Duffy appealed to Fay, Fay told him that a grocer was thinking of backing the show and had sent Fay some canned goods to prove his sincerity. Fay filled Duffy's arms with cans of corn and tomatoes to be taken home to his mother. On another occasion, when Duffy claimed that his mother was starving, Fay gave him a big cheese that looked like a spare tire. Duffy said his mother was hungry; she didn't have mice in the house. Duffy demanded money, but Fay had two things in his favor: he was adamant, and he was broke.

Fay's arrogance was eventually his undoing. John Golden and Winchell Smith, after seeing a rehearsal, agreed to finance the show; for their money they wanted fifty-one per cent of the stock to assure controlling interest. Fay refused. He had no consideration for the actors and chorus girls who had been rehearsing for weeks. It was Fay's idea, Fay's show; Fay was going to run it. *Fay's Fables*, with this cast, never opened. If Fay's ego had been acid, he would have consumed himself.

One thing often bothered me in the wake of this experience. At one optimistic period during rehearsals, Fay planned to open his show in Pittsburgh. Fay, Duffy, and I went down to the Penn Station one night to see the show's advance man off. The advance man had two three sheets under his arm, and a one-way ticket. He was going to publicize *Fay's Fables* and await the arrival of the company in Pittsburgh. I often wonder what became of that advance man.

I know what became of Fay. The last time I saw Fay he was walking down Lovers' Lane, holding his own hand.

The summer and my Broadway hopes vanished with *l'affaire* Fay. My salary had been $275; Leo Fitzgerald now told me that the Keith office would book me at $325. When I asked Mark Leddy's advice, Mark said that the Shuberts were going to start a vaudeville circuit in opposition to Keith. He added that the Shuberts needed acts, were paying higher salaries, and were guaranteeing twenty weeks. Arthur Klein, one of the leading Keith agents, had been engaged by the Shuberts to book their theaters. Mark spoke to Mr. Klein, and he offered to book me for $400. I signed the Shubert contract to open late in September. The Shuberts owned and operated theaters in New York City, Brooklyn, Newark, Philadelphia, Baltimore, Washington, Pittsburgh, Cleveland, Detroit, Chicago, Milwaukee, Hartford, Springfield, Buffalo, Toronto, and Boston. Their vaudeville shows were booked in each of these cities. The Keith circuit announced immediately that acts playing the Shubert theaters would be blacklisted for life. It didn't worry me. Most of my work in vaudeville had been done for Pantages, Loew, and independent bookers. The Keith blacklist didn't bother the Shuberts, either; they had many musical-comedy names and dramatic stars and comedians under contract. Arthur Klein knew his business and assembled a series of excellent vaudeville shows to tour the Shubert theaters.

I was assigned to a unit that starred Lew Fields in a condensation of *Snapshots,* a show he had done on Broadway. Featured with Fields was Lulu McConnell. Miss McConnell played the comedy scenes with Fields, and also did her vaudeville act in the first part of the show with her husband, Grant Simpson. The show consisted of five acts of vaudeville: the Arco Brothers, A. Robins, Yvette, Fred Allen, and McConnell and Simpson. Following intermission, Lew Fields's *Snapshots* presented an hour-long revue. The show opened at the Crescent Theatre in Brooklyn to critical acclaim. Acclaim in Brooklyn assured universal business; the Lew Fields unit played sixteen weeks to record-breaking success.

While we were on the road, Lew Fields's son Herbie graduated from Columbia and arrived to join his father's show. Herbie brought a friend who had also finished college; this boy's name was Dickie Rodgers. Mr. Fields made Herbie an actor, using him in the blackouts and the comedy scenes. Dickie was appointed the unit's musical conductor. All of the pit musicians out of town were middle-aged men, and most of them resented having the college boy guide them through their andantes and largos. Herbie and Dickie have been in the theater ever since. Fields, Rodgers, and Hart started auspiciously by writing the *Garrick Gaieties, Dearest Enemy, Connecticut Yankee,* and a number of early musical successes. Herbie starched his name to Herbert and, with his sister Dorothy, has continued to write Broadway musicals. Dickie gave up his feathered appellation and became Richard. As the melodic half of Rodgers and Hart and Rodgers and Hammerstein, Richard has made music that has festooned the acoustics of the world for more than thirty-five years.

*Snapshots* finished its career early in 1922. I was sent

with the Nora Bayes unit to return over the circuit. Miss Bayes was a great artist and a wonderful woman. Her company was one large happy family. She was interested in the welfare of every member of her show, and was eternally doing little things to brighten their days. With the Nora Bayes show, I met a Scottish comedian named Jock McKay. Jock had been booked from England. The jokes he had in his monologue were so ancient to American audiences that Jock went from city to city laying plaid eggs. I tried to help him freshen up his jokes, and did help him improve his act some. Jock gave me a joke he was afraid to tell; it concerned the "big-hearted Scotsman who donated two hundred dollars to the widow of the Unknown Soldier." As soon as Jock heard the scream it received in my routine, he asked me to give him his joke back. I did.

The opening of my act had now been changed. Before my appearance the orchestra played the heavy opening bars of *Lohengrin*. The music stopped abruptly. The theater went completely dark. One small spotlight focused on a sign as it shot down from the flies. The sign read:

Mr. Allen Is Quite Deaf
If You Care To
LAUGH OR APPLAUD
Please Do So
LOUDLY

The spotlight swooped to the entrance as I walked on the stage cupping my ear to hear if there was any applause. Early in the act, if a joke got no reaction, I raised my hand to my ear and listened to confirm the silence.

When our Shubert units were in New York, many of the acts made additional money playing Sunday Concerts. The Shuberts booked Sunday Concerts into their theaters that housed musical or dramatic shows during the week. One Sunday night I was booked into the theater where Al Jolson was appearing during the week in his show *Bombo*. When I told one of my jokes, the musicians in the pit groaned. When I asked them about this unfavorable reaction, they told me that Al Jolson was telling the same joke in his show. The joke was: "The man is so deceitful he puts salt on his toupee to make people think he has dandruff." I knew I had originated the line. I wrote Mr. Jolson a letter, and received this reply:

Al Jolson

October 13, 1921

Mr. Fred Allen
1493 Broadway
New York City

MY DEAR SIR:

I have your letter of the 11th regarding the "toupee" gag. In reply I beg to say that I have been using the same for the past three years.

I have no desire to use any one's material and would gladly give it up to save you any embarrassment of being accused of taking my material, but on the point of it being yours exclusively I think that is open for argument.

As one N.V.A. to another I send you greetings along with the "toupee" gag.

Yours truly,<br>AL JOLSON

Mr. Jolson must have dictated this letter. He couldn't have read it because he continued to use the "toupee" joke in his show for the rest of the season. Twenty years later, I met Mr. Jolson at the Hillcrest Golf Club in Beverly Hills. He told me that he used to see my act frequently and helped himself to my jokes. I thought the admission was flattering, but a mite delayed.

Shubert vaudeville did several things for me. Playing on the bill with big-name performers like Lew Fields, Nora

Bayes, William and Gordon Dooley, Nan Halperin, Bonita and Lew Hearn, and Stan Stanley and entertaining better audiences gave me confidence. I had been able to polish my act and improve the quality of my comedy. One week, at the Winter Garden, I followed Nora Bayes's act. At the matinee, after Miss Bayes had finished her final encore, I started my act at 5:45 P.M.; at night, I didn't get on the stage until almost midnight. The people stayed in their seats. For a single act, following such a long bill, this was considered a great achievement. At New Haven, the Yale students on three different occasions requested the manager of the Shubert Theatre there to book my act back; that one season I played New Haven four times, to the delight of the undergraduates.

Shubert vaudeville did another thing for me: it got me blacklisted for life in the Keith office. When I finished the Shubert contract, I went back to the smalltime and played independent theaters in Red Bank and Hoboken, New Jersey; Torrington and Ansonia, Connecticut; Watertown, New York; Stapleton, Long Island; and other whistle stops that puckered up and blew in my direction.

Shubert vaudeville did one final thing for me: it enabled J. J. Shubert to see my act several times when I was playing his New York theaters. And when, at one point, the outlook seemed as dark as 10 P.M. in the wintertime, Mark Leddy (good old Mark) called up to tell me that we had an appointment with Mr. Shubert. The following day, as the door of Mr. Shubert's office closed behind us, Mark said, "Congratulations! You are finished with vaudeville for a while!"

And I was. In my hand I had a contract to go into the next Winter Garden attraction: *The Passing Show of 1922*.

# 14

## The Life and Death
## of Vaudeville

THIS chapter is an autobiographical paren-
thesis. It is more about vaudeville than me. . . .

Vaudeville is dead. The acrobats, the animal acts, the
dancers, the singers, and the old-time comedians have taken
their final bows and disappeared into the wings of obscurity.
For fifty years — from 1875 to 1925 — vaudeville was the
popular entertainment of the masses. Nomadic tribes of nondescript players roamed the land. The vaudeville actor was
part gypsy and part suitcase. With his brash manner, flashy
clothes, capes and cane, and accompanied by his gaudy
womenfolk, the vaudevillian brought happiness and excitement to the communities he visited. He spent his money
freely and made friends easily. In the early days, the exact de-
gree of prosperity the smalltimer was enjoying could be determined by taking inventory of the diamonds that adorned
his person. If he was doing well, the smalltimer wore a large
diamond horseshoe in his tie and two or three solitaires or
clusters on his fingers; his wife, dripping with necklaces,
rings, earrings, and bracelets, looked as though she had been
pelted with ice cubes that had somehow stuck where they
landed. The smalltimer's diamonds didn't have to be good.
They just had to be big. What difference if the eight-karat

ring was the color of a menthol cough drop as long as the stone sparkled in the spotlight during the act? To the small-timer, a diamond represented security. It impressed the booker, the manager, and the audience, but, more important, the diamond was collateral. Confronted with a financial crisis in a strange community, the smalltimer didn't have to embarrass himself by attempting to convince a tradesman or a hotel manager that his credentials were valid. To obtain emergency funds, he merely stepped into the nearest pawn-shop, slipped the ring from his finger, and consummated a legitimate routine business transaction. When his diamonds were temporarily on location, the smalltimer avoided his friends and his usual haunts, knowing that the absence of his Kimberley gravel was an admission that the panic was on. The instant his luck changed, the diamonds were redeemed and returned to their customary places. Back in the spot-light, with the horseshoe pin and the rings sparkling, the smalltimer's necktie and his ring fingers resumed strutting their stuff.

The herd instinct was a dominant impulse in the vaude-ville actor's behavior pattern. When the season closed, the smalltimers congregated at vacation resorts to revel in each other's company. The smalltimer lived in another world. He thought and talked only about his act and about show busi-ness. Nothing else interested him. If you said to him, "Do you remember the Johnstown flood?" he would probably re-ply, "Remember the Johnstown flood? Are you kidding? I and the wife were playing Pittsburgh that week. Eva Tan-guay was the star. Walter Kelly was next to closing. After the first show the manager comes running back and says, 'You kids is the hit of the bill!' He moves us down to next to closing for the rest of the week. Kelly is blowing his top. All week long I and the wife murder them!" Everybody in

Johnstown could have been swept out of town: the small-timer wouldn't know or care. He had nothing in common with anybody who was not in his profession.

The two vaudeville centers of the country were New York and Chicago. During the summer layoff season — theaters had no air conditioning then, and many closed during the hotter months — vaudeville colonies were formed. The Chicago acts rented or bought cottages near the lakes in Wisconsin or Michigan; the New York vaudevillians huddled together in Connecticut and down on Long Island. The most famous of the actors' colonies was founded at Freeport, Long Island. The stars first established summer homes at Freeport, and then the smalltimers precipitated a real-estate boom fighting to buy property and houses to make their home in Freeport to let the stars see how the other half lived.

The Long Island Good Hearted Thespians Society was formed. This was a social club whose members reduced the name to the Lights. The first president was Victor Moore. One of the traditional Lights Club functions was the celebration of Christmas on the Fourth of July. In December, most of the vaudeville actors were on the road, away from their homes, their families, and their friends. They spent their Christmas Days on trains, in dingy dressing rooms, or in drab hotels. Members of the Lights ignored the conventional Yule season and saved their Christmas greetings and presents until the return to Freeport. On July Fourth, though the temperature be in the nineties, the Lights' Christmas tree was decorated and lighted, Santa Claus was dressed in his heavy suit with the ermine trimmings, presents were placed under the tree, and the members and their children arrived in their furs, mittens, and earlaps, some even clattering into the club on snowshoes.

A vaudeville actor could relax and enjoy himself only in

the company of another vaudeville actor. You could sit a vaudeville actor in front of a mirror and he would stay there contentedly for days on end. In cities on the road, the vaudeville performers congregated at the same boardinghouses or cheaper hotels. There was a time when the actor was *persona non grata* at the better inns, and this was especially true of vaudevillians, who were presumed to be irresponsible from the very fact that their profession was uncertain and their living precarious. It was generally understood that vaudeville performers went in for wild parties in their homes and that their domestic habits were rarely awarded the Good Housekeeping Seal of Approval. Accordingly it was deemed best for hotel clerks to smile blandly when they were asked for rooms and inform the vaudevillian that the hotel was "full up." Stage folk, except for those who had attained stellar rank, were pretty much pariahs around the decent hotels.

Duke Pohl, the manager of the Breevort Hotel in St. Louis, once told me that he was traveling in a special train to attend an annual convention of the Greeters of America, the official organization of the hotel men. Each man was asked to name his hotel and tell something about it. Duke later told me that when he announced that his Breevort catered to stage folks, "I could almost hear the gasp that went around the circle. I told them I considered stage people the most maligned persons on earth. I said that my experience with vaudevillians had been uniformly pleasant, that they paid their bills, were quiet in their rooms, were sober, sedate, and serious people trying to make a living."

Duke defended the profession at a time when many hotel and rooming-house owners were complaining that some vaudeville people were stealing towels. This practice was so common that jokes were being told about it. One joke was about the vaudeville actor who died and left an estate of eight hundred hotel and Pullman towels. Then there was the charge that actors checked into their hotels with heavy suitcases, stayed a week or two, then disappeared without paying their bills. Credit had been extended because the manager had seen the heavy suitcases; when, later, these were pried open, they were found to contain nothing but a collection of bricks and old telephone books. Indigent vaudeville actors were known to lower their suitcases out the window in the back of the hotel, then walk through the lobby empty handed, reclaim their cases, and leave town. An actor who had a trunk in his room received an extension of credit. When the bill mounted, the actor, anticipating that the manager would tip the trunk to ascertain its contents and to try to find out if clothing had been pawned, took the precaution of nailing the trunk to the floor. Ted Healy, a comedian, once owed a sizable bill at the Lincoln Hotel in New York. Ted brought the three stooges he used in his act up to his room and ordered each stooge to don two or three sets of his underwear, two complete suits of clothes, and an overcoat. Healy followed the stooges out of the Lincoln lobby wearing three suits and one topcoat, and carrying a raincoat with every pocket bulging. Healy left the Lincoln Hotel with two mementos of his stay: an empty room and an empty trunk. Things of this kind took place occasionally, and hotel owners were suspicious, but Duke Pohl believed in befriending actors, and they showed their appreciation. As Duke used to say, "I've never lost anything by it. They all paid me eventually."

Vaudeville could not vouch for the honesty, the integrity, or the mentality of the individuals who collectively made up the horde the medium embraced. All the human race demands of its members is that they be born. That is all vaudeville demanded. You just had to be born. You could be ignorant and be a star. You could be a moron and be wealthy. The elements that went to make up vaudeville were combed from the jungles, the four corners of the world, the intelligentsia and the subnormal. An endless, incongruous swarm crawled over the countryside dragging performing lions, bears, tigers, leopards, boxing kangaroos, horses, ponies, mules, dogs, cats, rats, seals, and monkeys in their wake. Others rode bicycles, did acrobatic and contortion tricks, walked wires, exhibited sharpshooting skills, played violins, trombones, cornets, pianos, concertinas, xylophones, harmonicas, and any other known instrument. There were hypnotists, iron-jawed ladies, one-legged dancers, one-armed cornetists, mind readers, female impersonators, male impersonators, Irish comedians, Jewish comedians, blackface, German, Swedish, Italian, and rube comedians, dramatic actors, Hindu conjurors, ventriloquists, bag punchers, singers and dancers of every description, clay modelers, and educated geese: all traveling from hamlet to town to city, presenting their shows. Vaudeville asked only that you own an animal or an instrument, or have a minimum of talent or a maximum of nerve. With these dubious assets vaudeville offered fame and riches. It was up to you.

Vaudeville families endured for generations. The female of the species foaled on trains, in dressing rooms, in tank towns, and in the big cities. The show must go on. At the theater the baby slept in the top of the trunk in the dressing room. At the hotel a crib was improvised by removing a large bureau drawer and placing it on the bed or between two chairs. A large blanket filled the drawer nicely; the baby, wrapped in its quilt, rested serene in his drawer bassinet. The vaudeville baby carried its own baggage. A small valise contained milk bottles, nipples, safety pins, and emergency diapers. On a sleeper jump, vaudeville couples with a baby always had the same routine: at 1 A.M., with the train thundering through the night, a tiny cry is heard. In two berths, an upper and a lower, lights snap on instantly. The husband jumps down from his upper berth into the aisle. The curtains of the lower berth part just a crack, muted voices are heard, the clasps on the miniature valise click open, and a nippled bottle, filled with milk, appears through the curtains. The husband steadies himself as he sways down the aisle on his way to arouse the porter to warm the precious quota of milk. In the lower berth, the sounds of the mother's soothing voice and the baby's cries persist until the husband returns. The warm milk bottle is passed in, the baby gurgles and stops crying, the curtains close, the husband crawls back up into his berth. The lights go off in both berths, and it is dark and silent once again; the train hurries ahead into the night.

Arriving in the next town, and safe in their room, the family goes to work. The husband removes a small drawer from the dresser, places a rubber sheet over the drawer, and pokes it snugly down into the four corners. Then he fills the drawer half full of tepid water. The mother lowers the baby gently into the drawer to enjoy its bath after the train trip.

The smalltime vaudeville mother had the endurance of a doorknob. She did three or four shows a day as part of the act. She cared for her baby on the road and prepared its food. She did the family washing: there was always a clothesline hanging and dripping away in the dressing room and the boardinghouse, and the sinks were filled with diapers. As the family grew larger, the kids were packed like sardines into upper berths. (Midgets often traveled in clusters in upper berths; an actor in a lower berth once complained that he had been kept awake all night by a midget with insomnia who had been walking up and down in the upper berth.)

Many wives cooked the family meals in the dressing room;

before electricity became promiscuous, vaudeville wives carried tin plates, cups, knives and forks, and prepared tasty meals over flaming gas jets and blazing Sterno cans in dressing and hotel rooms. Then there was a special theatrical trunk, made by the Herkert and Meisel Trunk Company of St. Louis, which was constantly adding new features to lighten the burden of the vaudeville wife. The H & M wardrobe trunk had such special innovations as a metal compartment in one drawer to hold an electric iron; a small rubber-lined compartment which enabled actors to pack wet sponges, washcloths, and soap on hurried closing nights; a hat compartment for man or woman; a flat drawer under the wardrobe section to hold shoes; a jewel box; an ironing board that could be attached securely to the trunk to enable women to iron in the theater. These, and many other features of this trunk, made life easier for the vaudeville mother.

Vaudeville families flourished. The babies teethed on greasepaint, and their sitters were other acts on the bill who watched the tots while the parents were on stage. When the babies were able to walk, they were led on stage to take their first bows. Later, they learned to imitate their parents and many other acts who played on the different bills. After completing their schooling, most of the children grew up and went into vaudeville, and had children who grew up and went into vaudeville.

The smalltimer plying his profession was exposed to many irritations. When his act laid an egg in one town, he couldn't wait to leave for the next town, where, he hoped, things would be better. When the audience was bad, the whole community was terrible; the hotel, the restaurants, the food, the newspapers, and the people all became impossible. When the smalltimer was a riot, his environment was perfect. Using the smalltimer's psychology, if his act went badly in Detroit,

Detroit as a metropolis was a bust. If his act went big in Eureka, Eureka was Utopia.

Next to the audience, in its importance to the smalltimer, stood the theater orchestra. If the orchestra could not play his wife's ballad properly, if the tempo of his dance music was too fast or too slow, if the drummer didn't catch his pratfalls with a well-timed roll and crash or tear the cloth on cue as he pretended to rip his trousers, the actor fought with his wife and sulked in his dressing room until the next show. Vaudeville orchestras varied from one piece — a piano — to seven or eight pieces. The usual smalltime theater had piano, cornet, and drums. The drums were very important: they accentuated the falls and crashes of the comedians and played long rolls for the aerialists' sensational slides. For his music, the smalltimer carried eight or nine parts in cardboard or leather covers. Playing the cheaper theaters, which had only a piano and drum, only the piano and drum parts were used. After the smalltimer had played several weeks in dumps, and was then booked into a big theater, he would occasionally brag at rehearsal in order to leave the musicians with the impression that he was accustomed to playing good theaters. He couldn't fool the musicians, however, because the minute they saw the smalltimer's music they knew where the act had been playing. The violin, clarinet, cornet, and bass parts were brand-new; the piano and drum parts were filthy. At rehearsal in a new town, the smalltimer, sensing that the orchestra wasn't too friendly, examined his music. It explained everything. The drummer in the last town had written on the drum part, "This act is lousy." The clarinet player had written, "He died here." The cornet player had summed everything up by simply writing one word: "Stinks."

The smalltimer's billing was a matter of great concern. Before the opening show at each theater he examined the front of the theater to check on the size of his name and his position in the list of acts. The vaudeville headliner often had a clause in his contract assuring him of top billing. The smalltimer's billing depended on the whim of the local manager or the man who printed or painted the theater signs. Seeing his name in runt letters could catapult the smalltimer into a three-day funk. His position on the bill was of major importance. If his act had been next to closing and he suddenly found himself second on the bill, wires were dispatched to the booking office and his agent, and the theater manager was summoned to the dressing room before the smalltimer deigned to do the first show. Headliners had clauses in their contracts that entitled them to the best dressing rooms. The smalltimer dressed where he was told. If he used the same dressing room as his wife, the smalltimer immediately examined all walls and connecting doors for holes. A few depraved actors carried gimlets and bits around with them, and drilled holes in the walls to watch the sister act or the single woman in the next room undress. If holes were discovered, the stage manager was notified and the apertures were filled with shoemaker's wax. One worry less for the smalltimer.

The censoring of his act also upset the smalltimer. When Paul Keith, after running a museum on Washington Street in Boston, opened his first theater, the Bijou Dream, he insisted on clean entertainment. Mrs. Keith instigated the chaste policy, for she would tolerate no profanity, no suggestive allusions, *double-entendres*, or off-color monkey business. As the Keith circuit grew, every theater carried a sign on the bulletin board:

## NOTICE
## TO PERFORMERS

Don't say "slob" or "son-of-a-gun" or "hully gee" on this stage unless you want to be cancelled peremptorily. Do not address anyone in the audience in any manner. If you have not the ability to entertain Mr. Keith's audiences without risk of offending them, do the best you can. Lack of talent will be less open to censure than would be an insult to a patron. If you are in doubt as to the character of your act, consult the local manager before you go on the stage, for if you are guilty of uttering anything sacrilegious or even suggestive, you will be immediately closed and will never again be allowed in a theatre where Mr. Keith is in authority.

Long after Mr. Keith's death the circuit was still waging its campaign against suggestive material. For many months *Variety* published a column called "You Mustn't Say That" which featured deletions in stage material ("Hell" or "Lord Epsom, Secretary of the Interior," or "An old maid taking a tramp through the woods," and so on) made by the Keith censorship bureau. As most of the gamy lines and jokes were his biggest laughs, the smalltimer would fight to the death to keep them in his act.

Many smaller acts who used one or two jokes, or a few comedy lines, and could not buy special material subscribed to *Madison's Budget*. For twenty years — from 1898 to 1918 — a man named James Madison published an annual collection of monologues, cross-fire jokes, sketches, minstrel-show afterpieces, and parodies. This assortment of humorous matter sold for one dollar and was known as *Madison's Budget*. If a comedian found six or eight jokes in the *Budget* that he could adapt to his act, his dollar investment had returned a hearty dividend.

Comedy acts were always the targets of the pirates. If a comedian was original and wrote his own material, or if he frequently bought new routines and songs to keep his act up to date, he soon found that other comedians were stealing parts of his act. For many years performers had no way to protect their gags, parodies, or bits of business. Copyright laws were ignored, and good gags spread like bad news. One blackface comedian on the big time stole so much material that he couldn't use it all in his act; he hired another blackface act and paid him a salary to play the smalltime using the stolen material he had left over. There was a young comedian whose father regularly attended the opening show at the Palace. If any of the acts had new lines, jokes, or song titles, the father copied them down and wired them to his son. The act continued convulsing the Palace audience in New York, little dreaming that its best jokes were being told in Omaha, San Francisco, or wherever the son happened to be playing.

Original material was spread around in many ways. For instance, when blackface acts and other comedy teams split up, many times the men or women took new partners, and both new acts continued to do the same routines. After a series of splittings it was not unusual to find four or five teams all doing the same act. Burlesque shows lifted scenes bodily from Broadway revues. Social directors at summer camps spent the winter copying down anything they found in the Broadway theaters which they thought they could use at the camps next summer. Johnny Neff, a monologist, used to explain to his audiences how crazy comedians were to buy jokes. Johnny would relate how Frank Tinney had paid a hundred dollars for a certain joke. Johnny would then tell the joke to prove that Tinney was insane. When Johnny had finished explaining how much money Raymond Hitchcock, Ed Wynn, Jack Donahue, Leon Errol, and Richard Carle had paid for their jokes, and after he had told all these jokes himself, Johnny had a hilarious monologue that hadn't cost him a penny. And Milton Berle for years has been bragging to audiences that he has stolen jokes from other comedians. There has been no reason to doubt his word.

When Mr. Albee founded the National Vaudeville Artists, Inc., after breaking the White Rats' strike (the White Rats had been the original vaudeville performers' association), one of the inducements to attract members was the new organization's Protected Material Department. Any member could protect his act. All he had to do was to enclose a copy of his material in a sealed envelope and deliver it to the N.V.A. office. The envelope was placed in the Protected Material files. Later, if a plagiarist was brought to bay, the act preferred charges, the sealed envelope was opened, and the N.V.A. officials dispensed justice. Hundreds of acts protected their material through this service. After Mr. Albee's death, vaudeville started over the hill and took the N.V.A. club with it. Before the members vacated the clubhouse on Forty-sixth Street, some official, by whose authority nobody will ever know, sold the entire contents of the N.V.A. Protected Material Department files to Olsen and Johnson.

Superstitions and irrational beliefs influenced the vaudevillian as he made his decisions and planned his daily activities. Many credulous omens the performer treated with respect. He thought bad luck ensued if he whistled in the dressing room, found peacock feathers anywhere in the theater, saw a bird on the window sill, threw away his old dancing shoes, and so forth. There were many other bad omens, but there were only two portents that assured the performer future happiness. Good luck was sure to follow if an actor put his undershirt on inside out, or if he touched a humpbacked person.

Vaudeville acts often assumed strange names to attract attention. An unusual name was easily remembered by bookers, managers, and audiences. A few uniquely named acts were: Fyne and Dandy (acrobats), Sharp and Flat (musicians), Willie Rolls (roller skater), Amazon and Nile (contortionists), Nip and Tuck (acrobats), North and South (musical act), Worth and While (sister act), Possum Welch (dancer), and Darn, Good, and Funny (comedy trio).

The early vaudeville performers were inventive; they had to create the unusual specialties they performed. Vaudeville grew, and new acts came along to help themselves to the ideas of the originators, and to elaborate on and embellish them. Many specialty artists, in constructing their acts, came up with some weird innovations. One of these was Orville Stamm. Not long ago I got a letter from Orville, asking if I remembered him. It was not easy to forget Orville. He billed himself as the "Strongest Boy in the World." To demonstrate his great strength, Orville played the violin; as he played, he had suspended from the crook of his bow arm an enormous English bulldog. The bulldog made graceful arcs in the air as Orville pizzicatoed and manipulated his bow. For the finish of his act, Orville lay flat on the stage and arched his back; in the better acrobat circles, this was known as "bending the crab." When Orville's chest and abdomen attained the correct altitude, a small upright piano was placed across his stomach. An assistant stood on Orville's thigh and played the piano accompaniment as Orville, in his "crab" position, sang "Ireland Must Be Heaven, 'Cause My Mother Came from There." This finish was a sensation, and I'm sure it was Orville's own idea.

Raymonde, a female impersonator, also originated an unusual finish. After doing his entire act as a girl, Raymonde took a bow and removed his wig. The audience, seeing man's hair, was amazed to find that the girl was a boy. As the applause continued, Raymonde removed the man's wig, and blond tresses tumbled down over his shoulders. The boy was now a girl again. The audience, again duped, was frantic. Raymonde took another bow or two to thunderous applause, then removed the girl's wig and was a boy again. Raymonde, emulating the manner of a female impersonator's conception of a truck driver, swaggered off the stage to absolute bedlam.

A man named Willard was billed as the "Man Who Grows." As he talked, he stretched his arms out a foot or more beyond their normal length. For his finish Willard grew four or five inches in height. I watched Willard many times backstage without being able to discover his secret. He must have been able to telescope his skin.

An inventive monologist in Chicago featured a singing goat. Following a dull fifteen minutes of talk, the monologist would introduce his partner, the Singing Goat. The orchestra would play "Mammy"; when the monologist finished the verse and started the chorus, the goat would join him in singing "Ma-a-a-a-my! Ma-a-a-a-my!" The act stopped the show. One matinee, a representative of the S.P.C.A. called at the theater and removed the goat from the premises. When the theater manager remonstrated, the S.P.C.A. man showed him the goat's lacerated buttocks; the monologist had been prodding his rump with a sharp-pointed nail.

This sort of thing often happened in animal acts. Trainers who exhibited lions and tigers could seemingly cause them to growl and snarl on cue. The audience little suspected that the beasts worked on metal flooring, and that the lions and tigers would naturally growl or snarl after this metal flooring had been charged with electricity. Similarly, dog acts often astounded audiences when the little white terrier climbed the ladder, rung by rung, hesitated on the top rung for a second, and then jumped into space, landing in its master's arms. Little did the audience know that the top rung of the high ladder was electrified. When the little white terrier hesitated on this top rung, he wasn't kidding; he was frightened. A short shock through the rung, however, and the dog jumped.

Another great inventive act was that of Will Mahoney, who danced to his own melodies by attaching xylophone hammers to the toes of his shoes, and then danced atop the xylophone. If Will had spent the same amount of effort in thinking that he did on his xylophone, he might have discovered penicillin. I am sure that if all the hours vaudeville performers spent trying to improve their acts had been donated to science, automation would have been here fifty years sooner.

Vaudeville old-timers may not be wallowing in affluence in later life, but each smalltimer has his store of memories that will help him to escape from the unhappy present into the happy past. When the time comes that I find myself confined to the rubbish heap of humanity, I can temper my plight by conjuring up random recollections from my smalltime years. I can recall . . .

The manager of the vaudeville theater at Sandusky, Ohio. The audience there was so bad that he felt sorry for the acts. He invented an applause machine and installed it in the back of the theater. The machine manufactured applause by slapping a series of wooden paddles together. When an act finished and the audience sat there in its customary silence, the manager turned on his applause machine. To the sound of the wooden clatter, the act returned, took one or two bows, and withdrew.

The manager at Sherbrooke, Ontario, who was in the raincoat business. I remember that on the last night of my stay there he tried to talk the actors into taking their salaries in raincoats.

The manager at Torrington, Connecticut, who, on closing

night, was driving me and a contortionist back to New York. Speeding through one small Connecticut town at midnight, the car was overtaken and stopped by the local policeman. The manager stepped out of the car to explain. He said, "I'm sorry, officer. I'm the manager of the theater at Torrington."

"I don't know nothin' about that," said the rube. "You was doin' sixty-five."

"I've got to get to New York," pleaded the manager. "I've got a contortionist in the car. He has to catch a train."

"You got what in the car?"

"A contortionist."

"A *contortionist?*"

"Yes."

"What's a contortionist?"

The contortionist couldn't stand it any longer. He jumped out of the car in the dark, ran around in front of the headlights, and ripped his coat off. He did a handstand, twined his legs around his neck, and ran around in circles on his hands.

The rube watched him for a few minutes and said, "That's a contortionist, eh?"

"Yes," said the manager.

"I'll be damned," the policeman said. "Go ahead!"

I can remember, too, the little theater at Lancaster, Pennsylvania, that had the bowling alley upstairs. Just as I came to the punch line of my joke, somebody in the bowling alley made a strike and the audience heard nothing but the awful crash.

And then there was the butcher in the small Ohio town who converted his shop into a theater at night and showed pictures and Gus Sun smalltime vaudeville acts. In the window of the butcher shop he hung a sign:

Hamburger — 10¢ lb.
Pork chops — 20¢ lb.
Veal — 25¢ lb.
Theater tonight — 20¢

There was a theater at Bayonne, New Jersey, where, during my act, a cat came down the aisle, emitted a series of blood-curdling cries, and delivered a litter on the carpet. An usher rushed down the aisle with a coal shovel, scooped up the kittens, and returned, followed by the mother, to the back of the house. The audience was in a tumult. All I could do in feeble rebuttal was to coin the line "I thought my act was a monologue, not a catalogue."

The Jefferson Theatre, on Fourteenth Street in New York, had a mongrel audience: the theater was going to the dogs. Situated between Second and Third Avenues, it attracted patrons of all nationalities. Third Avenue at Fourteenth Street was an uptown Skid Row, and should have been re-named the Bowery-Plaza. Alcoholics of all sizes and in varying conditions frequented the neighborhood and used the Jefferson as a haven from the elements and a slumber sanctuary. At some performances the Jefferson took on the appearance of a flophouse that had put in vaudeville. At one supper show, during my monologue I heard a sort of "clunk!" noise that was repeated at regular intervals. It sounded like someone dropping wet wedges into a bathtub. I'd talk for thirty seconds — then a clunk. Another thirty seconds — and another clunk. Finally I located the source of the clunks. On the aisle, in the third row, sat a simian-faced specimen. Between his feet he was holding a wooden bucket; on the seat next to him he had a bag filled with oysters. As I was struggling through my monologue, this combination bivalve addict and theater patron was shucking his oysters and dropping the shells into the bucket.

I can remember, too, *l'affaire* midget at the depot at Quincy, Illinois. The headline act, a midget troupe, was leaving to open at Galesburg. One midget on the platform was berating the manager of the act, and demanding in squeaky words that he be given a raise in salary. The train started, but the midget refused to get aboard unless he was assured of more money. As the baggage car went by, the manager calmly picked up the midget and threw him in through the open door.

When I try to clamp the lid tightly on the past, names keep popping up. There was Eddie Borden, who did an English act with a partner called Sir James Dwyer. Eddie read a magazine ad for a preparation guaranteed to cure skin blemishes. The ad claimed that you could save the expense of a trip to Hot Springs by buying a bottle of the company's elixir and taking your own curative baths at home. Eddie, who was concerned about an acne condition, mailed in the coupon. At Minneapolis, the fluid arrived with full directions. To enjoy the Hot Springs bath at home, the patient had to close the bathroom door tightly, fill the tub with steaming hot water, pour in a given amount of the magic fluid, and lie in the tub to soak for an hour or more. Eddie followed the directions implicitly, finished his soaking, and went to bed. The next morning he opened the bathroom door, and instead of the pure white bathroom he had entered the night before, he now found a room with a brown ceiling, brown walls, brown tub, brown toilet seat and bowl, brown medicine cabinet, and a brown door. The Hot Springs elixir had contained sulfur, and the steam had transformed Eddie's suite into mahogany.

Jack Inglis was a funny nut comedian. One season, work was scarce. Jack lived in a rented house in Jersey with his wife and four children. A butcher friend of his knew that things were bad, and that the family wouldn't have a very happy Thanksgiving. Early in October, he gave Jack a live turkey. He told him he could keep it out in the yard in Jersey, and when the time came, he could kill the turkey for the family's Thanksgiving dinner. Jack took the turkey — a plump specimen — home, and turned it loose in the back yard. Every day for six weeks Jack's kids played with the turkey and chased it around. By the time Thanksgiving arrived, the turkey, after running away from the kids for six weeks, had lost some twenty pounds. For their Thanksgiving Day dinner that year the Inglis family had what looked like a tall sparrow.

The Billy Doss Revue was a smalltime girl act featuring Bill, a blackface comedian. I played on the bill with this act in Kansas City, Florence, Topeka, and Wichita in Kansas, and some dry oil wells in Oklahoma. The last chorus number of the revue was sung on a Southern dock with a river boat tied up in the background. On the dock there were bales of cotton, and on one of the bales sat a buxom mammy. For the act's finale the mammy jumped off the cotton bale and did an agile wooden-shoe dance to great applause. The mammy was really a boy in blackface wearing a bandana and a well-stuffed calico dress. The boy sat on his bale for three or four shows a day, looking at audiences, and with audiences looking at him. The only thing unusual about this is that the boy was wanted by the police. When they finally caught up with the blackface mammy, he was washed up for ten years, which he spent in the Ohio Penitentiary.

Nelson's Cats and Rats were a big-time act. The cats and rats, traditional enemies, performed together to the astonishment of audiences. One time, on a bill in Chicago, Fanny Brice was the headliner. As she arrived at the theater one evening and opened her dressing-room door, she shrieked. The stage manager rushed over to her and said, "What's wrong, Miss Brice?" Fanny gasped, "A rat! There's a big rat in my dressing room!" The stage manager, no fool, called

Nelson, the cat and rat authority. Nelson rushed in, cornered the rat, caught him in a heavy towel, and took the rat out of the dressing room. A few weeks later, I was on the bill with Nelson's Cats and Rats. I asked Nelson what had happened to the rat he had caught in Fanny Brice's dressing room. He said, "The next show, watch the finish of my act." I watched the finish, and saw a big black rat walk across the tiny platform carrying an American flag. "That," said Nelson, "is the rat."

The smalltimer, as he trudged through the seasons, always felt that he was getting closer to his goal. Every vaudeville actor dreamed of his personal utopia. Weekly sums were banked or mailed home against the day the smalltimer "quit the business." Then he would open his restaurant, filling station, real-estate office, chicken farm, dancing school, or other project that he had envisioned supporting him through his remaining years. Very few smalltimers saw their dreams take dimension. As the vaudeville monologist would explain it, "A funny thing happened to my savings on the way to my utopia." Sickness, relatives, going into businesses he didn't understand, meeting real-estate salesmen, joining collapsible building and loan clubs, gambling, lending money to other actors who never repaid him, playing the stock market, and a thousand other mishaps dissipated the smalltimer's savings and shattered his hopes. The few that did realize their ambitions found that after the travel and excitement of vaudeville, the dull and sedentary routine imposed on them as they tried to run some picayune enterprise in a small town was boring.

One vaudeville actor I knew couldn't wait to retire and start his own chicken farm. After he had bought a farm in California and tried to operate it for a few months, he was very unhappy. I went out to visit him one afternoon and found him sitting out in the yard under a tree, griping.

Scampering around in a large wire enclosure were hundreds of White Wyandottes. The bottoms of these white hens had red circles on them; scooting by, they looked like little Japanese flags with legs on them. I asked the actor if his chickens had unusual markings. He said no, that he had seen an ad for Lay or Bust Feed that would increase the size of any hen's eggs, and that he had been giving his hens plenty of it. The hens started laying eggs that were too large for their disposal equipment. Laying the big economy-size eggs had sprung the hens' hips and split their sphincters. "That accounts for the red circles on the bottoms of the hens?" I asked. "Yes," he answered. "I had to catch every lousy hen and dab her with mercurochrome!"

The smalltimer was never happy in retirement. Had it been within his power, the vaudeville performer would have been a timeless wanderer, spanning the generations by using the bridge of his talents.

But vaudeville is dead. Vaudeville was more a matter of style than of material. It was not so much what the two- and three-a-day favorites said and did, as how they said and did it. For fifty years vaudeville's minstrels found their way into all lands, preaching their gospel of merriment and song, and rousing the rest of the world to laughter and to tears. A few diehards who knew and enjoyed vaudeville hover over their television sets, hoping for a miracle. They believe that this electronic device is a modern oxygen tent that in some mysterious way can revive vaudeville and return its colorful performers of yesteryear to the current scene. The optimism of these day and night dreamers is wasted. Their vigils are futile. Vaudeville is dead. Period.

# 15

## The Passing Show of 1922

SINCE that day in May when I walked out of the Shubert office with the contract in my hand, I had been writing material for, and worrying about, *The Passing Show*. During the summer I had designed a comedy curtain, and I had worked out four or five different monologue ideas in order to be ready for rehearsal. The monologist in a revue had to appear before the front curtain and talk just long enough to enable the stagehands to change the scenery. The writers who prepared revue comedy material concentrated, not on such a lesser light, but upon the stars, and as *The Passing Show* stars were Willie and Eugene Howard, I knew that they would receive all the attention during the rehearsal weeks.

Before the company was called, I was sent to talk to Mr. Harold Atteridge, who was writing the book for *The Passing Show*. Harold was a tireless, all-purpose author whom the Shuberts employed until they could invent a machine that could do the same amount of work. He wrote the books and lyrics for most of the Jolson shows and for most of the other musicals and revues the Shuberts produced in such profusion. If Harold had received royalties for the many successful shows he wrote during his fecund years, he would have been a wealthy man. Unfortunately for Harold, however, share the wealth was not the precept on which the Shubert domain had been founded. The Shuberts wisely had put him under contract, and instead of mounting royalties he received a weekly salary. Harold, with his various writing assignments, was busier than an octopus going through a revolving door.

Harold resided in a sumptuous apartment on Riverside Drive. That is, his quarters seemed sumptuous to me at the time: I was still living at the Stanley Hotel on Forty-seventh Street, where the plumbing was held together with twine. When I arrived at Harold's, by appointment, he showed me into his study and invited me to have a drink. I declined, and he accepted his own invitation. He opened the door of a breakfront, where the whiskey bottle had apparently taken temporary refuge, and a cascade of *Tit-bits, Pearson's Weeklies, Answers,* and other English comedy magazines tumbled onto the floor. As he placed the bottle on the table, I smiled, knowing I had discovered two sources of Harold's inspiration.

After he had picked up the magazines and tossed off a junior flagon of straight whiskey, Harold got down to business. He explained that he had been so busy working on comedy scenes for the Howard Brothers and George Hassell that he hadn't had time to think about my material at all. He added that he hoped I had some ideas. I showed him a drawing of the comedy curtain I had developed, and explained two of my monologues: one an impression of Will Rogers, the other involving a man reading a letter from home. I also told him that I had some sight gags. One was the business of carrying a feedbag and explaining that I had a date with a girl who "ate like a horse." Another involved my holding a coat hanger under my arm during an entire monologue and remarking at the finish that I had to go down to the courthouse, where I expected to win a suit. I also suggested a device which would enable me to appear in and out throughout the whole show. I would first appear early in the show and announce that I had written some jokes on the cuff of my dress shirt, but the shirt had been sent to the laundry by mistake. The Chinese laundry was just around the corner. I would add that while the show resumed I would hurry to the laundry, get the shirt, return, and carry on; then, as the next number started, I would leave the theater through the audience. A few numbers later, I would return, running down the aisle, and arriving winded back on the stage, carrying a bundle; when the bundle was opened, I would discover that the laundry man had given me the wrong shirt. I would have to return to the laundry. Back again with the right shirt, I would show the audience the jokes written on both cuffs, up the sleeves, all over the bosom, and down the back of the bottom of the tail.

Harold, who had been listening attentively, stood up and gulped another beaker of whiskey, shuddered a bit as the shot passed his epiglottis on the way to its internal target, said that it all sounded great, and that I actually had more material than I needed for the show. This seemed to remind Harold that he was trying to find an opening gag for Willie and Gene's first entrance; if I didn't mind, he said, he would give them my "feedbag" bit. Eager to be cooperative, I didn't mind.

Mr. J. J. Shubert supervised the production of all the Shubert musical shows. "J.J.," as he was called, was a small ball of a man. With his short neck and pudgy body he looked like a turtle who had somehow got out of its shell and was standing upright and walking around.

Rehearsals were held every day at the Century Theatre. For the first four weeks of rehearsal I was ignored. I had nothing to rehearse, and nobody with whom not to rehearse it. Every day on the Century stage the chorus went through the dancing numbers under the practiced eye of Allen K. Foster. The singing principals learned their numbers in one of the smaller rehearsal rooms. The comedy scenes were being perfected in a large bare dressing room. Hour after hour, Willie and Gene repeated their comedy lines, with the director, J. C. Huffman, and Harold Atteridge looking on and making occasional suggestions to improve a joke or enhance a bit of business. When Willie and Gene left to rehearse their songs, George Hassell took over and belabored the acoustics with his strident sallies. Every morning, J.J. arrived and sat watching the comedy scenes: a quiet, inscrutable, soft-looking lump. While Willie, Gene, and George Hassell read their comedy lines, J.J. sat in a little human tuft, looking more like a turtle than ever as he blinked and gave the impression that his mind was miles away under a lily pad somewhere, and that he wished he were there with it. J.J. rarely smiled. When he did, it was considered a bad omen. Comedians who worked for the Shuberts swore that any comedy lines or funny business that J.J. laughed at during rehearsals were invariably taken out after the show had opened. To a joke, J.J.'s laugh was the kiss of death.

After I had attended rehearsals as a bystander for four weeks, on Monday of the fifth week things picked up. The entire cast was called on the mammoth Century stage, J.J. turtled in, and Mr. Huffman announced that Mr. Shubert was going to put the entire show together for the first time. J.J. sat down at a wooden table. On this he placed several sheets of paper on which he had listed a tentative running order of the scenes and numbers. Mr. Huffman said that I wouldn't have to do my monologues aloud. When my specialties were called, I was to stand at Mr. Shubert's table and go through my routines in a low voice. Mr. Shubert was going to time the show and wanted to see and hear all its ingredi-

ents. The piano player pounded out a few introductory
chords, and the rehearsal started. When I was called on, I
stood in front of J.J. and explained the shirt with the jokes
on the cuff, the Will Rogers imitation, the comedy curtain,
and the letter from home. J.J. sat there, ignoring me completely. He didn't laugh and he didn't smile: to me he began
to look like a mummy that had been suddenly unwrapped
and didn't know quite what to make of his surroundings.
If J.J.'s laugh doomed comedy material, my routines had
come through unscathed.

*The Passing Show of 1922* was booked to open on Labor
Day at the Apollo Theatre in Atlantic City. The Saturday
morning before, the entire cast and crew left New York by
special train. On Sunday afternoon, the company was to be at
the Apollo to unpack personal trunks and prepare for a dress
rehearsal on Sunday night. Coming down on the train,
George Hassell asked me to share an apartment with him.
Later, I discovered why. George was so fat he couldn't bend
down to tie his shoelaces. That was my morning chore. I had
to guide George's ample feet into his enormous shoes, tie the
laces, and inform him when he was ready to amble. George's
stomach protruded to the point where his feet were only a
memory, and during the time his shoes were being serviced I
was reduced to a sunken, invisible voice. Once George was
launched, he was busy all day with working, drinking, clean-
ing and stoking his briar pipe, and filling the air with his
favorite oath: "God's trousers!"

All day Sunday, backstage at the Apollo was bedlam.
Endless lines of trucks shuttled back and forth from the railroad station to the theater carrying bulky scenery flats,
electrical equipment, prop boxes; the show's stage manager
seemed to be everywhere, shouting instructions to his men
and to the local stagehands, who were busy hauling the trunks,

stacking scenery against the back wall of the theater, tying drops on the battens that had been lowered from the flies, and helping the wardrobe women unpack the chorus costumes and hang them in the dressing rooms. Dress rehearsal was called for 8 P.M., but when the time arrived, the stage was still a shambles. J.J. canceled the dress rehearsal, dismissed the company, and called everybody for dress rehearsal the next morning.

Monday was Labor Day. Atlantic City was jammed, and the Apollo was sold out for the opening show. The stage crew worked all through the night, but on Monday morning there was still work to be done. Al Goodman, the musical conductor, was busy rehearsing the orchestra; Mr. Huffman was lighting the sets; and the stage manager was darting around giving last-minute instructions to his crew. The cast sat around out front in the theater. When three o'clock came and still the stage was not clear, Mr. Huffman informed J.J. that it was too late to have the rehearsal and advised him to cancel the opening performance and have the dress rehearsal that night.

With the theater sold out, suggesting to J.J. that he return the money was like hinting to a small boy that he give you his ice-cream cone as he is raising it to his mouth to take the first bite. J.J. decided that the show would open, on schedule, and without a dress rehearsal.

And it did. The curtain rang up at 8:30 and came down for the end of the first act at 1:30 A.M. The show finally ended at 3:30. Curtains were fouled, light cues were missed, props didn't work, actors forgot their lines: the whole night was a colorful nightmare. Mr. Huffman made me sit with him on the stage in the first entrance; we were both perched on campstools. When anything went wrong, Mr. Huffman pushed me out on the stage to fill in until the crisis had been surmounted. During this *première* performance of *The Pass-ing Show*, I made eighteen appearances.

The next morning J.J. called a meeting of the show's princi-pals at the theater to read a revised line-up of the show. Mr. Huffman cautioned us that nobody was to interrupt J.J., as his word was final. As J.J. read, entire comedy scenes, dance numbers, song and production numbers were deleted; spe-cialty acts, bit actors, and female secondary singers vanished from the show as J.J. droned on. Most of Willie and Gene's scenes survived. George Hassell still had three or four skits. When J.J. had finished, I found that, in the future, my partic-ipation in the extravaganza would be confined to three ap-pearances.

In its final form, *The Passing Show* opened with "The International Circus." Miss 1922 sang about the political figures in the news as they appeared in replica: leaders of India, the Irish Free State, Japan, Germany, Lloyd George, the Prince of Wales, Uncle Sam, and so on. The scene led into a chorus number climaxed by the Mackweys, a fast acrobatic act. The act finished with all of the scenery falling and the curtains, drops, and borders covering the stage and burying the Mackweys. It was a surprise blackout and started the show with resounding applause. I immediately appeared, stepping through the front curtain in a white spotlight. I was wearing an oversized black astrakhan coat, held on down the front by a series of frogs, and a small black derby; and I was carrying a shovel. My first line was: "You remember me from moving pictures — the man who followed the Four Horse-men?" As self-styled prologue, I explained the nature of the show, read burlesque opinions of H. G. Wells, Thomas Edi-son, Lydia Pinkham, and other important figures of the day who had supposedly seen *The Passing Show*. This hilarious interlude *segued* into an impersonation of Will Rogers. Before starting this, I reminded the audience of the great difference between our salaries, adding that for a man of my picayune stature, receiving a starvation wage, to impersonate Will Rogers, a great star who was paid a thousand dollars a week (a fortune in 1922), was not only an insult that teetered on the brink of audacity, but was an impudent gesture that struck a blow at free enterprise in this country. To impersonate Will properly, I added, it was necessary for a man like myself to have two men to help me. As I did a topical monologue, these two men appeared, dressed as cowboys. One — clad in full regalia with chaps, guns, and Stetson hat — stood on my left, spinning a lariat. The other, similarly clad, stood on my right, chewing a lumpy wad of gum. Will Rogers was very popular, and the impersonation came off extremely well. But after a few days in Atlantic City, J.J. discovered that my gum-chewing cowboy, who had been in some of the comedy skits that had been eliminated after opening night, now had nothing remaining in the show but his appearance with me. It went against J.J.'s instincts to pay an actor a weekly salary just to stand around on the stage chewing gum. The inevitable ensued. My Will Rogers imitation was done with the one cowboy spinning the rope.

The "Old Joke Cemetery," my second appearance in the show, exceeded everybody's expectations. Using the trite rejoinder "That joke is dead" as a basis, I drew a crude cemetery and took the idea to Mark Leddy. Mark had booked Martin Branner in vaudeville before he abandoned the theater to turn cartoonist and launch his highly successful *Winnie Winkle*. Mark took me to him, and he liked my idea and drew his professional version of an Old Joke Cemetery. The graveyard, situated on a hill, contained forty-six headstones, mausoleums, assorted cenotaphs, and tombstones, on each of which was written an old joke. Some of the interred jokes and puns were: "Lost, a Ford — Lizzie, Come Home — All Is Forgiven"; "An Icicle Is a Stiff Piece of Water"; "A Prohibitionist Lies Here — His Ails Are Over — He's on His Bier"; "She Broke My Heart, So I Broke Her Jaw"; "The Church Is On Fire: Holy Smoke"; "It Is Easier to Say a Mouthful Than to Get One"; "A Husband Is Something No Respectable Family Should Be Without." Under the arched entrance to the cemetery a sign read THIS IS A ONE WAY STREET; a hearse, passing under the arch, was labeled: "Who Is That Lady in the Hearse? That Is No Lady — That Is My Wife."

The Old Joke Cemetery was exposed to the audience gradually. The orchestra play a soft, toe-tapping, rustic melody, and the curtain in front of the cemetery was raised slowly. As the jokes on the tombstones came into view, the audience started to laugh, the curtain continued to rise slowly, and by the time the entire cemetery could be seen the theater seemed to be a huge percolator top holding down hundreds of happy, bubbling shrieks. The curtain just hung there for almost five minutes with nobody on the stage. There were forty-six old jokes lying in state, and no two people in the audience looked in the same direction. As the laughter mounted, men nudged their wives or girl friends to call attention to one particular joke, and strangers were prodding their neighbors and pointing to others. At the peak of the cachinnation the theater was blacked out, a white spotlight swept to the left entrance, and I walked on, carrying a banjo. This second specialty consisted of topical gags and stories, and finished with some banjo imitations and a song for which I played my own accompaniment.

My final monologue came late in the second act. As I rushed on the stage wearing an enormous walking suit, I apologized for appearing in my street clothes. I then explained the baggy suit by saying that I lived in New Rochelle and that the suit had been made for me by a tailor there. That was why the suit looked too large: I was a much bigger man in New Rochelle than I was in New York. Then I took a letter out of my coat pocket, saying that it had just come from home. The stamp was attached to the envelope with a safety pin. I explained that this meant my father had mailed the letter: since Prohibition, his mouth had been so dry, he couldn't wet a stamp. When the envelope was opened, the letter unfolded until it became a large piece of Manila wrapping paper. "My mother always writes on this kind of paper. It saves time. As soon as I know what the family is asking for I can wrap it up and send it right home." The letter read:

MY DEAR SON:

A few lines to let you know about our new neighborhood. The man next door has bought pigs; we got wind of it this morning. Your father had a terrible fight with him about it, but the man hit your father with a rock in the left ear. It didn't bother your father; he is stone deaf in that ear. The policeman who took him away said he would get his hearing in the morning. The other man, the one who owns the pigs, was arrested for fragrancy. Your brother Pete has taken his Civil Service Examinations, but he is too ignorant for the Police Department. They will probably put him on the School Board. I've tried to give him advice but it is like pouring water on a duck's back — in one ear and out the other.

The new cook has arrived. [At home we always have two servants — one coming and one going.] The man upstairs sent down for his wash boiler this morning. Your father had to put the home brew he was making back into the bathtub. Nobody will find it there. Your father read last week that a carrier pigeon will go farther than any other bird. We tried one out for dinner on Sunday — but it didn't. The baby has had something in her eye all week. The doctor says it is a foreign substance. She will have to stop playing with those wop kids if it is going to ruin her eyesight.

Your sister has a new beau and judging from his actions when he calls on her, he is no gentleman. He always hangs his hat over the keyhole — possibly a Yale man. He is an ugly boy. He is so cross-eyed everything he looks at he thinks is double-breasted. He is so bald he has to carry his dandruff around in his hand. But in spite of this I am afraid he will make her a good husband. He is in business for himself. He puts peroxide on sparrows and sells them for canaries.

There is no other news except that our oil stove exploded yesterday and blew your father and me out into the back yard. It is the first time we have been out together for twenty years. I am sending your Spring overcoat to you separately — I have cut off the buttons to make the package lighter. You will find them in the inside pocket.

God bless you and keep you from your loving
MOTHER

After Atlantic City, the show moved to New Haven. Rehearsals were called every day, numbers were changed, scenes were tightened, and the Howard Brothers brought on a comedy writer to strengthen their routines. The show was taking form. On closing night in New Haven, everybody associated with *The Passing Show*, from J.J. down to the theater doorman, was convinced that it was going to be a big hit in New York.

But we were all fooled: the show ran only ten weeks at the Winter Garden. Most *Passing Shows* survived a full season; ours established a new record for abbreviated engagements. Some Broadway sages diagnosed the anemia at the box office as resulting from the too-frequent New York appearances of the Howard Brothers. Others, speaking bluntly, stated that the show itself was mediocre. Compared to the *Ziegfeld Follies*, the Tiffany revues of the era, the average Winter Garden show looked as though it had stepped out of a Sears, Roebuck catalogue. The 1922 edition of *The Passing Show* was rumored (and I think the rumor may have been started by J.J.) to have cost eighty thousand dollars. Later, it developed that the show had cost only thirty thousand dollars. Most of the scenery was secondhand. Walking backstage on opening night, I saw scenery stenciled *The Last Waltz, Blossom Time, Sinbad,* and the names of other shows that had long since closed and gone to the Shubert storehouse, that lumber heaven which was the final resting place for all departed Shubert attractions.

Very few of our *Passing Show* costumes were new. The Shuberts also maintained a massive wardrobe limbo where thousands of costumes, uniforms, and suits that had come to the end of their sartorial days hung in splendor, waiting for the day of reincarnation when, every garment knew, they would return to the theater in some other form and shine again in the spotlight of another Shubert show. The wardrobe department was in the hands of the efficient "Ma" Simmons. Nobody ever seemed to know Mr. Simmons's first name. The chorus boys had christened him "Ma," and this maternal sobriquet served him through the years. Ma's memory was uncanny. In August, when the new Shubert shows were in rehearsal and the older shows were being readied to go on the road, Ma might be supplying wardrobes for eight or ten different shows. This entailed supervising the making of new gowns for the women stars in the modern shows and period costumes for the principals in operettas; remodeling old costumes for the chorus girls and boys; and furnishing such items as shirts, ties, and shoes for each show. Working around the clock during his hectic season, Ma knew the name of every chorus girl who had torn her farthingale at the *Passing Show* rehearsal in New York, the name of the *Blossom Time* principal whose peruke was too tight, how many buttons were off the chorus boys' trousers in the road company of

*Bombo,* and how many moths were flying around at any given hour in the Shubert wardrobe building.

Our ten weeks at the Winter Garden passed minus incident. When the stoplight made its first appearance on the automobile, I added a joke to my monologue: "Ford is making a new car for the Y.W.C.A. — the stoplight is inside." After a few shows the audience suddenly stopped laughing at it. I couldn't understand why until I watched the show from the beginning one night, and heard Willie telling the "stoplight" joke in his café scene, earlier in the show. Also, in 1922, jokes about girls walking home from automobile rides headed the Wit Parade. I had a line saying, "My girl has walked home from so many automobile rides, I gave her a road map for Christmas." Shortly after this second joke appeared in the café scene, I spoke to Willie. He told me the jokes had been given to him; he and Gene were so busy making changes and doing scenes that they never had time to watch the rest of the show, and so he never knew that the jokes were mine. Willie Howard was a great artist. He was a fine comedian, an accomplished dramatic actor, an excellent singer, and a versatile mimic. Willie wasted most of his professional life impersonating actors who didn't have a fraction of the talent he possessed. Gene was a Beau Brummel. He was the first actor I had ever seen wear a scalp blowout patch: a penwiper-sized toupee to cover a small bald spot on the top of his head. Gene was an excellent straight man who dedicated his life to Willie's advancement.

But Willie and Gene together couldn't save *The Passing Show of 1922.* Early in December we closed in New York. We left the Winter Garden, and began our tour on the road.

In 1922, a road tour was important to a show. The Shubert Theatre in Boston was our first stop. We left the Winter

Garden a failure, but we played to capacity business for four weeks in Boston. The Boston papers hailed me as a local boy who had made good. My Aunt Lizzie and Aunt Jane came to the show, and after seeing the nude chorus girls probably went home to pray for me. My brother Bob and all the old gang around Hodge White's in Dorchester gave a royal welcome. This called for tickets for everyone, which I supplied.

News of my appearance in *The Passing Show* had somehow seeped through to the Savin Hill section of Dorchester where Bob and I had lived with my Aunt Lizzie when we were kids. Long after we had left the neighborhood, the Savin Hill Associates had been formed. Most fraternal organzations are founded to espouse a cause or to uplift a community. The Savin Hill Associates owed its existence to a handful of indolent advanced adolescents who loitered on the street corner all year long, and during the winter months wanted to get in out of the cold. Monthly dues were assessed and a small room was rented on Savin Hill Avenue. When the club got under way, members used the room principally for card games and drinking conclaves. When the wassail elixir ran out, one or two of the members were dispatched to visit John the Baptist. John the Baptist was a Polish bootlegger who had acquired his trade name because his house was situated behind the Catholic church on Dorchester Avenue. Sending two members of the Savin Hill Associates to bring back a ewer of whiskey was akin to deputizing two hungry cannibals to bring back a fat boy. On numerous occasions the members started back from John the Baptist's and fell by the wayside, figuratively and literally. Apart from the monthly rent, the club's overhead was small. The tables had been brought from the members' homes, the chairs borrowed from the neighborhood undertaker. If you entered the club and saw most of the members standing, you knew that somebody had passed on and the undertaker had taken his chairs back to use at the wake. For some time, the club paid no light bill. One of the members worked for the electric light company. He drove his truck around one day and ran a wire into the club that was spliced to the main feed line of the street light that stood outside on the corner; for many months the club was lighted through the courtesy of the city of Boston. As the membership grew, the club faced a recurring and irritating problem: the treasury kept growing. The minute the treasury contained a sizable amount of money, the members couldn't wait to spend it. Kegs of beer were tapped on birthdays, fishing trips were organized in season, and local political candidates were supported and banqueted. When its treasury was bulging, in an emergency there was no person too obscure or no event too insignificant to be cited, honored, or feted by the Savin Hill Associates.

The arrival of *The Passing Show* came at an opportune time for the club. The treasury was pregnant with pelf. It was December, and the entertainment committee was having difficulty trying to fabricate an event that would enable the members to turn the treasury funds back into circulation. I solved the problem. A Savin Hill boy returning to Boston with a Broadway show merited a home-town salute. A theater evening was planned and some forty club members descended on the Shubert Theatre. I cannot prove that every member was lit on arrival, but when the show got under way, a nimbus of light hovered over the corner of the theater where the Savin Hill Associates had clustered. Every time I came on stage, I stopped the show. During the evening I made three speeches. The theater porter told me later that the record for empty whiskey bottles being abandoned during intermission in the men's room — a record formerly made on the Saturday of a Harvard-Yale football game — was broken that night.

After the performance, the Savin Hill Associates tendered me a dinner at Healy's Hotel. I invited George Hassell to join me. As George and I came up Washington Street at midnight, even with the windows of Healy's Hotel closed we could hear the tribute to me taking place a block away. When the dinner was served, the members threw the food back at the waiters and at each other. After the waiters had fled, quiet was restored, under duress. The toastmaster, Duke Dunegan, made a speech and presented me verbally with a traveling bag. He reached under the table to produce my gift and discovered that his hand was gripping empty air. The traveling bag had been stolen. Accusations were hurled, recriminations volleyed back and forth, invective filled the air, fights broke out all over the banquet room, humanity was effervescing. Just as the turmoil attained its peak, the door flew open and Mr. Healy, the Boniface, charged in. Mr. Healy drew himself up to the height of his Irish fury and announced in bellicose words that the guest of honor and the members of the Savin Hill Associates were bums, and if we jointly did not quit his premises, he would call the police, and have me, the tribute to me, and all the invited guests removed in a municipal vehicle. This dinner was the social highlight of my Boston visit.

The Howard Brothers were very popular on the road; the show did excellent business in Philadelphia, Baltimore, Washington, Pittsburgh, Cleveland, Detroit, and all the other principal cities visited. When we opened in Indianapolis, J.J. arrived to prepare the show for its Chicago run. Chicago was a wonderful theater city. Conventions and tourists made it possible for successful musical shows to run from six months to a year there. It was important for a show to open well in

Chicago, since the critics' reaction would determine the length of the show's stay. J.J. had come on to have the scenery freshened, the costumes checked, and also to engage in another old Shubert custom — cutting the cast.

The Shuberts had a process of reduction which enabled them to operate any show under any given circumstances and still manage to show a profit. A Shubert musical show always opened in New York with a top cast. If the show was a smash hit, after it had been running for a few weeks some of the minor principals were replaced with cheaper actors. When the show finished its New York run and left for the road, high-salaried principals who could be spared were replaced, scenes were eliminated, and occasionally the chorus was cut down. Names were needed in Chicago itself, but when that run was finished and the show started on split weeks and one-nighters around the Middle West, chorus boys and girls replaced dancing and singing principals in the sketches. After these dates, a Shubert musical leaving for California was again cut down until only one or two of the stars remained; their names were needed to draw business. *The Passing Show of 1922*, upon leaving the Winter Garden, had lost Mlle. Alcorn, Arthur Margetson, the Fooshee Sisters, and Janet Adair. When J.J. finished preparing the show for the Chicago opening, we had lost George Hassell, Sam Ash, Nat Nazarro, Jr., and the Mackweys. Willie Howard was playing all of George Hassell's parts, and cheaper people and chorus boys and girls had replaced the others. The Howard Brothers were still the stars, but of the others only the Lockfords and I had survived the traditional Shubert replacement system.

The show opened well in Chicago. Willie and Gene were favorites there, and we stayed for six months, all through the summer, at the Apollo Theatre. In Chicago I became very friendly with Ethel Shutta and her husband, Walter

Batchelor. Ethel was a very talented girl who sang two of the show's production songs and worked in most of the comedy sketches with Willie and Gene. Walter Batchelor was assistant manager of the show. He was also a fine cook: he had the heart of a chef, and the body of a man who could keep a chef busy. When we saw that our notices were good and that our show was assured of a long run, many of the married couples, as well as groups of chorus girls, moved into furnished apartments where they could enjoy home cooking and a change from hotel life. Ethel and Walter rented an apartment. Walter started looking like the Mystery Chef; his stove became a magic cabinet from which, at mealtimes, he caused tasty viands to appear. I was Walter's closest friend in the show, and was frequently invited to dinner. Ethel had an attractive girl friend, one of the chorus girls in the show, who often came to dinner. The girl's name was Portland Hoffa.

During the summer months, Ethel, Walter, Portland, and I became a foursome. The girls did the marketing, Walter did the cooking. When there was no matinees, we spent the days at the beach. On rainy days we went to the movies and later visited one of the excellent restaurants in the Loop, or one of the tea shoppes on the North Side. After the shows at night we investigated different speakeasies and other nocturnal points of interest that Chicago boasted. They were days of laughter and happy times.

In October, *The Passing Show* left the Apollo Theatre and Chicago. The apartment life, the home-cooked meals, the excursions, and the happy times were soon memories as Ethel, Portland, Walter, and I returned to the split weeks and the one-night stands. Ancient theaters, opera houses, auditoriums, towns that all began to look alike — Bloomington, Galesburg, Springfield, Fort Wayne, Toledo (where the chorus girls had to make their changes in an alley in back of the theater), Lima, Ohio (where the stage was too small to hold the scenery: every time I started to talk in front of the curtain, the stagehands opened the big back doors to bring in the next scene and the gusts of wind would billow the curtain and nearly blow me out into the audience) — dirty trains, drafty sleepers, rickety hotels, and greasy restaurants fused into a montage that contained all the ingredients of a nightmare. I always seemed to be running to the train, the hotel, the restaurant, or the theater. I rarely knew what day it was or what town I was in.

To augment the confusion, a rumor persisted that *The Passing Show* was going to California. If the rumor was true, I didn't have to be psychic to know that the company was going to be preshrunk before starting the cross-country trip. I didn't suspect that I was expendable until one Saturday morning when we arrived in Williamsport, Pennsylvania, to play a matinee and an evening performance. The manager of *The Passing Show* presented me with a railroad ticket and advised me that I was to report to Mr. Shubert in New York on Monday. I told him that I thought this was rather short notice, and that I would require a trunk in order to take my Old Joke Cemetery curtain back with me. He said that Mr. Shubert had made no mention of this curtain. He added that he didn't know whether I owned the curtain or not, and that even if he did know, he had no authority to let me have it; therefore there was nothing he could do about it. After the matinee I went over to the sheriff's office with my copyright papers and the bill of sale for the curtain. In Williamsport, however, it appeared that all crime ceased on Saturday afternoon to enable the sheriff to relax his authority and quit his office for the half day. After the night show, the manager paid me my salary and advised me to talk to Mr. Shubert about my curtain. The stagehands told me I could overpower them and force them to carry the curtain out into the alley, where I could take it away from them, but I had no trunk nor any transportation to carry the bulky curtain onto the train. I thanked the stagehands and left the theater. Ethel, Portland, and Walter came down to the depot to see me off. After playing eighty-three weeks with *The Passing Show*, I was going back to New York, and my Old Joke Cemetery was on its way to Scranton and Wilkes-Barre.

On Monday morning, back in New York, Mr. Shubert was too busy to see me. I left a note saying that if the office would pay me fifty dollars weekly, they could continue to use the curtain and return it to me when the show closed. To replace the curtain in the show would involve a principal's having to learn a song, a new dance routine for the chorus, and costumes for the principal and chorus. But to the Shubert office, actors were actors and costumes were costumes, and fifty dollars was fifty dollars. My request for the weekly royalty was ignored. On Wednesday, when it appeared that the Old Joke Cemetery had been stolen, I consulted a lawyer. I explained the circumstances, produced the copyright papers and the bill of sale, and the lawyer promptly had an injunction served which prohibited *The Passing Show* from leaving Wilkes-Barre, with the curtain, until my claim had been settled. A telegram came back from the manager agreeing to send the curtain back to New York on the night train. What he didn't mention in the telegram was the fact that he planned to call in a local photographer at Wilkes-Barre and have him photograph the Old Joke Cemetery curtain before he sent it back that night. He could then have another curtain made from the photograph, and all would be well. I would have my curtain back, *The Passing Show* could go to California with the duplicate, and J.J. would both have the curtain and save fifty dollars a week. One trivial oversight, however, occurred:

when the picture was developed the following day, it came out too dark for anyone to read the inscriptions on the tombstones. Without sufficient light in the theater, the photographer had goofed. The Old Joke Cemetery had not been copied. J.J. had been thwarted. Justice had triumphed.

My contract had three more years to run, but Shubert contracts contained one-year options. With a five-year contract, the Shuberts could cancel at the end of any one year. On the other hand, the actor, if he had better offers and wanted to cancel, could not; if the Shuberts took up his annual options, he was bound for five years. After getting out an injunction against his molting turkey, I was sure that J.J. had no future plans that included me, and so I made a few plans of my own. Two weeks later, I had Mark Leddy book me in Norwich, Connecticut, to break in a new vaudeville act. Because I was still under contract to Shubert, I used the pseudonym "Benjamin Franklin." Mark, the booker, and I were the only three people who knew where I was and what name I was using. On the last day in Norwich, the phone rang at the hotel. New York was calling. It was the Shubert office. How they ever found Benjamin Franklin in Norwich I could never understand, but there were so many things I could never understand about the Shuberts that I dismissed the Norwich incident rather than learn that J.J. had occult powers. The call ordered me to return to New York and join the *Artists and Models* show at the Shubert Theatre. A comedian in the show, given to alcholic lapses, had succumbed to temptation and vanished. His disappearances were frequent and followed a pattern. When his bibbing reduced him to tremens, he withdrew from society and took inventory of all the men in the world until he came to himself. His understudy substituted for the comedian in his sketches; I was now to replace him in two monologue appearances.

*Artists and Models* was the first American revue to copy the Folies Bergère vogue and exhibit chorus girls with their breasts exposed. Twice during the show, I had to come on following these nude tableaux. When the curtains closed, women in the audience were busy gasping and the men were not in the mood to listen to me. After I had spent two unhappy weeks posing as an antidote for sex in *Artists and Models*, the comedian I had replaced must have heard the distant rumble of a Salvation Army drum. He suddenly materialized in J.J.'s office with Sen Sen on his breath, and he was accompanied by his father and a priest. A pledge, signed by the comedian, was produced and examined by the Shubert lawyer for loopholes. Everything seemed to be in order. I was removed from the cast, and the comedian turned his back on Wine and returned to Women and Song in *Artists and Models*.

And so once more I was separated from the Brothers Shubert. But not for long.

# 16

## The Greenwich Village Follies

THE Shubert empire was ruled by two brothers, Lee and J.J. I mentioned earlier that J.J. produced the firm's many musical ventures. "Mr. Lee," as he was called, ran the theaters and supervised the vast real-estate holdings the brothers controlled. He also financed the dramatic shows. In the spring of 1924, J.J. went on his annual trip to Paris. (All the prominent American revue producers made annual trips to Europe. They visited London, Paris, and other continental cities to view the new musical shows and to either buy or steal costumes, scenery, lighting, or comedy ideas for their forthcoming shows in New York.) This year, after J.J. had departed, Mr. Lee did something special. It had always rankled him that his brother had enjoyed such success in the musical field. Subconsciously, way down at the bottom of his mind, under the money-thought layer, Mr. Lee had a suppressed desire to produce a musical show. With J.J. away, this seemed an opportune time. By the time J.J. returned, Mr. Lee hoped to have a big musical hit running, and be in a position to laugh up his brother's money belt at him. Mr. Lee went into action. He engaged Clifford Grey and Fred Thompson, two British authors and lyricists, to write the show; Herbert Stothart was to write the music, Dave Bennett to create the dances, and J. C. Huffman to direct. The show was to be called *Vogues*. The star was Odette

Myrtil, a talented musical-comedy actress supposedly imported from Paris.

As a blue-ribbon cast to support Miss Myrtil, Mr. Lee engaged J. Harold Murray, Charles Judels, Irene Delroy, Betty Compton (who later married Mayor Jimmy Walker), the Swanson Sisters (one of whom later married Mr. Lee), Jimmy Savo, and myself, and a number of specialty acts. To insure the success of his first musical venture, Mr. Lee announced that no money was to be spared. The costumes and scenery were to be brand-new, and *Vogues* was to be a class show. When J.J. returned from Paris, he would see how a musical show should be presented. Mr. Lee was in such great haste that the show went into rehearsal on the Century roof before the authors had completed the book. Clifford Grey and Fred Thompson were writing night and day. The show was not to be just another revue: it was to be part musical comedy, with a story running through it.

At the early rehearsals, the star, Miss Myrtil, apparently was not impressed with Jimmy Savo's potential or mine. As the comedy scenes arrived from the writers, she insisted that Mr. Judels be given the male parts. Jimmy Savo had a very funny vaudeville act with his wife that was to be used in the show. I had some new monologues. As the days went by, Miss Myrtil and Mr. Judels did all the rehearsing, while Jimmy and I sat around watching. The director, Mr. Huffman, wasn't happy with the scenes that had been written, and complained several times about the slowness of the writers. At the end of the first week I realized that the authors were ignoring Jimmy and me and were concentrating on material for the star and Mr. Judels. As things were progressing, I knew that Jimmy and I would be unveiled on opening night with nothing but our two specialties in the show.

One afternoon, as Miss Myrtil and Judels were rehearsing

one comedy scene after another, I enticed Jimmy Savo into a corner. Jimmy had never been in a show before, and didn't realize that the handwriting on the wall wasn't any dialogue that was going to be given to us. I explained to Jimmy that the director wasn't any too pleased with the comedy scenes that the authors had written up to now, and added that if Jimmy wanted to work with me, I would try to write four or five short comedy bits. If they turned out well, and complications arose, we might be able to do them in the show. Jimmy thought it might be a good idea. I worked out two characters for us: we were to play the authors of the show. After the opening chorus number, the second scene would show the front gates leading into the grounds of an insane asylum. A guard opens the gates; Jimmy and I enter. Jimmy is wearing an oversized fur coat; I have on a Palm Beach suit. I explain to the audience that we are the authors and have permission to leave the asylum for two hours to witness our show. We would go on from there. As the evening progressed, the author-characters would not interfere with the main plot; they would confine their comedy to themselves, popping out between scenes to comment on people, songs, costumes, or anything else that had comic possibilities.

Every night Jimmy and I rehearsed this at his apartment. We didn't have to wait until opening night to rehearse our comedy bits. One routine morning, as the show was starting its third week of rehearsals, Mr. Huffman exploded. He delivered a scathing address to the ceiling that ridiculed the authors for the paucity and quality of their comedy scenes, he heaped aspersions on the cast, and in conclusion predicted that the show would be a colossal flop with which he didn't care to have his name associated. While the reverberations of his caustic diatribe were still rattling around the acoustics, Mr. Huffman jammed his felt hat on his head and charged into the elevator. The door slid closed with a bang, and through the glass his silhouette was seen submerging. Mr. Huffman was making his final shadowy gesture to *Vogues* and the Century roof.

The rehearsal stopped. Some hungry actor had an idea and suggested that the cast go to lunch. Back from lunch, we all sat around wondering what was going to happen. The silence was compounding as the minutes tumbled into eternity's bin. Finally the silence was broken. From the bowels of the Century Theatre we heard the sound of the elevator, moving slowly on its way up to the roof. The actors, sensing that their destinies were about to be determined, turned their collective eyes to the elevator. The door opened; Mr. Huffman was back, and with him was Mr. Lee. Mr. Lee didn't waste any time. He asked the actors to give him their attention. When he felt that he had it, he said that Mr. Huffman was disappointed with the way things were going with the show. Mr. Lee assured us that *Vogues* was "his baby," and that no money or effort would be spared to make the show a hit and provide us all with a long run. In closing, Mr. Lee asked if any of the actors had any suggestions. I answered and said that Jimmy and I had been attending rehearsals for two weeks and hadn't been given anything to do. I explained the "authors" idea, that would enable us to add some comedy to the show without upsetting the plot as conceived, or adding any appreciable cost. Mr. Lee thanked me, and some of the others had suggestions. Mr. Lee said that Mr. Huffman was returning to the show and would discuss these new ideas with the sponsors. Assuring us all again that *Vogues* was going to be a smash hit, and thanking us all, Mr. Lee exchanged a few final words with Mr. Huffman, hurried into the elevator, and was gone.

When I explained my idea to Mr. Huffman, he seemed to

like it very much. He said that Jimmy and I could rehearse by ourselves. I told him that we would need an insane-asylum curtain with practical gates in front, and also a large, sloppy-looking fur coat for Jimmy. Mr. Huffman assured me that these trivial details would receive his personal attention, and signaled Miss Myrtil and Mr. Judels to start one of their scenes.

Mr. Lee must have given the authors a pep talk; they had a creative reawakening which resulted in a batch of new comedy scenes, all of which were for Miss Myrtil and Mr. Judels. Before *Vogues* left to open in New Haven, Mr. Lee ordered a run-through of the entire show. The comedy interludes that Jimmy and I had rehearsed fell into place and worked out well. I spoke to Mr. Huffman again about the insane-asylum curtain, and he said that it would be at New Haven for the dress rehearsal. I spoke to Ma Simmons about Jimmy's fur coat and was assured that it, too, would be at New Haven. Sunday night, at the dress rehearsal, these promises were not quite kept. Instead of an insane asylum with practical gates, the Shubert organization had spared no expense to prepare an elevator door, with the word *Asylum* scrawled over the top. At our cue, I was to slide the door open and have Jimmy follow me out onto the stage. Ma Simmons had also economized. Instead of spending the twenty dollars it would have cost to buy a mangy secondhand fur coat, Ma informed us that his chauffeur had a fur-lined coat. If Jimmy wore the chauffeur's coat inside out, he said, it would be fur.

At the dress rehearsal, Miss Myrtil did several singing and violin numbers as well as ten or twelve comedy scenes. Actors and material are unknown quantities in the rehearsal hall. Experienced actors and competent directors will rehearse dramatic and comedy scenes and agree that they are technically perfect; when these same scenes are performed before an audience, they fall completely flat, and nobody can explain why. Some actors scintillate at rehearsals, but in front of an audience they have no warmth or personality. Jimmy and I weren't too impressive at rehearsal. On opening night, however, we were working to an audience. Our first scene was played as written:

ENTRANCE INSANE ASYLUM. *Man in uniform unlocks and opens gates. Allen and Savo enter from asylum grounds hurriedly. Savo wearing baggy fur coat; Allen, Palm Beach suit.*

ALLEN: Ladies and gentlemen, please pardon the intrusion. We are the authors of this extravaganza. As a rule the authors wait until the audience calls for them at the end of the show. We are not taking any chances. This is Mr. Savo, who wrote the music. My name is Allen. We always dress this way. We are inseparable companions, so no matter what the weather is, one of us is always comfortable. Many of you assembled may say, "Who are these men? What have they ever written?" Replying bluntly to these carpers, may I say that we are the authors of the drama that had the shortest run of any show ever presented on Broadway. This drama had four acts, and only three of the acts were seen. On opening night, the critics left at the end of the first act. The audience left at the end of the second, and the cast left at the end of the third. For the inquisitive many who may wonder why we are in the asylum, I claim that we have no reason to be in there. We simply stated that this revue could be a success despite the fact that it contains no suggestive jokes, and has no song you will remember tomorrow or that you can whistle on the way out of the theatre. This show has no jazz band, and the only part of the feminine anatomy displayed is that with which the chiropodist is familiar. Everybody says we are crazy.

(*Savo whispers in Allen's ear and exits.*)

Ah, yes! Mr. Savo recommends that we give you a sample of some of the jokes we have written. A cunning suggestion. If you are in the mood, Mr. Savo, carry on!

(*Savo enters carrying large wooden dumbbell.*)

ALLEN: Mr. Savo, why are you carrying that one dumbbell?

SAVO: These always come in pairs.

(*Savo exits.*)

ALLEN: You see how you are going to be convulsed during the evening.

(*Savo enters carrying two suitcases.*)

ALLEN: What have you there in that suitcase? (*Pointing.*)

SAVO: Ten pounds of sugar for my coffee.

ALLEN: What is in the other suitcase?

SAVO: Ten pounds of sugar for my tea.

(*Savo puts down suitcases and removes hat. Allen hits him over the head with club.*)

ALLEN: There is a lump for your cocoa.

(*Savo replaces hat, picks up suitcases, and exits.*)

ALLEN: This being an English revue, some of the better jokes will be told two or three times during the evening. Another service this show provides: if you have gotten into the wrong theatre and came expecting to see a motion picture, during the next scene Mr. Savo will illustrate the story in pantomime. If you are a theatre-lover, a devotee of the spoken word, look at me. If you wonder how the same story would look as a motion picture, watch Mr. Savo.

(*Savo enters, and during next monologue illustrates jokes and story with gestures.*)

ALLEN: When the curtains open you will see a rural drama in three acts. The story has been translated from the language of ancient Greece, way back in B.C., or even before B.C. In "A," I think it was. The opening scene of the story is laid in Italy, and concerns an old Italian peasant, Launcelot Ginsberg by name, who is a retired female impersonator. So seldom you

see a retiring one, but this one has retired, and lives
at home with his two daughters, Marie and Florence.
As the curtains part, you will see the old man kill
his daughter Marie, and leave Italy without touching Florence. That is the end of the first act. In the
second act he starts to swim his way over to this
country. He swims quite well, having for years been
a pallbearer in Venice. One day while swimming he
accidentally runs across his wife in the middle of the
ocean. It seems that she is lighthousekeeping at the
time. Eventually he arrives in this country, an alien,
but at Hoboken he buys a package of Bull Durham
and takes out his first papers. That is the end of the
second act. In the third act, as I remember, the Civil
War breaks out. In the year of 1812, to be exact.
You remember Pocahontas and one of the Smith
Brothers — the trouble they had. However, the Civil
War insists on breaking out and the old man, having
no Union Suit, is forced to join the Southern Army.
Everything is hunky dory and the goose hangs high.
The goose starts hanging so high they have to send
for a tall butcher. The old man turns out to be an
inventor and is finally put into jail for inventing the
pretzel. The authorities claim that the old man has
made the first crooked dough in this country. The
moral that this little drama tries to bring out is
that . . . "A knock is as good as a boost, unless you
are trying to look over a transom."
(*Guard enters — blows whistle — Allen and
Savo return through insane asylum gates — curtains close.*)

The audience laughed all through our opening. Jimmy and
I looked very funny together; there was a contrast in height,
and our comedy methods were entirely different. I depended
on talk, Jimmy on pantomine. Everything that we did in the
show — a series of blackouts and a number of short comedy
scenes — went very well. Jimmy's vaudeville act, with his wife,

came late in the show and was the applause hit of the evening. After the opening night most of Miss Myrtil's and Mr. Judel's scenes were taken out of the show. Before we finished at New Haven, Mr. Judels had departed *Vogues* and returned to New York to start rehearsing with a new show.

*Vogues* opened at the Shubert Theatre in New York on Friday, March 28, 1924. Mr. Lee had high hopes for his first experiment in the musical field. The reviews were favorable. The *New York Times* critic headed his report:

NEW SHUBERT REVUE
BRIGHT WITH COMEDY

———

LESS GORGEOUS THAN SOME OTHERS
BUT WITTIER — ODETTE MYRTIL
DOMINATES "VOGUES"

After speaking highly of Odette Myrtil's talents and contribution to the show, and divulging that he recalled Miss Myrtil as a minor *chanteuse* and violinist who had appeared in *Ziegfeld's Midnight Frolic* years before she had gone to Europe, where she had made her reputation, the critic came to Jimmy and me:

> Next to Miss Myrtil, the honors go to two comedians named Fred Allen and Jimmy Savo. "Vogues" leans heavily on Mr. Allen for his comedy and it does not lean in vain. He is a droll young man who was evident about a season ago in a Winter Garden revue and probably came from the burlesque circuits before that. Mr. Savo, now and then, was frankly a burlesque comedian, but legitimately comic none the less. As for Mr. Allen he reached his high point of the evening in an algebraic demonstration: Let "X" equal my father's signature. Then too, there was the story about how he left the building hoi polloi . . .

The notices in the other papers were all complimentary, but *Vogues* was not a smash hit. Nobody knew why. Alibis ran the gamut: Odette Myrtil was not known to the New York audiences; the people who came to see *Vogues* didn't like it as well as the critics; the show wasn't dirty enough, and so on. To stimulate business, Mr. Lee added Roger Wolf Kahn's orchestra to the show. Roger was the son of Otto Kahn, the millionaire. Otto Kahn loved the theater, and for many years had helped finance impresarios bent on raising the cultural standards of the New York theater. Roger, the son, was interested in popular music, and was conducting an orchestra that had been taken up by the social set. To equip himself for his musical lark, Roger had rented an excellent band owned by Eddie Elkins. Eddie was also engaged for the show, either because he owned the baton, or because Roger wanted Eddie to handle all of the band's rehearsals. But even the Roger Wolf Kahn Society Orchestra couldn't help *Vogues*. The show ran fourteen weeks and closed for the summer. I guess they had to close until J.J. stopped laughing at Mr. Lee's first musical attempt.

In September, we started out on the road hoping to get a run in Chicago. It was the same story in every town. When we stepped off the train and saw the buzzard hovering over the theater, we knew business was dead. I never did discover how the buzzard knew where *Vogues* was heading from week to week. In big cities or small towns, the buzzard was always there first, outlining figure eights in the sky. An actor in a flop show develops complexes. He goes from city to city, knowing that the notices are going to be bad. When the curtain goes up, and he sees the audience's expectant faces, he knows that as the show progresses the look of anticipation on every upturned face is going to gradually change into disappointment, and that at the final curtain the faces that remain will register anger. A person who has paid to see a bad show feels that he has been robbed of both his time and his money, and holds every actor on the stage to be an accessory to the crime.

The road trip with *Vogues* was depressing. I had worked out the "authors" idea and had given Savo the additional comedy bits that he was doing. After the New York opening, all of his vaudeville friends told Savo that he was the star of the show, and he believed them. If I suggested changing a joke, he suspected that I was trying to take advantage of him. On one occasion he invited me to "step out in the alley and fight like a gentleman!" An example of one of his annoying pranks involved an entrance I had given him to follow a band specialty. Savo appeared with his hand caught down the bell of a French horn. We sat at a table in a café to discuss his problem; then I suggested that perhaps, if a certain note could be blown on the horn, it might release his hand. After we had gotten a number of laughs, talking about algebra and music, I worked it out with a pencil and piece of paper and proved to him that blowing an E-flat would loosen his hand. He doubted me; I adjusted my fingers and blew a note on the French horn, and his hand flew out. This scene had been in the show for several weeks, always getting plenty of laughs. One night, as I finished talking and reached over to sound the E-flat, Savo blew the horn himself and released his hand. When we came off the stage and I asked him why he had done this, he said that some friends of his had seen the show and told him that, since he came on the stage with the French horn, the audience naturally assumed that he was the one who played it. Then, when I put my lips on his mouthpiece to blow the note, as Savo quoted his friends, "it ain't sanitary." After two or three similar episodes I stopped talking to Savo except on the stage. *Vogues* eventually arrived in Chicago. The buzzard was outdoing himself high above the theater. The show ran but a few weeks. It was the first time I had ever been happy on a closing night.

Back in New York, Ethel, Portland, Walter, and I renewed old acquaintances. Ethel was in *Louis the Fourteenth*, a Ziegfeld show; Portland was in a small musical, *Tell Me More*, still a chorus lady; and Walter was working as a film salesman for Universal Pictures. Walter and I were stage-door Johnnies, meeting the girls after their shows every night to take them out for a snack. The first time Barnum and Bailey got together they had a circus; every time the four of us got together we had more laughs than Barnum and Bailey had on the day they pooled their hyenas. Portland I were going together now. I think Ethel's ambition was to see me hooked. But, as an actor who had obligations at home and an indefinite future, I wasn't inviting anyone to jump into that future without a lift from the springboard of security. I had seen enough insecurity at home. Most of my people lived not only from hand to mouth, operating with short arms; they also had to go through their years paying ten and fifteen cents weekly on insurance policies. The insurance policy was a guarantee that, no matter how many necessities a person had to forego all through life, death was something to which he could look forward. It was the only luxury he had ever known that he could afford. It seemed to me that when a male invited a female to share his nest, the nest should contain a good-sized egg. If I was ever going to acquire an egg for my nonexistent nest, I had to work.

I assembled a monologue and started to break in another act for vaudeville. The Keith office had blacklisted me for playing Shubert vaudeville, but three years had passed and I had been in two Broadway shows. When my act was submitted to the Keith bookers, they made no mention of the blacklist. But the Keith ritual never changed. I was booked again in the cut-salary theaters — the Hamilton, Fordham, Proctor's One Hundred and Twenty-fifth Street, Proctor's

Fifty-eighth Street, and so on — to break in the act; later I
would show it at the Fifth Avenue Theatre and the bookers
would see it and set a salary. By the time my act was acceptable to the booking office, I would have played most of
the New York theaters at a cut salary. I was spared this
financial indignity by a call from the Shubert office. I still had
two more years to go on my contract, assuming the options
were taken up, and the Shuberts had to guarantee me twenty
weeks every season. To make up my twenty weeks for the
current year the Shuberts were sending me to talk to A. L.
Jones and Morris Green, who produced *The Greenwich
Village Follies*.

The *Follies* was an annual revue that had started on a
small scale down in Greenwich Village and had been brought
up to Broadway. John Murray Anderson assembled and
directed the first *Village* versions, and it was to his taste, skill,
creative and directorial abilities that the *Follies* owed its
initial success. Ushered into the presence of Messrs. Jones and
Green, I was informed that the current version of *The
Greenwich Village Follies* was undergoing radical changes.
The show had opened at the Shubert Theatre, starring the
Dolly Sisters, Vincent Lopez and his band, Moran and
Mack, Don Barclay, Ludmilla, and a host of minor luminaries.
The show had opened badly, and Murray Anderson and the
producers had been trying to improve it ever since. The Dolly
Sisters and Vincent Lopez were leaving, and the show was
about to move to the Winter Garden. Jones and Green were
planning to add to the cast Mordkin, the famous Russian
dancer; Toto, the clown; and me; they would then advertise
a "new version" of the *Follies*.

Don Barclay, an excellent comedian, was doing all of the
comedy sketches. My only function in the show was to
provide two monologues before the front curtain, one in

each act, to enable the stagehands to set Modkin's scenery. The *Follies* opened at the Winter Garden, and ran until March. The show finished the season on the road, playing Boston, Providence, Springfield, New Haven, Newark, Brooklyn, and Philadelphia. After I had been in the show for a few weeks at the Winter Garden, Don Barclay left the cast, and I was asked to replace him in all his comedy skits. This was my first opportunity to play scenes and work in a musical. Before, I had been purely a monologist. Being a monologist is a lonely occupation: you stand on the stage talking to yourself, being overheard by audiences. In scenes, the comedian works with other people. If a scene is bad, the comedian has somebody with him to share the blame. I enjoyed this new experience. In addition to my two monologues, I was in Scene Three, "Service," a telephone episode featuring a series of wrong numbers, in which I played "A Jewish Gentleman"; Scene Six, "Up in Mary's Room," in which I was "1st Policeman"; Scene Fifteen, "An Horror-toria," featuring a small-town choral group, of which I was the musical conductor. In the second act, I was in two scenes, in one of which I sang and danced. The experience was very helpful, and any doubts I had about making good in the new roles were silenced by the producers and everybody associated with the company.

The success the *Greenwich Village Follies* series enjoyed was due to the men who were responsible for the shows. In addition to John Murray Anderson, who wrote, edited, directed, lighted, and supervised the preparation of every show, there were Jones and Green themselves, the producers, who handled the financial and business affairs; Alfred Newman, their musical director; and Saul Abrams, the company manager. Each man knew his business thoroughly and performed his chores quietly and efficiently. As a group they were kind and considerate of actors, and in a day of pompous charlatans, no-talented self-proclaimed geniuses, shoestring and conniving managements, all so prevalent in the theater, it was a joy to be associated with the men responsible for *The Greenwich Village Follies*.

As the weeks went by, I improved as an actor. In a sketch called "Neighbors" I impersonated an intoxicated husband. When my Aunt Lizzie saw the show in Boston, she complimented me on my toper delineation. Coming from my aunt, this was high praise, for she had seen many inebriated relatives, under assorted circumstances, down through the years.

*The Greenwich Village Follies* closed in June. I was through with the theater until the fall; meanwhile, I would spend the summer months at home, in Boston.

# 17

## Summers Back Home

EVERY summer, when I went home to live with my Aunt Lizzie in Dorchester, I tried to accomplish something that would help me in the theater. I knew I didn't have any great talent, but in vaudeville, and in revues, a comedian who could do a variety of things had more scope for comedy. A comedian who sang and danced might some day star in a musical comedy. A comedian who played a musical instrument well had a finish for his vaudeville act; if he played it poorly, the instrument could be used for comedy purposes. During each summer vacation I always augmented the swimming, baseball, and gang diversions by studying one subject. Since the time I had bought my first banjo in New Zealand, I had used the instrument in the theater. I didn't know anything about the banjo, and could play in only one key, and so one summer I decided to take lessons. The only teachers I could find in Boston were the McGrath Brothers. The brothers, Fred and Dick, had been one of the first double banjo acts ever to appear in vaudeville. By the time I caught up with them, the boys were rather advanced in years and a trifle outmoded. As a direct result of my studies with the McGrath Brothers, I went through my entire banjo career using the original five-string tuning that was popular back in the slave days, and I always strummed the banjo backwards. However, the brothers did teach me the chords in the various keys, modulations, chromatic runs, and a number of basic exercises that were very helpful.

The next summer, I studied the clarinet. My teacher was a Mr. Herrick. Mr. Herrick was probably the busiest clarinetist in Boston. He played the morning shows at the Orpheum Theatre. The Orpheum played Loew vaudeville and the acts did four shows daily. The theater employed two different orchestras. A small group played the 11 A.M. vaudeville show and background music for the silent feature picture. At 1:30, the morning musicians departed, and the full orchestra, directed by Charlie Frank, took over to play the entire matinee. At 5, the complete orchestra withdrew and the morning ensemble returned to play until 7:30, when the augmented orchestra again took over and finished the day.

Mr. Herrick was a sort of Jekyll and Hyde of the clarinet. At the Orpheum morning shows, he sat slumped over in the sparsely filled orchestra pit, tooting away on his clarinet with complete indifference. But at 2:15 P.M., every day but Sunday, Mr. Herrick took his place with the orchestra at the Old Howard to play the matinee for the burlesque show. When the curtain rose and the chorus girls pranced down to the footlights, Mr. Herrick's clarinet was raised to attention, his fingers danced merrily over the keys, and his shrill notes jumped for joy as they were released from the instrument. The burlesque show finished at 4:40, which gave Mr. Herrick twenty minutes in which to pick up his B-flat breadwinner and return to the Orpheum, where, at 5 he joined the skeleton orchestra. At 7:30, Mr. Herrick left the Orpheum to return to the Old Howard, where, at 8:15, he started playing the evening burlesque show. At 11 P.M., lip tired and lark happy, Mr. Herrick packed away his clarinet for the last time that day and returned home.

I don't remember who originally sent me to Mr. Herrick.

Our meeting took place on a Sunday at Mr. Herrick's Back Bay apartment. Mr. Herrick first impressed me as a man who could be very busy doing nothing. He looked like a toy that some child had wound up and forgotten to play with. I didn't realize that I was seeing Mr. Herrick in his relaxed state, on the day he didn't have to work. When I confided in Mr. Herrick that I wanted to learn to play the clarinet, he asked me if I owned an instrument. When I confessed that I didn't, he opened a closet door and took down a clarinet case from the shelf. Before I knew what had happened, I was the owner of a B-flat clarinet complete with case, had made an appointment to meet Mr. Herrick at the Orpheum Theatre stage entrance the following morning, and was shaking Mr. Herrick's hand, halfway out the door.

The next morning I met Mr. Herrick after his first show at the Orpheum and ran beside him as he trotted down Tremont Street, through the square to Howard Street, and then up Howard Street to the Old Howard stage entrance. As Mr. Herrick pounced up the stairs, I followed him and kept on his heels through the stage door and down another short flight of stairs that led to the cellar where the musicians assembled and tuned up before entering the pit. At my first lesson, we were early and the cellar was empty. Mr. Herrick showed me how to assemble the instrument, how to moisten the reed, and how to hold the clarinet. Then he told me to practice blowing the reed to get a steady tone. Now that I was occupied, Mr. Herrick opened a brown paper bag he had been carrying, extracted a jumbo sandwich, lifted the top piece of bread to check on the contents, replaced the top slice, and started eating his lunch. For my first four weeks of lessons, I met Mr. Herrick at the Orpheum stage entrance on Mondays and Thursdays. As we jogged together to the Old Howard, he questioned me about the number of hours I had practiced the exercises he had given me, and about my general progress. Now that I had mastered the art of assembling my own clarinet, Mr. Herrick started eating his lunch as soon as we arrived in the cellar. We always had the same routine. I would place my lesson on a music stand, and repeat the scales, finger exercises, and simple pieces as Mr. Herrick munched on a lumpy sandwich, occasionally taking a swig from a bottle of milk. Mr. Herrick always carried a pint bottle of milk in his brown paper bag to keep his sandwich company. When I made a mistake, Mr. Herrick would lower the sandwich from his lips and correct me through a mouthful of semimasticated bread and meat. As it neared show time and the other orchestra members straggled in, Mr. Herrick would say, "That's enough for today. You're doing fine." As I dried my clarinet and packed it away in the case, Mr. Herrick finished his lunch and folded up the brown paper bag. We usually both came out even. Before putting my hat on, I handed Mr. Herrick three dollars for my lesson, he marked a new set of practice exercises for me in my instruction book, and we walked to the cellar steps, where we said good-by.

Even as I studied, two things told me I would never be a clarinet virtuoso. The first was that, after running to the Old Howard from the Orpheum, I was always out of breath through most of my lesson. I was sure that if I learned to play the clarinet winded, I wouldn't know what to do when I was relaxed and had plenty of breath. The other reason concerned the life expectancy of a practicing clarinet pupil in my Aunt Lizzie's neighborhood. Every time I practiced in the house, irate neighbors shouted over from their three-decker houses in back, or stepped on their cats in rebuttal. Somehow, I lived to acknowledge my indebtedness to Mr. Herrick. I made good use of the clarinet in vaudeville and in shows for many years. Mr. Herrick told me, years later, that I had become his most famous pupil — but not because of my mastery of the clarinet.

During one vacation, I studied voice. With my nasal range, I guess I should have taken singing lessons from a nose specialist. It didn't occur to me at the time, however, and I became a pupil of Professor Reddin. I didn't know anything about the Professor's background. He didn't ask me any questions, and I treated him with the same deference. Professor Reddin had a studio in a wedge-shaped building just off Copley Square, on Huntington Avenue. The Professor was a thin, rather white-faced individual. At our first meeting I deduced that the Professor's debilitated appearance had been induced as the result of breathing the dormant air that lurks in choir lofts. After my second lesson, the Professor told me that he had been ill; I am sure that listening to me vocalizing didn't help his convalescence.

My first few lessons were dull. The Professor sat at a piano striking a variety of notes which I attempted to reproduce vocally, mi-mi-mi-ing up and down the scale. Whenever I climbed up high into my nasal passage and broken sinus barrier to render a top note, I could see the Professor wince at the piano. When he got to know me better, the Professor just sat there and trembled. To vary his aural discomfort, after his studio acoustics and his eardrums had been pockmarked by the pointed ends of my pear-shaped tones, Professor Reddin one day suggested that I lay the cornerstone for a repertoire and master a popular song. The most popular song at the time was "When You and I Were Seventeen." With my nose crammed with lyrics, I went to town. Guided by the Professor at the Steinway, my vocal tones were properly placed in the mask, my vowels were wide open, and my volume was increased. The results were amazing. The Professor's studio was on the fifth floor of a ten-story office building, and its windows faced on an areaway. On the hottest days, when the Professor started thumping his piano and I started baying "W-h-h-h-e-e-e-n Y-o-o-o-u a-w-w-n-e-d I-e-e-e W-a-a-a-r-e S-e-e-e-v-a-a-w-n-t-e-e-e-n," we could hear the areaway windows slamming up and down the entire ten floors.

I had scarcely mastered the song when the Professor asked me if I would do him a great favor. The favor involved stepping across the street to the S. S. Pierce building and singing "When You and I Were Seventeen" for an acquaintance of his. I didn't know whether the Professor's landlord had told him to get me out of the studio or the acquaintance wanted to break a lease. Then the Professor explained. The acquaintance was a successful middle-aged businessman who had been a boy soprano. The boy's voice had been beautiful, and he had sung in churches and had been in demand at the most important functions held in New England. The boy liked to sing and enjoyed the popularity and acclaim his voice brought him. When the boy grew older, his voice changed. The beautiful soprano was gone. His singing days were finished. Many years later, when he had become successful in business, he often thought back to the good old days when he and his voice were the toast of the town. The businessman had an idea. Perhaps, if he studied singing, his magnificent voice would return, and he could again enjoy the triumphs he associated with his childhood. The businessman consulted Professor Reddin, and began to take vocal lessons. For several years, the middle-aged businessman took his lessons regularly and practiced at home religiously. His voice improved, but he was unhappy. He had given up hope that his soprano voice would return. He called Professor Reddin and advised him that he was discontinuing his lessons. This came as a prime blow to the

Professor. The businessman had become sort of an annuity in the Professor's scheme of things. I suspected that I was to be the Professor's trump card. A one-man recital by me might convince the businessman that Professor Reddin could do anything with the human voice.

On the appointed morning, Professor Reddin and I crossed Huntington Avenue, entered the S. S. Pierce building, stepped into the elevator, and ascended. The businessman stood up and welcomed us to his office, then sat back down at his desk. Professor Reddin took his place at a grand piano that stood in a corner of the room. I removed my hat and stood directly in front of the businessman. The Professor pommeled out the introduction with his concrete touch, I adjusted my sinus diapason, and nasaled into "W-h-h-e-e-e-n Y-o-o-o-u-u a-w-w-n-e-d I-e-e-e-e W-a-a-a-r-e S-e-e-v-a-w-n-t-e-e-e-n." During my entire song the businessman sat transfixed. When I finished, he seemed stunned; he looked as though somebody had told him that his body had become obsolete and that he was no longer a part of his generation. I put on my hat. Professor Reddin got up from the piano, and said a few words to the businessman. Good-bys were mumbled, and the Professor and I departed. I never did learn if my solo influenced the businessman to continue his singing lessons or not. That solo must have been my swan song. Since that day I have never had a request to sing "When You and I Were Seventeen." Or any other song, for that matter.

The summer I returned from *The Greenwich Village Follies* I spent in the hands of another professor. It happened in this way. Joe Kelly, the only fellow I knew in our neighborhood who was going to college, worked during his vacations as a lifeguard at Carson Beach. When I came home every year, Joe would let me row the lifeguard boat to enable me

to get a good tan in a hurry. In June, 1925, when I came
back from the *Follies,* Joe told me that this year he couldn't
take the lifeguard post; he had to take a summer course at
Boston University to make up some credits. He suggested that
I take a summer course, too. It sounded interesting. I wasn't
much of a scholar; it had almost taken extradition papers to
get me out of the High School of Commerce. The subsequent
years I had spent in vaudeville and in shows. I had never
been to college; I didn't need any credits; I hadn't been near
a school for fourteen years. All my qualifications were nega-
tive, but, after looking over the Boston University catalogue
and selecting a course that was given by Professor William C.
Hoffman and included English Vocabulary, Rhetoric, Oratory, Public Speaking, and a few other subjects, I agreed to
accompany Joe on enrollment day just to see what would
happen.

When we crawled through a hole in the ivy and entered
the Boston University building at Boylston and Clarendon
Streets, Joe went upstairs to enroll for his courses; I was left
alone at the door to locate Professor Hoffman. I found the
proper room on the ground floor, and got into line. When it
came my time to sign, the Professor looked up and blinked.
Then he looked away, looked back, and blinked again. He
couldn't believe his eyes. He had seen me in Boston only a few
weeks before with *The Greenwich Village Follies.* He
couldn't understand why I was posing as a college student. He
thought it was some sort of gag. I explained my presence by
saying that I came from Boston and couldn't be traveling
around the country in show business making grammatical
errors in other cities that would reflect on the high cultural
standards of Boston's educational institutions. The Professor
fortunately had a good sense of humor. After learning that I
had only graduated from high school, he said that permitting

me to enroll for his course would be highly irregular. However, he added, if I really wanted to spend six weeks studying, he would permit me to join his class as a stowaway. When I got to know Professor Hoffman better, he told me that as a boy he had wanted to be an actor, and when he had graduated from college, he had gone to New York to try to get into the theater. With shows closing for the summer, he had found no jobs available. He had, however, met one actor-manager named Corse Payton, who was known as the "World's Best Bad Actor." Payton was apparently impressed by young Hoffman, and had advised him to return to Boston until the season opened. In September, Payton promised, he would send the boy a telegram telling him to come on and join the Corse Payton Company. When Hoffman arrived home, his parents suggested that he teach school temporarily until he left to become an actor. Finishing the story, Professor Hoffman said, "That was twenty years ago, and I am still waiting for that telegram from Corse Payton!"

Professor Hoffman's summer course was very popular. The class was filled and consisted of English and Public Speaking teachers from small schools throughout the country who considered Professor Hoffman the authority in his field. The teachers gladly gave up their summer vacations to come to Boston and study Professor Hoffman's methods. In this class, I was as out of place as a diabetic football player in the Sugar Bowl. I studied along with the others, trying to improve my vocabulary, preparing my subjects for the Public Speaking assignments, and taking my homework seriously. None of my classmates knew who I was, and occasionally, during a discussion period, the Professor would look up at me, over the tops of his steel-frame glasses, with a twinkle in his eye, as if to let me know that we were putting something over on the others.

The last week in class, I am afraid that I took advantage of the Professor. I had no contract to return to *The Greenwich Village Follies* for the coming season, and had written a new monologue to start back in vaudeville with. I thought that, instead of preparing a talk for my next Public Speaking appearance, I could accomplish something by trying out my vaudeville monologue, which I called "The Misconception of Man." The monologue was in lecture form, and proved that Man's anatomy in concept had been bungled badly. Man's nose stuck out in front of his face where it could be easily punched and where it had to smell everything. If Man's nose were on the top of his head, it could be covered by his hat. If Man didn't want to have his nose punched, or didn't want to smell anything, he could keep his hat on. Man had two ears, one on either side of his head. This was duplication. Man should have one ear in the middle of his forehead. The other ear should be at the nape of his neck. With this arrangement, Man could hear people who were talking behind his back. The finish of the monologue explained that Man's two eyes in the front of his head were a complete waste. One eye in the center of the face, where the nose used to be, could do the job. The other eye should be put on the end of the middle finger of the right hand. The advantages of this arrangement were obvious. If you lived in a boardinghouse and wanted to take a bath, you might find the bathroom occupied. You wouldn't want to knock on the door. There might be a lady in the tub; you might embarrass her. With the eye on the end of Man's middle finger, all he had to do was poke his finger through the keyhole and take a look.

During this monologue, the class laughed at every joke. When I sat down, Professor Hoffman looked speechless. He removed his glasses and wiped them thoroughly, taking his time; then he replaced them and, embracing the class with

one forlorn look, said, "There is a time and place for everything." Professor Hoffman and I parted good friends, however. He was interested in my progress through the years, and
we corresponded until his death in 1955.

*The Greenwich Village Follies* company went into rehearsal in August. The New York run, with the adverse
critics' reviews and the added expenses incurred through the
many cast changes, had put the show in the red. The *Follies*
always did well on the road, and Jones and Green hoped to
assemble a cheaper cast and recoup their losses during the
second season. My salary, with the Shubert option being
taken up, was six hundred dollars a week. I was to be replaced
by a less expensive monologist. I had forgotten all about the
show and was busy trying out my "Misconception of Man"
in a small theater in Melrose. One night I came home to find
a telegram asking me to phone the Jones and Green office
in New York. I called Morris Green, and he said that when
they started to put the show back together, they realized that
I had been doing two monologues and five scenes, and they
also realized that instead of hiring two or three less expensive
actors to replace me, it would be cheaper to put me back in
the show. Morris knew that I was going with Portland, and
said that if she wanted to go on the road, he had a place
for her with the company.

We both opened with the *Follies* in Buffalo. Moran and
Mack, Toto, and Ludmilla were the stars. Moran and Mack,
two blackface comedians, were billed as the "Two Black
Crows." The boys had made a record of one of their comedy
routines that had swept the country. Audiences screamed at
Charlie Mack as he drawled out a discovery that he had made
on his farm: "Black horses eat more than white horses." Charlie's explanation followed: "I think it's because we got more
of the black horses than we got of the white horses." Toto the

clown had a number of very funny pantomimic scenes, and
Ludmilla, a lovely ballerina, did a John Murray Anderson
interpretation of "Liebestraum" that added grace and beauty
to the show. Lew Seymour and his partner had taken over
the parts in the comedy sketches. This version of *The Greenwich Village Follies*, with the laughs predominating, proved
to be a great show for the road. It did excellent business in
every city, and enjoyed a profitable five-month stay in Chicago.

During this road trip I blossomed as a writer. I had
written a number of smalltime vaudeville acts. The vehicles
had not been profitable, because most of the acts had been
written for vaudeville actors who had no talent. I wrote
monologues and a number of talking acts for various couples.
I liked to write and to see ideas take form and come to life.
When I finished their acts for them, none of my clients ever
paid me. I was lucky when they didn't borrow money from
me to go out of town to break in the acts. I became a joke
philanthropist. Every time I walked down Forty-seventh
Street some actor pinned me to a wall and held me there
until I had listened to his routine and had promised to try
to fix it up. The light in my front room at the Stanley Hotel
was a beacon for the smalltimer. If he knew I was awake, even
if it was 3 A.M., he would drag his wife up to my place to
run through the act to see what I could suggest: a funny line
for the wife as she did her split, a sock gag for his exit as
the wife went into her song, a new parody, an idea for an
opening, a few song titles. There were a number of good
comedy writers in New York, but writing was their business.
They had to be paid. Writing, with me, was a hobby, a
side line.

One good actor who encouraged me to write was Jack
Donahue. Jack was one of the most popular comedians of his

day, and one of the best eccentric dancers the theater has ever known. Before Jack became a great Ziegfeld star, I wrote the first monologue he ever did in vaudeville. Jack and I spent weeks working on his comedy part in the first book show in which he appeared, *Molly Darling*. In his later shows — *Angel Face*, *Two Little Girls in Blue*, *Sunny*, and *Rosalie* — we always discussed his comedy scenes, and I tried to improve them with odd lines and jokes. Jack always wanted me to stop trying to be an actor and concentrate on writing. I was always afraid to take the risk. As an actor, I could make a living and always have enough money to send home. As a writer, I knew that my relatives couldn't eat my words. A number of my show-business pieces had been published in *Variety*, and for three of the annual editions I had written "The Acrobat's Christmas," "The Smalltimer's Diary," and "The Sharpshooter's Revenge."

I began to write more or less regularly shortly after Tommy Gray died. Tommy was a well-known comedy writer in the nineteen-twenties who specialized in vaudeville material. Tommy prepared the act for the famous Cherry Sisters when they made their first appearance in New York. The sisters were so bad that Tommy had them perform behind a net. The net hung down from the flies and covered the entire stage, protecting the Cherry Sisters from impulsive members of the audience who had come to the theater laden with throwing tomatoes and sundry passé fruits. When the fame of the Cherry Sisters spread, society people used to come from Park Avenue to toss avocados. Tommy Gray also wrote a weekly column for *Variety*. He was very popular with the performers, who were always quoting his lines. "I wouldn't say he is effeminate: all I know is I saw him staggering out of Huyler's!" or "Is that a red tie or is your tongue hanging out?" were samples of Tommy's cracks. When Tommy died unexpectedly, Sime Silverman, the *Variety* editor, asked me if I would write a weekly column for the paper. I explained to Sime that I could not hope to replace Tommy Gray. Sime said that he wanted me to write my way, and that while I was away on the road with *The Greenwich Village Follies* I could do anything I wanted with the column. I thought that having a weekly deadline might stimulate me and force me to think and write; I told Sime that I would like to try it.

Near Beer was a favorite comedy subject during Prohibition. My *Variety* column was called "Near Fun." It was a conglomeration of random thoughts, and every week it showed up in *Variety* looking approximately like this:

### NEAR FUN
### by
### Fred Allen

#### A Fable

Once upon a time there was a little man whom we shall call Hal Fpint. He stood 36 inches in his bare feet — he rarely wore stockings. Hal was very short and there was a reason. He was forever worrying about something. At grammar school he said, "I'll never be able to go to high school. If the school is too high I will get nosebleeds." At high school he said, "I can't go to college. I have no raccoon coat." At college he said, "I can never be a big man in business: I'm only 36 inches tall." Let this be a warning, kiddies, never worry. Hal was so busy worrying all his life that he never had time to grow. Today Hal is 88 years old and 36 inches tall. He is nothing but a yardman in a dry goods store.

#### The Moral

Parents! If you want to have tall sons and daughters never let a child grow up with a weight on its mind.

#### Observations

An actor has three salaries: the one he thinks he ought to

get; the one he really gets; the one he tells the Income Tax Collector he gets.

The reason some chorus boys wear flowers in their lapels is because they can't wear them in their hair.

The height of deceit: a bald man wearing a toupee when he calls on his mother.

### Our Novelette

#### Chapter One

Many years ago there was a boy who wanted to see America from coast to coast. He had no money to satisfy his urge to travel and so he became a motion picture operator. This enabled him to see different cities in the Pathé News. Looking at the pictures through that little hole in the operator's booth, the boy's eyes finally gave out. Wanting to see more of America, he joined a circus. But the circus traveled at night and for many years, while his journeys took him from Portland, Maine, to Ditto, Oregon, peering into the darkness he saw nothing. Through constantly living he became an old man, and lost his job with the circus. Gradually he had no money. One night, tired and hungry, he climbed into a freight car and fell asleep. Two months later, the old man awakened and crawled out of the freight car only to find that he had again crossed the entire country, while asleep, and was back in his home town. The old man was broken in health and spirit and was nothing but a tramp. His boyhood dreams had been realized: he had traveled America from coast to coast — but he hadn't seen anything.

#### Chapter Two

Aesop once said: "A boy who is fond of scenery should become a stagehand.

### Poem
Hush little bright line
Don't you cry
You'll be a cliché
Bye and bye.

Song Titles

You're Cross — Your Eyes Have Told Me So

I Walked Her Down To The Meadow And She Listened To My Bull

Married Men Have Better Halves — Bachelors Have Better Quarters

I Held Her Hand And Melded 40 Pinochle

Passé News

Energine, Ill. — Hi Tom Minstrel Show had to close here. Both end men had fights with the interlocutor and stopped talking to him.

Liverpool, England — American dramatic actor leaves the country. Being left-handed, the actor found it impossible to keep replacing monocle in right eye.

Butte, Mont. — Glass blower with carnival was stricken with hiccups and blew 200 percolator tops before he could stop.

Layoff, Fla. — Old actor who retired to start raising rabbits has gone out of business. Learned too late that the two rabbits he started with were brothers.

Every day I was busy running around, trying to dig up ideas, making notes, and typing my items to meet my weekly deadline. I wasn't getting any salary, but seeing "Near Fun" in *Variety*, with my name under it, seemed to be worth all the effort. I wanted to write, and this was a start.

After the column had been appearing for a few weeks, people in the show started to tell me how much they enjoyed certain gags or ideas. Vaudeville actors in different cities stopped me on the street to volunteer jokes and comedy experiences for use in the column. John Murray Anderson came on to rehearse the show and told me that he never missed my column. He suggested that I start writing in earnest. The encouragement and flattery were gratifying, but the decibels generated from a resounding slap on the back never appeased an empty stomach. I reasoned that as an actor I made a living speaking words. Until such time as somebody offered to pay me for writing words, I had better be satisfied with my present status.

*The Greenwich Village Follies* was thriving. Lew Seymour, Jesse Howard, Portland, and I went sight-seeing in the various towns, ate together, and had a lot of fun, but my mind was always on the column. I was concerned about the future. I felt that an actor faced a lifetime of insecurity. A humorist with a column on a newspaper, or one who wrote for syndication, enjoyed a greater security, it seemed to me, and had a much more satisfying life. As the writer masters his craft, his value increases. Acting has never appealed to me. An actor, to spend his entire life as an actor, has to have the mind of a child. A writer at sixty can be a Steinbeck, a Faulkner, or a Hemingway. An actor at sixty can make a funny face or do a creaky dance. The actor lives a reasonable-facsimile existence while cavorting in an unreal world. The value of an actor's services are determined by the needs of another person. An out-of-work actor, whose salary has been fifteen hundred dollars per week, cannot earn fifteen dollars in any other business, and cannot ever earn fifteen hundred dollars again until some producer or author needs him badly enough to pay that fifteen hundred dollars. Of course, there are a few exceptions: stars who finance and produce their own shows, and others who have built up loyal audiences over the years. With the coming of radio and television, the actor finds both his success and his oblivion accelerated. Confronting the mirror, the average actor discovers that Father Time is the make-up man responsible for the physical changes that determine the parts he is to play. These changes diminish his value, and finally, crowded out of the spotlight by the new generation, the actor finds himself reduced to an offstage voice as he arrives at the end of his career. With the coming of the Machine Age, however, the writer has become a vital force. The newly invented printing presses, radio microphones, and television cameras, left to their own devices, can do only one thing — they can collect rust. Without the writer these brave new ominous monsters would be silent metallic Mongoloids. The satisfaction and the feeling of accomplishment I derived from writing, as well as the writer's future, appealed to me.

*The Greenwich Village Follies,* after playing as far West as Kansas City and Des Moines, started back east. The show was to play a return date in Philadelphia, late in May, and then close permanently. During the final week in Philadelphia, Al Newman, the musical conductor, gave a farewell party for the cast, the newspapermen, the musicians, and anybody who happened to be in the neighborhood and was thirsty. While the din was in its embryo state and voices could still be distinguished from each other, Al introduced me to Linton Martin, the dramatic critic of the *Inquirer.* Linton mentioned that he had been enjoying my columns in *Variety.* I told him that I would like to learn to write, and that if I could just get enough money to live on, I would begin writing some sort of column. I told him that since the *Follies* was closing, I would have to give up my *Variety* column when I went back into vaudeville. Getting an act together, doing two or three shows daily, and traveling would leave no time to turn out a weekly column. Linton suggested that before I made any definite decision, I should explain my ambitions to Sime Silverman when I returned to New York. Linton said, "If the column is important to *Variety,* Sime will pay you. If it isn't important, you might as well forget about it."

I took Linton's advice. The show closed, we went back to

New York, and I called at Sime's office. I explained to him that I had obligations at home and that I had to work steadily. I told him that I wanted to become a writer, and that if *Variety* would pay me sixty dollars a week, I would give up the theater, continue to do my weekly column or anything else he wanted me to do, and study to learn how to write. I told him that my aunt's expenses at home were small, that I could live cheaply in New York, and that all I required was a small weekly salary. As I talked, Sime was busy rummaging around in a mound of editorial debris that littered his desk; from time to time he looked up to see if I was still there. When I mentioned small salary the second time, Sime stopped foraging, looked up again from his rubble, and said, "Do you know *Variety's* advertising rates?" I said I didn't. "You get two columns a week," Sime continued. "If you took a two-column ad, you'd have to pay for it." Picking up a pencil and salvaging a small pad of paper from the desk litter, he said, "Let me show you." He started scrawling away at some figures; when he had finished his calculations, he looked up with a wry smile and said, "It seems to me, at current advertising rates, *Variety* is paying you about two hundred dollars for this column you're writing."

That was final. It was also the end of my writing career. Sime was the mortician who embalmed my ambitions. As my hopes were lowered into the open grave, I made two hasty decisions: I resigned as a *Variety* columnist; I returned to Boston.

# 18

## Bert Yorke, Straight Man

WHAT Capistrano was to the migratory swallow in the spring, Boston was to the home-town actor in the summer. Late in June actors started flocking back home to spend their vacations. The musical-comedy performers and the vaudeville acts who had enjoyed good seasons rented cottages at one of the nearby resorts. Revere, Nantasket, and Nahant beaches were popular with the gregarious set. On week ends, being accessible by trolley car, these vacationing actors were swamped with relatives and friends. The kibitzing hordes arrived on Friday night. Over the week end they consumed great quantities of food and liquor; soiled all available bed, bath, and table linen; saturated the rugs and puddled the floors with their dripping bathing gear; and departed Sunday night, leaving the host with his premises littered and his sinks overflowing with defiled china.

The prosperous actors who were allergic to friends fled to small incognito towns on Cape Cod. The Boston actors who had no money spent their summer days in the city, promoting passes to ball games or, on stifling hot days, going over to L Street, the free municipal beach in South Boston, to swim and sprawl around in the sun. By 1926, the Boston show-business fraternity had moved across town. The Rexford Hotel clientele had established a new frontier at the Hotel Clarendon in the South End. Smalltimers no longer gathered at the Daisy Lunch on Howard Street; the popular meeting place was now the Waldorf Lunch on Tremont Street, across from the Majestic Theatre. The Waldorf was a white-tiled, self-service lunchroom that featured good food and reasonable prices. Actors sat at the table by the hour, sipping cold coffee, swapping conversation, and keeping their eyes on the door to appraise each new arrival. At the Waldorf, tab owners (a tab — condensation of "tabloid" — was an abbreviated burlesque show that usually boasted a line of chorus girls, a sexy prima donna, a good-looking straight man, and one or two comedians) booked comedians and principals for their attractions; song publishers hired pluggers to sing at theaters, banquets, ball games, and political affairs; old acts were broken up and new acts formed; gossip was dispensed; and jokes were bought, sold, and exchanged over the calories.

One afternoon, two tab comedians were discussing a blackout that ended with a gunshot. The comedians were wondering aloud about the gun, and where they could get it. One thought that he might be able to borrow a gun from a friend; the other felt that they should buy it at a pawnshop. As they got up to leave the restaurant, two calloused hands descended on the shoulders of the hapless funsters. They were walked around the corner to the La Grange Police Station. A detective sitting behind them at the Waldorf had heard their conversation about the gun and had apprehended the comedians, positive that he had two potential burglars.

Back home that summer, I knew how the average Russian citizen felt at the expiration of the first Five Year Plan. I had just finished my five-year contract with the Shuberts. Like the Russian citizen, I was breathing easier for the moment, but didn't know what the future had in store for me. I had no plans. I was living at my Aunt Lizzie's, spending the sunny days at the beach or at the ball games, and the rainy days in the house, reading. One sunny afternoon, armed with two passes to the Red Sox game, I stopped in at the Waldorf to find somebody to take along. At the first table there was a man who seemed to be in the process of interring his head in a plate of Boston baked beans. I didn't know whether he was nearsighted and was looking for something he had dropped in his beans, or if he had a short nose and was trying to smell something on his plate. When the head ascended from the actor's caviar — as beans were called by the Boston actors — I saw that it belonged to Bert Yorke. (Faces are all important. Without faces it would be impossible to identify our friends. If we had to recognize people by their bodies, we could only tell men from women. With career women, in many cases this would be impossible. But I had identified Bert Yorke's face, and hanging down from his face was the rest of him.)

I had known Bert for years. I first met him at the Hamilton Theatre in Dorchester, one of the theaters I had booked myself before I retired permanently from the hardware business and Chandler and Farquhar's. At that time Bert was fourteen years old and was doing an act with his father called Yorke and Yorke. The father was an English comedian, with the red nose and the baggy full-dress suit. Bert was dressed exactly like his father. They sang, told jokes, and danced together. To foment enough applause at the finish of the act to enable them both to come back for a bow, Bert executed a series of rapid back somersaults. At the Hamilton, I had envied Bert. He was already an old-timer in vaudeville. He knew how to put on a funny make-up and could sing, dance, and do acrobatic tricks. As we were growing up, I met Bert many times in the city. Bert and his father lived in a rooming house on Bulfinch Street. When the act wasn't working, the elder Yorke spent his days and nights drinking ale and helping a group of senile cronies keep a bar from falling over by propping their puffy stomachs against it for hours on end. While his father was working overtime to enable sundry breweries to stay solvent, Bert, instead of going to school, was acquiring a delinquent's education in the Bucket of Blood, the poolroom on Howard Street. Here Bert learned the Three R's: Reading, from the Racing Form; Writing, from tracing the names of horses on slips he later gave the bookmaker; and Arithmetic, from adding the points he made as he played pool. Bert grew up and married Maybelle Killeen. Maybelle, a very pretty girl, had been singing illustrated songs and working in various tab shows; after their marriage Maybelle and Bert did a comedy and singing act together known as Yorke and Maybelle. When this act had played all of the smalltime, Bert went to work with another comedian named Eddie Lord, and as Yorke and Lord they played the big time for two seasons.

The boys had recently split up, which brings us up to date on Bert as he sat in the Waldorf, armed with a fork and a piece of buttered bread, attacking a defenseless plate of baked beans. Every summer, when we met in Boston, Bert laughingly suggested that he and I do an act together. I always had future commitments, and our act became an annual gag. This year, as we went out to the ball game together, Bert made his summer suggestion that we do an act, and now it seemed like a good idea. Bert had no obligations. I was free. We agreed to meet the next day and discuss the project.

Bert owned an antiquated Dodge that was half vibrator and half conveyance. Driving with Bert was an oscillating experience: when you arrived at your destination, your watch was ten minutes fast and you knew how a milk shake felt as it was being poured out of the mixer. The following morning Bert picked me up at my Aunt Lizzie's house and we drove out to Waltham, where Maybelle's mother owned a small grocery store on Lake Street. The lake for which the street had been named was a mucky-looking economy-sized puddle that offered swimming and boating for the less discriminating vacationers. Arriving at the lake, Bert and I trembled for a while after stepping out of the Dodge, then rented a boat and rowed out to the middle of the lake for privacy. After three days of these floating conferences, and exchanges of countless ideas, Bert and I agreed on an act.

It was more than an act, it was a series of acts. The Palace Theatre in New York had been booking masters of ceremonies for extended runs. Frank Fay, Lou Holtz, Eddie Cantor, and Georgie Jessel had been great Palace successes, presenting the acts, and working through the shows. It seemed to me that if the innovation was so popular with New York audiences, two comedians who could speed up a show and weave the acts together would be accepted by audiences in any big-time theater in the country.

Vaudeville acts were always slowed down when stagehands had to set and remove props between acts. The stage was blacked out, the orchestra played *agitato* music, shadowy figures could be seen tugging at pianos, benches, hall trees, and other objects. The audience waited patiently in the dark until the figures scurried off, the lights flashed on, and the next act appeared. If Bert and I could assemble enough comedy bits and take over the stagehands' chores between acts, moving the pianos and props, the lights would never have to be darkened, and the show would run without interruption from overture to exit march. Added to this masters-of-ceremonies stint, we planned to do a complete comedy act, next to closing. To allow sufficient time for the extraneous high jinks between the acts, we planned to bill ourselves as two acts: Yorke and Allen, and Fink and Smith. On an eight-act bill, Yorke and Allen would be the third act, Fink and Smith the seventh. As a selling point, the manager would have a stronger comedy show and save the cost of one act.

As Bert and I sat out in the boat in the middle of the lake at Waltham, it sounded perfect. All we had to do now was assemble the fun and sell the idea to an agent and the bookers. I agreed to try to prepare the material. The most important ingredient was the Fink and Smith act. That had to be written, rehearsed, and broken in; the other interruption bits we could worry about later. I started thinking and writing, fortunately in that order. I owned no typewriter; I had to sharpen my pencil along with my wits. During the day, I sat around the house, writing. At night, I took a long walk, stopping at Hodge White's on the way home to buy my Aunt Lizzie and my Aunt Jane some ice cream. My Aunt Lizzie could eat a quart of ice cream before retiring. I used to think that she had frosted nightmares, but she never mentioned them. My Aunt Lizzie hated to go to bed at night. She sat until all hours in her rocking chair in the dining room, with the oil lamp on the table, reading the evening papers and digesting the news of the day. When she finally succumbed to the blandishments of the sandman, she went to sleep well informed.

After two weeks of concentration I finished the Smith and Fink routine. Bert liked it, but thought that, since the other comedy bits would be all talk, it might be better if the Smith and Fink act opened with a song and dance. He donated an old English song called "Gravy and Bread." The lyrics couldn't be used, but we salvaged the music and wrote some new lyrics. When we added the final touches to Fink and Smith, Bert and I opened the act walking on in a white spot, wearing silk hats, black Inverness coats, white gloves, and white spats; we sang:

> We don't care much about working
> To employment we're not averse
> We think that labor is vulgar
> Our idea of a job could be worse.

> Chorus

> On Monday, we'd never start working
> On Tuesday, we'd finish at two
> Wednesday we'd have half-a-day off
> Thursday there'd be nothing to do
> Friday would be early closing
> We'd put all the things on the shelves
> Saturday, we'd have a bit of a rest
> And the rest of the week to ourselves.

The song *segued* into the chorus of "Tea for Two," to which we did a double soft-shoe dance and exited. I returned, minus the silk hat, Inverness, and gloves; I was now carrying a clarinet. In the act, I was to announce that I would give an impression of Ted Lewis, playing the clarinet; each time I began, I would be interrupted by Bert, coming on stage in various disguises. Each time he came on, he interrupted my playing to announce that he was the representative of a different company to whom I owed money; he had come, he said, for purposes of repossession. Each time he went off, he took something of mine with him: a watch, my coat and vest, my pants, and so on. Originally, there was no girl in this skit; later we wrote in a part for Bert's wife. She joined briefly in the cross talk, and then, to give Bert and me a chance to change our wardrobes, she sang a song. Following Maybelle's song, I came back on stage with a banjo, and told a few jokes. Bert then came on, carrying a large folding blackboard. He explained that he had given up his job as an installment collector for various firms because he was worked too hard. This led us into another bit:

ALLEN: Did you ever stop to think how little you work in a year?

YORKE: I work like a horse. Instead of underwear, I have to wear harness.

ALLEN: You don't work at all — even in Leap Year. Set up that blackboard. I'll show you.

YORKE: (*Arranges blackboard, and prepares to write figures as they are explained to him.*) Okay!

ALLEN: In Leap Year there are 366 days. Put that down: 366. Now, you sleep 8 hours a day. That is one third of the day — 24 hours — that you sleep. You sleep one third of the year, or 122 days. That gives you 244 days left. Now, another 8 hours of the day you have for rest and recreation. That is another 122 days you don't work. Which leaves you 122 days remaining. Of these 122 days — you don't work on Sunday. There are 52 weeks each year — 52 Sundays from 122 days leaves you 70 days. You get a half holiday every Saturday. Half of 52 is 26; take that from 70 and it leaves you 44. How long do you take for lunch every day?

YORKE: About an hour and a half.

ALLEN: An hour and a half. During the week you spend more than half a day eating. About 28 days you do nothing but sit around and eat. 28 days from 44 — that leaves you 16 days. Every year you get two weeks vacation. That's 14 days from 16. That leaves you only 2 days. Those 2 days are the Fourth of July and Labor Day. Have those 2 days off. So you see — you don't even work one day in the year!

The act finished with me playing the banjo while Bert did an acrobatic dance. Now that the act was all assembled, we had to rehearse. Charlie Van, the property man at the Shubert

Theatre in Boston, was a friend of mine. When I told him that Bert and I were looking for a place to rehearse, he said that the Majestic Theatre was closed for the summer. Charlie spoke to the watchman, who agreed to let us use the Majestic every day for rehearsal purposes. For two weeks Bert and I met every morning and went through our lines and our opening song and dance. Meantime, I had been working on other comedy bits, to have them prepared.

The Fink and Smith act was finally ready to break in; all we needed was some comedy wardrobe. To insure his comedy entrances, Bert had to have seven funny coats of assorted sizes and materials and a collection of ludicrous vests, hats, wigs, false noses, and additional grotesque items. When a vaudeville or burlesque comedian required bizarre wardrobe, he automatically thought of Guttenberg's. The Guttenberg family for years had been selling and renting secondhand clothing, costumes, hats, and shoes to stock companies, burlesque shows, musical-comedy companies, amateur groups, and vaudeville acts. The Guttenbergs also stocked new clothing, and if the price was right, would sell anything, including the fixtures in the store. When I first went to New York, I bought all my juggling hats at Guttenberg's, which was then on Third Avenue at Fourth Street. The original store was a dirty, cluttered repository for used merchandise. Bales of cloth were stacked to the low ceiling, tinseled dresses, minstrel suits, red and green dress coats were hung on lines strung from wall to wall. Cartons filled with shirts, hats, and shoes were strewn around the floor. A customer entering Guttenberg's for the first time got the impression that Guttenberg was a giant spider who was displaying his fusty wares in an enormous web.

The juggling hats were kept in the cellar. A juggler who was known to Guttenberg could open the bulkhead doors on Third Avenue and step down the shaky wooden steps into a muggy cavern filled with silk toppers. There were hundreds of hats of every age, size, and style. When the juggler had found ten or twelve hats he could use, he closed the bulkhead doors, carried his selections into the store, and deposited them on the littered floor. Guttenberg, smelling a sale, would suddenly appear from the back of the store, his shoulders draped in a mantle of soot, his hands clad in gauntlets of grime. Appraising the juggler's pile of hats, Guttenberg would say, "My friend, you've got a bargain. Take 'em for thirty-five dollars." Having spoken, he would start to fit the hats one inside the other to facilitate the packing. The juggler would immediately remonstrate; the price was too high; he would say, "I'll give you ten dollars." Guttenberg would dash the hats to the floor and launch into withering vituperation involving thieves who came into his store, stealing merchandise. The juggler, refusing to budge, would answer, "Ten dollars." Guttenberg would throw the hats down again and order the juggler out of the store. As the juggler started to go, Guttenberg would call him back and say, "All right, I'll lose a little. Take the hats for twenty dollars." The juggler, with his hand on the doorknob, would say, "I'll give you twelve dollars." Guttenberg would be stunned. He would look up at his dirty ceiling as though to summon help from the calcimined regions above. Wringing his hands and describing the members of his immediate family who had fatal and costly ailments, the amount of money the store had lost in recent months, and glossing over his dizzy spells and the doctor's advice not to get excited, he would shout, "Eighteen dollars!" The juggler would open the door. Guttenberg would shrug his shoulders, admitting defeat, and would say wearily, "All right, cut my heart out! Take the hats for fifteen dollars!" The juggler would close the door and say, "It's a deal!" At this, Guttenberg's face would light up, the routine rancor and acerbity would be diffused into a tentative smile. The sale had been made. The hats would be wrapped up and the juggler would depart; Guttenberg would disappear into the back of the store and, chameleonlike, lose his identity against a background of dust.

Guttenberg, senior, was a versatile actor. He could manipulate his ducts and cause avocado tears to well up in his eyes, roll down his cheeks, and spatter on a garment as he was dickering with an obstinate customer over its price. Abandoning a dramatic high light, with the sale consummated, Guttenberg would turn to comedy. When a comedian appeared in the store to buy a funny suit, as he donned the suit and stepped to the mirror to get the effect, he could see Guttenberg looking over his shoulder, convulsed with laughter. When the comedian selected a funny-looking derby, Guttenberg would put on the derby first to model its laughter potential. When the comedian put on the derby, Guttenberg would double up shrieking, and would call his wife, who came in and joined the laughter. Many a comedian found that the only laughs his comedy attire ever obtained were those he heard in Guttenberg's rubble emporium.

Bert and I drove to New York in the pulsating Dodge, and spent two days selecting comedy wardrobe. After a riotous guffaw display, as Bert tried on the fur coats, Invernesses, droopy pants, jungle helmets, tiny hats, and big shoes, we left Guttenberg laughed out, loaded the Dodge with our newly acquired rummage, and drove back to Boston. Following one more week of rehearsal, with Bert wearing his comedy habiliments, and a piano player engaged to drum out "Gravy and Bread" and "Tea for Two," we agreed that Fink and Smith were ready.

Lou Walters, now the owner of the highly successful Latin

Quarter in New York, started with a closet-sized office in Boston, through which he booked a number of smalltime theaters. Bert and I explained the new act to Lou, and he booked us for a week at Nipmuc Park. The park, an alleged amusement resort, was situated at Lake Nipmuc, at Milford, Massachusetts, and consisted of a cluster of tall trees, a few food and game concessions, picnic grounds, rowboats for hire, and an outdoor theater. Like the other New England parks, Nipmuc was operated by the local streetcar company. The theater, a primitive wooden contrivance, boasted a tin roof, six or eight bare dressing rooms, a weather-beaten curtain masked in by faded wings, and a skimpy row of footlights. These footlights were too weak to brighten any part of the stage; their sole function seemed to be to attract moths and night-flying insects who had better than twenty-twenty vision. During the summer months, Nipmuc played six acts of vaudeville for a full week, and Bert and I felt that after a week of work we would know if the act had merit.

On a Monday late in August, we drove up to Milford in the agitated Dodge and a driving rain. The matinee was canceled; this augured well. The matinees were filled with children, and at night, an adult audience would be more inclined to react to the jokes. Late in the afternoon the rain stopped. Bert and I hung up our stage clothes in the dressing room and rehearsed our music. We ran through the dance and the jokes; I limbered up my banjo and clarinet. After dinner, we both started to get nervous. When the show got under way, and we heard the other acts getting laughs and applause, we steadied down. It sounded like an easy audience. Fink and Smith were the fifth act on the bill. The show was going well. The fourth act finished and took its bows; Bert and I shook hands and wished each other luck. The orchestra started our introduction. As we walked onto the

stage, the clouds burst. Rain started pounding on the theater's tin roof. Bert and I sang, but we couldn't hear the
orchestra; we danced, and the orchestra couldn't hear us; we
told jokes, and the audience couldn't hear anything. The rain
clattered on the tin roof all through the act. When we finished, we hadn't heard one laugh. After our opening show, we
didn't know whether the act was good or bad.

During the rest of the week, however, the reaction of the
audiences told us that we had a good comedy vehicle, and
we tried new jokes and lines every show to improve the routine. After the Nipmuc Park junket, we returned to Boston
and decided to go to New York to break in the other bits.
Bert was friendly with Dave Gordon. Dave had opened an
office with Joe Woods. Dave's brother Max was the head of
the Orpheum circuit, and Joe's sister Mae was an influential
booker in the Keith office. Bert told me confidentially that
Dave and Joe had an "in," and the acts they represented were
booked solid. We turned our Yorke and Allen and Fink and
Smith enterprise over to Gordon and Woods. I explained to
Dave our masters-of-ceremonies idea, and he predicted it
would be very successful. He booked us into some Proctor
theaters — at Yonkers, Elizabeth, Mt. Vernon, and elsewhere
— to perfect Fink and Smith, and to try out the other interludes. When the entire program was assembled, our first
appearance on the bill was self-explanatory:

ALLEN: Ladies and gentlemen, I do hope you will pardon
the intrusion. It won't take a moment to explain our
mission. Every big business has efficiency experts,
and since Vaudeville is now one of the largest rank-
ing industries in the country, Vaudeville surely
needs efficiency attention, too. We are an Efficiency
Committee sent from the Keith Offices by Mr.
Albee to investigate and remedy the evils existing

in this theatre. This is my associate, Mr. Yorke.
Mr. York is a self-made man.

YORKE: Showing the horrors of unskilled labor.

ALLEN: Let us not give way to our lighter natures, Mr.
Yorke. Many things are wrong in this theatre both
from the actor and audience standpoints. These
things must be looked into.

YORKE: Coming downstairs just now, I noticed that the keyhole in one of the dressing rooms was broken.

ALLEN: We must look into that. Now, there are other
things we hope to check on this week. (*Consulting
notes.*) Oh, yes. The Fly Menace. We have it on
good authority, ladies and gentlemen, that flies have
been coming into this theatre without tickets and
not only seeing the show, but also those flies are
causing untold trouble. Many an actor thinks he is
being applauded when the hand-slapping is only a
fly being swatted on a bald head. In order to keep
these germ-carrying insects out of the building,
these signs . . .

(*Yorke holds up sign which reads:*
*FLIES ENTER AT YOUR OWN RISK*
*POSITIVELY.*)

ALLEN: These signs will be placed at every doorway and
from now on flies coming into this theatre will
suffer the consequences. This is no joking matter as
the word "Positively" at the bottom of the sign
will show the trespassing little fly.

Item Number Two: The Gum Situation. Oh, how
many people there are who come into this theatre,
night after night, put their gum under their seats
when the show starts, and then go home when the
show is over, forgetting to take their gum with
them. They come back the following week and
get the same seats in the hope of finding the gum
which is rightfully theirs. How many are disappointed?

YORKE: Four out of five at the age of forty.

ALLEN: That is pyorrhea.

YORKE: Pyorrhea is in the gums.

ALLEN: Consider yourself ignored. And watch your cigar. You won't have to catch fire to be put out. Now, the management has received many complaints about gum. Some of our best patrons have come in here and left Spearmint and have come back later and got Blackjack. In order to remedy this situation we are installing a parking system for your gum:

> *(York holds up sign with numbered squares. A hook is in each square with a number hanging from it. Several of the hooks are covered with great wads of gum that have been checked.)*

### GUM PARKING

| 1 | 2 | 3 | 4 | 5 | 6 | 7 |
|---|---|---|---|---|---|---|
| 8 | 9 | 10 | 11 | 12 | 13 | 14 |
| 15 | 16 | 17 | 18 | 19 | 20 | 21 |
| 22 | 23 | 24 | 25 | 26 | 27 | 28 |

ALLEN: As you come into the theatre at night, you stop at the Coat Room and check your gum. This gum is placed on one of these little hooks, you receive a number, and we hold the gum for you until you call for it. After thirty days, of course, if the gum is not called for, we have to return it to the Used Gum Department at the Wrigley Factory, where it will be reflavored and simonized.

Item Number Three. (*Consulting notes.*) Oh. Program Conditions. These are simply atrocious in this theatre. You people coming into the theatre get programs at the door. By the time you get to your seats the lights go out and you cannot see the names of the artists on the bill. We shall see that every act on this program is properly explained and introduced.

Another joke or so with Yorke, and we would introduce the first act and go off stage. Between succeeding acts, we had shorter bits. One was a dissertation on applause, and the harmful effects caused by sitting on the hands. In vaudeville, if an audience was not responsive, the people were said to be "sitting on their hands." We proved that people who sat on their hands not only flattened out their rings and enjoyed lumpy sitting during the show, but they also cut off the blood supply to the hands. In time, the hands just withered and hung there. The person in the audience who applauded slapped his hands together, started his circulation, stimulated his entire body, and, after applauding all through the show, left the theater a much healthier specimen. For the stubborn patrons, who insisted on sitting on their hands, we supplied a sofa pillow on which two white canvas gloves had been sewed. Slipping his hands into the gloves, the person placed the pillow on his seat and sat down. For another interruption, we used the "Old Joke Cemetery." And for others, we commented on the acts that had just finished. One bit we did is fairly familiar now, but it was funny at the time. It had Bert walking on, carrying a sign:

ALLEN: Where are you going?
YORKE: I have to go next door to the Fish Market.
ALLEN: What for?
YORKE: The man asked me to make a sign for him. It's finished. I'm taking it to him.
ALLEN: What kind of a sign?
YORKE: Here it is.
 (*Holds up sign to audience.*)
ALLEN: (*Reads.*) FRESH FISH FOR SALE HERE. It's all right, but you have too many words there.
YORKE: Where?
ALLEN: Well, you don't need the word FRESH. If a man is selling fish, they have to be FRESH, don't they? You

don't think the man could do any business with
stale flounder, do you?

YORKE: That's right. I'll rub that out.
(*Rubs out word* FRESH.)

ALLEN: Why do you say HERE? He's not selling them any
place else, is he? You see the fish HERE and you
know that he is selling them HERE. You can leave
that out, too.

YORKE: I never thought of that. (*Rubs out* HERE.) It's all
right now, isn't it?

ALLEN: Let me see. (*Studies sign.*) FOR SALE is superfluous
as well.

YORKE: What does that mean?

ALLEN: It means you can rub out FOR SALE. The man isn't
renting the fish, is he? He wouldn't have the fish
there unless they were FOR SALE. Why, it's silly!
He isn't keeping them as souvenirs. It is understood. The man has a store full of fish and they are
FOR SALE.

YORKE: (*Rubs out* FOR SALE.) Now, it can't be any shorter
than that. Nobody can find fault with the sign now.

ALLEN: No. The only thing is — I don't see why the man
needs a sign on the store when you can smell his fish
a mile away!

After four weeks of work, Fink and Smith, the Efficiency
Men, and all the interruption bits were working smoothly.
Dave Gordon booked us into the Palace. We opened on
October 4, 1926, and the idea was so well received at the
Palace that Bert and I were held over for a second week.
This was very gratifying, because the Palace was the most
famous vaudeville theater in the world. The Palace patrons
were supercritical. Week after week, they saw the finest
talent, and when a new act was accepted by the Palace, it
meant that the act had arrived. *Variety*, in reviewing us,
listed us under —

## NEW ACTS

York and Allen
Comedy, dancing
18 min. One.

Freddy Allen, formerly in vaudeville as a "single," has taken unto himself a male partner, half of the former Yorke and Lord team. Both worked throughout the entire Palace vaudeville program last week, Allen doing comedy announcing and "interruptions" until down next to closing when the pair did their own bit, billed as Fink and Smith.

Allen did similar work in a musical comedy with Jimmy Savo opposite. Allen as a single was strictly for the intelligentsia and as a result led a hectic vaudeville career. His current act is aimed at the collar bone, and those who miss parts of the fly talk will have a chance to laugh at the physical absurdities when Yorke, as a collector, makes frequent appearances demanding various portions of the Allen apparel until he is down to his undies and an umbrella. When the umbrella is collected, they black out.

The bits are punctuated by Allen's running fire of comment, probably the brightest talk ever heard on a vaudeville stage. Allen also contributes half of a comedy double dance and plays a bit on a clarinet. Yorke does an efficient bit of contrast and contributes a solo dance.

Yorke and Allen are an important addition to vaudeville bills. Allen is unique inasmuch as he doesn't have to depend on layoffs for gags, and writes his own ultra-smart delivery. He has a keen sense of comedy and a big league delivery.

As a "single" Allen was too fast and refused to compromise. With his present partner the act contains all the necessary elements for the poets and peasants, and is geography proof. They'll like Yorke and Allen, from half a buck up to $5.50.

During the second week at the Palace, Dave Gordon stopped in at the dressing room and said that he had booked us on the Keith Time for thirty-five straight weeks. Vaudeville was always full of surprises. Five weeks after we broke this new act in at Nipmuc Park, with the clatter of rain on the tin roof drowning out the jokes, we were at the Palace and booked for a solid season to play the best vaudeville theaters in the country. There was always hope in vaudeville. An actor could be out of work for months. By changing his partner, trying a new act, or altering the finish of an old act, he could suddenly find himself in demand.

Bert, Maybelle, and I started on our tour. The act's salary was $1150 a week. I paid the agent's commission and the railroad fares; Bert and Maybelle received $450 net. My salary fluctuated, depending on the train and Pullman costs; some of the weeks Bert and Maybelle did better than I. In the big-time theaters, with the eight-act bills doing two shows a day, the act went very well. The shows ran smoothly, and the double masters-of-ceremonies idea was new to the audiences.

In the three-a-day theaters, with five acts billed, we were two of the acts; this was not so good. Following the first act, Allen and Yorke were second with the Efficiency Men. We then introduced the third act, and when that was over, we were back again as Fink and Smith. Unless we had seven or eight acts on the bill, our idea was a liability. On a five- or six-act bill we had to run our bits together to stretch the vaudeville section of the show out to its programed time. In many of the smaller theaters, the audiences had never seen a master of ceremonies. People didn't know what we were trying to do. After they had seen us doing three or four unrelated bits all jumbled together, the audience had had enough of Yorke and Allen. And, when Fink and Smith turned out to be Yorke and Allen again, some of the audience looked as though they were ready to pull the theater up by the roots.

At the Academy Theatre, in Norfolk, Virginia, the manager had but two other acts on the bill. The show opened with a hand-balancing act and closed with a diving act; the rest of the show was us. In rapid succession we did all the comedy routines, finishing in a blaze of silence with Fink and Smith. After the opening matinee, Bert and I were sitting in front of the large make-up mirror in the dressing room, spreading cold cream on our faces to remove the make-up. We were both dejected and were looking into the mirror as though to blame our reflections for our predicament. A violent knock sounded on the dressing-room door. In the mirror, over our shoulders, Bert and I could see the door open. When it opened fully, we saw, framed in the doorway, the manager of the theater. He didn't speak. He just stood and glowered. Using the mirror, he seemed to be trying to kill us both with a cold and dirty look. Finally, in a gesture of despair, he moved his head slowly from side to side as if to say, "No! No! I refuse to believe what I know I saw!" The door closed and he was gone. We didn't see him for the rest of the engagement; the last night our salaries were brought by an usher.

In Toledo, the Keith Theatre had been reduced to playing three shows daily. The orchestra leader, a little bald, acid-looking man, was so sick of looking at Bert and me that every time we walked on the stage he hung his head. To accommodate his drooping head he had to take his violin from under his chin and play it down around his naval. At one of the many shows we did I said to him, "What would you charge to haunt a house?" This line has since been said by many comedians, but I said it first, on a really trying day in Toledo.

At the old Broadway Theatre, in New York City, the vaudeville started at 11 A.M., with the acts doing four shows a day. Bert and I did three bits and the complete Fink and Smith act every show. We were making sixteen appearances every day. For one entire week Bert and I left the hotel at Forty-seventh Street every morning at 9, on our way to the theater on Forty-first Street. We came back to the hotel at midnight. We ate all our meals in the theater, and spent the days running from the stage to the dressing room.

There were times when vaudeville actors who worked too much together got on each other's nerves. Traveling on the same trains, living in the same hotels, eating in the same restaurants, and spending their days cooped up in the same dressing rooms, vaudeville partners found themselves saturated with companionship. As we trouped from town to town, I marveled at Bert. If we arrived in a strange city at 6 in the morning, shortly after I had checked into the hotel, Bert would appear, announce that he had left our baggage checks at the theater, looked at the dressing rooms, and found the name of a bootlegger and the phone number of a bookmaker — all before 7 A.M. Bert played the horses regularly and confined his reading to the Racing Form. Bert had no traffic with banks. His entire wealth was always on his person. The cash was carried in a grouch bag. When Bert had a good day, the grouch bag bulged out, resting in the V of his vest, and he looked as though he had a honeydew concealed high up in his underwear.

I guess I bothered Bert at times. After one show, in Cleveland, when we had come off the stage, Bert followed me into the dressing room. He had a red nose on and a funny facial make-up, and was wearing a dirty streetcleaner's helmet, a yellow Inverness in the lapel of which he had a large sponge posing as a chrysanthemum, and on his hands he had red rubber gloves. He was wearing sailor pants with a watch fob that was the handle of a toilet chain; he had soiled spats over a pair of big shoes, and was carrying a cane, the ferrule of which reposed in a rubber plunger. Arrayed like a thrift shop come to life, he said, and I quote, "I ain't going to be no straight man for nobody!"

# 19

## Portland and I

IN April, Yorke and Allen came back from the road to play another week at the Palace. Portland was working in George White's *Scandals*. When I returned to New York, I found that all winter she had been taking instructions to become a Catholic. Portland's father was Jewish; her mother was a part-time Presbyterian. Friends of ours from Boston, Benny Drohan and his wife Marty, lived at the same hotel on Forty-seventh Street, and many Sundays, when the Drohans and I attended the Actors' Chapel, Portland joined us at Mass. Shortly after Bert and I had left New York, Portland divulged her religious intentions to Mrs. Drohan, who took her to meet the Reverend Father Leonard.

Father Leonard was the pastor of St. Malachy's Church, on West Forty-ninth Street, in the theatrical section. Many of the vaudeville actors attended St. Malachy's — the Actors' Chapel — and as Father Leonard got to know them, he began to understand their problems and to become interested in the actors as people. He knew that vaudeville acts which closed out of town on Saturday night didn't arrive in New York until all hours. Therefore he started the Actors' Mass at 12:15 P.M., and a later Mass at 12:30 P.M., to enable the actors to get some much-needed sleep on Sunday mornings. Father Leonard was a twinkly little man who became a great influence in the theatrical profession. He founded the Actors'

Chapel. He counseled, consoled, and encouraged actors. He settled their domestic squabbles. He talked actors who were drinking too much into signing pledges. He comforted the sick and he aided the poor. He had vaudeville singers and instrumentalists perform at Masses. He delivered his sermons in the jargon of the actor. He told hilarious stories from the pulpit. Many a non-Catholic, passing St. Malachy's on Sunday and hearing the congregation screaming with laughter, would look again to make sure that the building was a church and not a theater. Father Leonard told me that one day he had been summoned to the Astor Hotel. He found an actor who thought he was going to die. The actor had abandoned his religion, but now he wanted to return to the Church. To impress Father Leonard with his good intentions, the actor gave him a Masonic card and a pint of whiskey. After completing his spiritual task, Father Leonard started back to the rectory with the Masonic card in his vest pocket and the pint of whiskey on his hip. As he stepped off the curb to cross Forty-ninth Street, a truck swerved around the corner and missed hitting him by the proverbial hair. As Father Leonard told the story, he smiled and said, "If the truck had hit me, I could see the headlines in the tabloids: 'Priest found in gutter with Masonic card and whiskey in pockets'!"

By the time I overtook the events that had occurred during my absence, Portland had been confirmed and had received her First Communion. The next Sunday, Father Leonard stopped me, coming out of church, and told me what a wonderful girl Portland was, and that at her confirmation he had given her his favorite name — Mary. The next thing I knew I had bought the ring, and Father Leonard was marrying Mary Portland and me at the Actors' Chapel. The bridesmaid was Kate Starner, a chorus-girl friend of Portland's, and the best man was Charlie Lane, a vaudevillian friend of mine from

Boston. The best man had bad feet and wore white socks with his blue suit. The wedding wasn't one of the social events of the year. As the services started, Portland's family and a few of her girl friends from the *Scandals* were seated in the church, and I was represented by Joe Woods, one of my agents, and Sam Krauss, the owner of the Hotel Coolidge, my new home, on Forty-seventh Street. As for the honeymoon, it was spent partly in Waterbury, Connecticut, where Bert and I opened the following Monday at the Poli Theatre. In Waterbury, Bert bought a new car, and we all drove up to Springfield, where the act played the last three days of the week.

The next week, Bert and I finished our season at the Keith Theatre in Boston. Bert was tired of being a "straight man," and wanted to do an act with his wife the following season, so Yorke and Allen and Fink and Smith, who had been born in Boston in August, came back to Boston to die in June. During the Boston week I had to take Portland out to my Aunt Lizzie for inspection. My Aunt Lizzie and my brother Bob approved of this addition to our family. Also, at this time, Benny and Marty Drohan were home and wanted Portland and me to spend our vacation with them on Cape Cod. I had no act or any immediate plans, and Portland had never been on the Cape. We decided to rent a cottage at Onset.

Onset had quite a large summer theatrical colony. The days and nights were filled with laughs; the beaches and the cars were filled with actors. There were week-end visits from my aunt and my brother. Portland broke the culinary barrier and used my stomach as a laboratory for her oven experiments. (Her early successes were a salmon loaf and macaroni and cheese.) During the summer, I wrote an act for Portland and me. In the theater, Portland had been a herd thespian: as a member of the chorus she had participated, unnoticed, in group singing and bevy dancing. As half of a vaudeville act, however, she would be isolated. It was the accustomed practice in vaudeville: when an actor married, he moved over and made room in the act for his wife. An acrobat's wife tossed him his handkerchief; a magician's wife passed him his rabbits; a musician's wife handed him his trombone; and the monologist's wife helped him with a few jokes. Vaudeville actors married pretty girls, so the wives were usually decorative. Augmenting his vehicle enabled the vaudevillian to ask for more money; the increase bought his wife's wardrobe and paid her fares and expenses. Working in the act also occupied the wife's time on the road. A wife who was not in the act had to wait around in the hotel or in the dressing room until the husband finished his artistic chores. With a vaudeville act, Portland and I could be together, even if we couldn't find any work.

I wrote an act called "Disappointments of 1927." Big girl acts were popular that season, and "Disappointments" was intended to be a satire on that type of act. I opened as a prologue, entering center stage through a baggy satin curtain to sing an introductory song. When I announced my dancing chorus, the Tiller Girls, the spotlight went to the opening of the curtains. Set back in the opening there was a pedestal on which stood a telephone. As I swept off my hat and bowed low to welcome the Tiller Girls, the phone rang. I answered and discovered that it was Mrs. Tiller. After exchanging two or three jokes with Mrs. Tiller, I learned that the girls could not appear. That was my first disappointment. The music started again, and I welcomed my next star, Eva Tanguay. Again the spotlight went to the center opening, and the phone rang. Eva Tanguay was on the phone; *she* could not appear. This was another disappointment. I then sang a welcome to my greatest star, Paul Whiteman and his orchestra. The spotlight, the phone, a few jokes with Whiteman, and my final disappointment.

I then announced that I had decided to do the act alone, and wheeled out a trunk which contained my banjo, clarinet, ventriloquial dummy, and juggling props. These things were concealed in the trunk, which kept the audience from anticipating the comedy sequences. I told a few topical jokes about Chicago, which was very much in the news at the time: "I'm a little hoarse tonight. I've been living in Chicago for the past two months, and you know how it is, yelling for help on the way home every night. Things are so tough in Chicago that at Easter time, for bunnies the little kids use porcupines. I was reading about a boy, seventeen years of age who killed his father and mother, and then asked the judge for clemency on the grounds that he was an orphan." (This last joke, incidentally, had been originated by Artemus Ward, fifty years before I got around to it. Dead men tell no tales, but dead men's tales can be told by others.)

After the Chicago, I told some other jokes: "I knew a girl who ate nothing but Hershey bars and ice cream for six months, and had to be operated on for Eskimo Pies" or "If Noah had forgotten to put two herrings in the Ark, half of Far Rockaway would have starved to death years ago." Then I started my clarinet solo — "When the Roll Is Called Up Yonder, What Shall We Dunk in Our Coffee" — and Portland entered. . . .

ALLEN: Don't you realize that acting is going on here? This is no Symphony Concert where one runs in and out at will. You're not Joan of Arc, are you?

PORT: No.

ALLEN: It's funny — I smell a horse around here some place.

PORT: (*Hands Allen note.*)

ALLEN: (*Reads.*) This will introduce Miss Ann Howe. She

lives around the corner and has had a fight with her folks and wants to do something in the neighborhood to disgrace them. So, I thought it would be nice if she could be seen up on the stage with you. (*Looking at letter.*) I thought that was a period. You really should have a screen door on the house at this time of year. You must never rely on the little insects for your punctuation. Some day you will want a question mark and look in vain for a round-shouldered gnat. Are you looking for work?

PORT: Yes, sir.

ALLEN: What character do you portray?

PORT: I'm a chorus girl. I have no character.

ALLEN: Have you been in any of the big shows?

PORT: I was in the *Follies* until . . .

ALLEN: Until what?

PORT: I was vaccinated.

ALLEN: Boy, that's painful. It's like getting tattooed except that you have no ship left when the man goes home. Where were you vaccinated?

PORT: In Detroit.

ALLEN: I'll just tip-toe around so I don't wake you up mentally while you're here. Do you dance?

PORT: Spring dancing.

ALLEN: I should sit around all winter until you get ready to dance in the spring. Do you sing?

PORT: No, sir.

ALLEN: You mean you have no bathtub in your house? Where I live, everybody sings in the tub. We have to. There is no lock on the bathroom door, and naturally . . . What is in that little box?

PORT: My costume.

ALLEN: The one you dance in?

PORT: Yes.

ALLEN: Would you rather put the costume on first, or shall we get right in the patrol wagon?

There was more of this banter and then, following Portland's exit, I put the clarinet back in the trunk and took out some rubber balls and did a few juggling tricks. The juggling props were deposited in the trunk and a ventriloquial dummy was produced. A short routine ended with my exposing my duplicity and explaining that the dummy was not really talking but that I, a deceitful cad, was doing both voices. This was a very funny bit. The dummy, returned to the trunk, gave way to a banjo. While I was strumming away, Portland re-entered, in costume; she danced, and we told a few jokes. Then, when she left the stage, I had a few gags on topical matters; Florida real estate, for example, was a popular subject of the day. ("I may have to go to Florida tomorrow. I've just had word that somebody has found land on my property down there. Real estate is so expensive in Florida. I know a man who sold his dog down there for six hundred dollars — three hundred dollars a front foot.") Then some additional jokes led to a treatise on applause that alerted the audience to put down their hats, wraps, and packages in order to have their hands free to applaud when I finished. I played a banjo solo to conclude the charade.

When the act was ready, Portland and I did our rehearsing in the cottage and at the beach. In the middle of August I went up to Boston to try to find some theaters to break the act in. Lou Walters came to the rescue again. He booked us for a full week at Nipmuc Park, starting on Labor Day, and also gave us three days in Malden, Massachusetts. When we arrived at Nipmuc, a Labor Day throng mobbed the park. Portland started to get nervous about her debut. Her surroundings were a bit different. Accustomed to the comforts of the Apollo Theatre in New York, she now found herself in a rustic theater that looked as though the back of it had been eaten away by woodpeckers. Formerly surrounded by the rest of the *Scandals* to bolster her morale, Portland now found herself surrounded by me. To help her cope with this

radical readjustment to environment and association, I told
her that I would do the two Labor Day shows alone; then, at
the matinee the following day, she could make her World
*Première*.

And it came to pass. I did a monolgue at the two Monday
shows. Tuesday, after lunch, we went to the theater early and
rehearsed the act on the stage two or three times. Then Portland put on her make-up. As matinee time approached, we
joined the other acts who were sitting on benches at the side
of the theater. The park seemed rather quiet. Labor Day was
the final holiday of the season, and naturally we expected the
rest of the week to be a letdown. The theater piano player
arrived; he reported that there was not a soul in the park. At
matinee time, the theater manager appeared carrying a cloth
bag containing change for the box office. He said that since
there was no audience to see the show he was going to hold
up the matinee until the arrival of the three-o'clock trolley
from Milford. The manager left, and the actors relaxed to
await developments. At 3:05 P.M. we saw the manager coming
back down the path through the trees toward the theater.
When he came up to us, he announced that the three-o'clock
trolley had arrived empty, and he was calling off the matinee.
Thus Portland's first vaudeville appearance was actually a
nonappearance. That night, however, a handful of people
showed up, and our act was christened. During the rest of
the Nipmuc and Malden dates the routines got plenty of
laughs. Portland looked pretty, and I was confident that with
a few weeks of work we would have a good act. After Malden,
we stayed in Boston for a few days, visiting my Aunt Lizzie,
and then Portland and I returned to New York.

Back in New York we played any smalltime theater we
could book, for three reasons: to keep working, to give Portland confidence, and to improve the act. At Ansonia, Connect-

icut, we worked on the bill with an act called the Yale Collegians. In the saxophone section was the adolescent version of Rudy Vallee. When Rudy got out of college and formed the Connecticut Yankees, for years he used parts of our act while giving imitations of me. Using my material finally caught up with Rudy. When he appeared in George White's *Scandals*, Mr. White asked Rudy to eliminate his impression of me. Words were bandied, and Mr. White punched Rudy in the nose: the larynx of his singing equipment. Fortunately, Rudy stopped impersonating me in time, or Mr. White might have punched me in the nose, to get at the source.

When I thought our act was ready to show to the Keith bookers, I spoke to Dave Gordon. Dave hadn't seen us, but after several attempts to book the act he told me that the office wasn't interested. The bookers had liked Yorke and Allen, and thought that breaking up the act had been a great mistake. Despite the fact that nobody in the office had seen Portland and me, the act was taboo. I told Dave that we were playing in Patchogue, Long Island, and asked him to come and see us; I promised him that if he didn't like the act, I would retire Portland to the kitchen. Dave came to Patchogue on Saturday night, saw the late show, and waited to return to New York with Portland and me. Coming back on the train, he said, "Well, I've got to tell you frankly. I came down here tonight expecting to see a Bolivar." He stopped to light a cigarette, then said, "But this is a great act. Portland looks beautiful, the material is funny, you both have class, it's big time." A week later, he booked us into the Fordham Theatre.

This new theater, uptown on Fordham Road, was situated in a good neighborhood and attracted a high-class audience. Before the Monday matinee, Dave called me at the theater and said that he was bringing Eddie Darling to see our act that night. Mr. Darling booked the Palace, and if he liked us, our troubles would be over. At night, we were on next to closing, the audience laughed at everything, and we stopped the show. When I came off the stage, after making a speech, Portland stood in the entrance with tears streaming down her cheeks. She was crying for joy. Mr. Darling was in the audience, we had just stopped the show, he would surely book us into the Palace. The next morning I strutted into Dave's office and found him sitting dejectedly at his desk. I said, "We stopped the show." He said, "I know, but we didn't see it."

Then he explained. He had taken Mr. Darling to dinner at a fish place. Apparently Mr. Darling had been served a clam that was not up to its physical peak. Mr. Darling had swallowed the clam and had come uptown with Dave and the clam to the Fordham Theatre. Mr. Darling managed to dominate the clam until the act just ahead of ours was finishing; at this point he advised Dave that he and the clam had to part company immediately. Dave escorted Mr. Darling out of the Fordham Theatre and curbed him. His sense of loss at bidding the clam adieu weakened Mr. Darling, and Dave took him home. But that was vaudeville: a bad clam could stop a good act from playing the Palace.

On Wednesday night, Dave and Mr. Darling returned to the Fordham. Again our act stopped the show, and two weeks later "Disappointments of 1927" opened at the Palace. *Variety*, as usual, reviewed the show:

> Aside from Fanny Brice and the Gus Edwards Revue, the outstanding turn was Fred Allen, doing a new solo line of patter, 20 minutes of as sparkling a monologue as can be found hereabouts. Allen is one of the exceptional comics who can get honest laughs without hokum. The material is meaty with witty surprises. Portland Hoffa, nice looking

girl, does assistant for brief interruptions, but otherwise Allen alone sustains an amusing interlude.

A week at the Palace to a vaudeville act was like the Good Housekeeping Seal of Approval to a food product. The minute Portland and I did well at the Palace, Dave was able to book us through the winter at all of the Eastern big-time theaters. In April, Dave said that we could go out on the Orpheum circuit and work through the summer. Portland had never been to California. She had been born in Portland, Oregon, and had been named for that city. The family had moved to New York when she was a baby, and Portland had never really seen Portland. We accepted the Orpheum Time to enable Portland to visit the city of her birth and to let her see Hollywood. We started the Orpheum tour in Chicago, and went to Milwaukee, St. Louis, Minneapolis, and so on. By the time we arrived in Seattle, the hot weather had set in, and the Portland Orpheum had closed for the summer. After all that traveling, Portland did not get to see Portland. She hasn't seen it to this day.

The Orpheum circuit, when we started on it, was abandoning its straight vaudeville two-shows-a-day policy, and was advertising a feature picture and six acts of vaudeville, three shows a day. The big time was doomed. The motion-picture companies were erecting theaters in every city. Millions of dollars were being spent to advertise motion pictures and the stars who were being developed in the new medium. Hollywood was soon to consign big time to the horse and buggy era. Big-time vaudeville theaters in most cities were antiquated buildings run by local managers who never tinkered with tradition. The matinee started at two-fifteen. The night show started at eight-fifteen. The music was supplied by an eight-piece orchestra composed of paunchy, middle-aged men who played a "Stars and Stripes" overture and then provided the music for the acts. The big-time stars came back year after year with their same songs, dances, and jokes. The big-time theater mellowed its audiences, but it didn't pamper them.

The motion-picture theaters, on the other hand, were cathedrals that made the vaudeville theaters look like privies. The movie theater opened at nine in the morning; the housewife out shopping didn't have to wait until two-fifteen to see a vaudeville show matinee. The motion picture was available at any hour of the day. Trim, gold-braided lackeys stepped ahead with flashlights to show the housewife to her seat. The show started with a mighty Wurlitzer shooting out of the wall. Mounted on the Wurlitzer, a dress-suited organist provided the accompaniment for the housewife as she sang the lyrics of the popular songs thrown on the screen. Hardly had the housewife's voice died down when a forty-piece orchestra rose from the bowels of the theater to regale her with a classical selection and to play for the presentation that followed. Then came the feature picture, starring one of Hollywood's brightest stars. Hollywood had stars to suit every taste. There was an assortment of sexy females from which the male patron could take his pick. There was an army of he-men or coxcombs, any one of whom was guaranteed to start a housewife drooling in the second balcony. In the motion-picture theater, the housewife was Queen for a Day. Popcorn, candy, soft drinks were available if her tapeworm reared; coffee and tea were served in the lounge. One picture theater in Oakland advertised a "Glassed-in Crying Room," where mothers could watch the picture while pacifying their turbulent infants.

The big-time vaudeville theater couldn't stand off this competition. The vaudeville-circuit heads had their money stacked so high they couldn't look over it to see what was happening to the big time. In 1926, when the Palace Theatre in Cleveland installed the grind policy and declared a cut-salaried week, there were but seven full-salaried weeks of big time in the East. For over fifty years, as I mentioned earlier, vaudeville had been the popular entertainment of the masses. The first time the Orpheum-circuit theaters billed the pictures above the acts, the picture men claimed that it was an admission that vaudeville had lost its drawing power and had become secondary to the picture.

At the time, Portland and I didn't realize that we were part of a crumbling profession. We were happy playing the Orpheum circuit, sight-seeing on the way. At San Francisco, we played on the bill with the great Nazimova. From San Francisco we went to Los Angeles. Sunday nights at the Orpheum in Los Angeles were social events. The Hollywood stars swarmed to the theater to see each other and the new vaudeville show. Many of the silent stars who were present on the night we opened little suspected that, even as they sat there, Brynie Foy, with a few actors and a band of technicians, was busy on the Warner lot experimenting with talking pictures. The talkies would eventually silence most of the silent stars permanently.

During our act Portland and I were properly awed in the presence of the celluloid aristocracy out front, and while we were in the city, we drove out through Hollywood to see the studios and the homes of the stars. The weird stucco abodes perched on the sides of hills, or coyly hiding behind clusters of palm trees, gave the impression that the chefs had overpowered the architects and had baked the community's houses in a pastry oven. We ate at Victor's, where the stars dined, and saw Laura La Plante. She may have seen us. We will probably never know until Laura writes her autobiography.

After the Los Angeles week, Portland and I returned to

San Francisco to play the Golden Gate Theatre. The Golden Gate, with a three-a-day policy, played six acts of vaudeville and a feature picture. Our next stop was across the bay, at Oakland. The headliner there was Elsie Janis, and Portland and I were assigned the dressing room next to Miss Janis. On opening day, as we were unpacking, Elsie's mother came in and asked us if we would mind taking a dressing room upstairs. Mrs. Janis said that Elsie had so many friends in Oakland, she had to have another room in which to entertain them. We abdicated, and Mrs. Janis, in gratitude, gave us a bag of cherries.

It was while we were in Oakland that I received a telegram from Dave Gordon saying that Arthur Hammerstein wanted me for his new musical show. Mr. Hammerstein had produced *Rose Marie*, *Katinka*, and many musical successes. For me, it meant another chance on Broadway. I wired Dave to cancel the rest of our Orpheum booking and to break our jump back to New York. He did this, booking us into Chicago for one week, and into Fort Wayne for three days. During the three-day train trip from Oakland to Chicago, Portland and I discussed the Hammerstein opportunity. If he wanted me for his Broadway show, perhaps he would have a place for Portland; we couldn't wait to get back to New York.

In Chicago, the week dragged as though the days had weights on them. At Fort Wayne, our act was featured with the *WLS Showboat*. The *Showboat* was a radio program broadcast weekly from WLS, the Sears, Roebuck station in Chicago. It was very popular in the Middle West. The cast, poorly paid in radio, was now learning what money was in their personal appearances. The company consisted of a ratty-looking drove of hillbillies of assorted sizes who sang sinus songs and played fiddles, harmonicas, jew's-harps, and empty bottles. They sweated through sets of square dances, gave barnyard imitations, and exchanged rustic antiquated wheezes at which they laughed themselves. There was no silo big enough to hold the corn these meadow minstrels dispensed. If the *WLS Showboat* had ever worked out of doors, it would have had to use a scarecrow for a master of ceremonies; otherwise the crows would have made off with the entire cast.

In the Fort Wayne theater, Portland and I were presented in the middle of the *Showboat* to inject a little class into it. (The idea must have worked well. The radio show came to New York some months later, and in our place the company had Bob Hope. I think this was Bob's first appearance in the East.) I didn't know anything about radio and I had never heard of the *WLS Showboat*, but a lot of other people apparently had. Fans came from all over Indiana to see their favorites in person at the theater, and to bring them home-made pies, cakes, pickles, preserves, and other edible tributes. The Fort Wayne theater manager had found that people in his area were listening to radio and would pay to see their favorites in the flesh. He had found this out the hard way. The previous year he had been to Chicago, booking his shows. Theater business was always bad during Holy Week, and the manager, thinking to economize, asked the booker about a cheap act he could book and feature for Holy Week. The booker said that none of the big vaudeville stars would cut their salaries to play Fort Wayne, but that he had two boys available who were doing a piano act on the radio. The manager spoke to the two boys, explained the poor Holy Week business in Fort Wayne, and asked their lowest salary to play the date. The piano boys said they would take a chance to protect the manager: instead of a salary, they would play Fort Wayne on a percentage basis. The manager laughed to himself at the sharp bargain he had driven, and gave the act a contract for a percentage of the box-office receipts.

Holy Week arrived, so did the piano act, and so did the audience. The manager advertised the act as a radio attraction. Radio didn't mean anything to him, but thousands of families in the Fort Wayne area were hearing radio programs in their home every week. These families knew the piano act. At the first show, and at every show during Holy Week, the theater was packed. When the manager realized that his feature act was playing on percentage, he offered the boys a new contract at a good salary. They laughed at him. The manager called up the booker in Chicago and instructed him to threaten the boys and make them agree to take a salary. The boys laughed at the booker in harmony. Holy Week passed, day by day, and at every show the theater was jammed. The manager was beside himself, which made him doubly mad. Finally, on the last night, when he saw a line of people outside his theater waiting to see the show, the manager couldn't stand it. Walking along the line he said, "Don't go in to see the show, it's rotten! You're wasting your time! Go home! Next week I've got a great show! This show stinks! It's lousy!"

The manager found that picketing his own theater didn't help. The piano act finally left Fort Wayne with several thousand dollars. The manager, then, learned the hard way that radio attractions did business. This explained why he had booked the *WLS Showboat*. It did good business, but Portland and I weren't too interested. All we were thinking of was getting home.

# 20

## June in January

NEW YORK looked good after seven months on the road. Portland and I took an apartment at the Hotel Coolidge on Forty-seventh Street. Portland didn't like the neighborhood and was already making plans: if the show was a big hit, we were going to move uptown. I didn't even know what the show was until I found myself in the presence of Mr. Hammerstein. Arthur Hammerstein was a good-looking, rough-and-ready type of man whose classic features and white hair gave him a dignified and rather formal appearance that his dancing eyes and friendly manner belied. I liked Arthur the first time I met him, and liked and respected him more the longer I knew him. He was one of the old-time producers of the Ziegfeld, Dillingham, Sam Harris school. These men engaged the best creative talent — writers, musicians, actors, and directors — let them alone to prepare their shows, and hoped for the best. A producer was a gambler at heart, and took success and failure in his stride. Arthur Hammerstein had just built a combined office building and theater at Fifty-third Street and Broadway. The theater was called the Hammerstein, and was conceived as a monument to perpetuate the family name. Today, thirty years later, the theater is leased by the Columbia Broadcasting System and is known as Studio 52.

The elaborate Hammerstein offices were in the new building. At our first meeting Mr. Hammerstein told me that he had seen me at the Palace and had a part for me in his new show. It was to be a musical version of *Polly with a Past*, a play originally written by Guy Bolton and George Middleton, and produced by David Belasco. In 1917, Ina Claire had starred in *Polly with a Past*, and the play had enjoyed a long run. It was 1928 now, and Mr. Hammerstein was calling his musical simply *Polly*. Guy Bolton and George Middleton, the original authors, were doing the new book; Herbert Stothart, Phil Charig, and Irving Caesar were writing the music and the lyrics. The star was to be an English girl named June. Mr. Hammerstein had seen June in a London revue called *Clowns in Clover*, and had thought that she would be a great success in America, and especially in *Polly*.

If Mr. Hammerstein had stepped into a gypsy tearoom before he started to produce *Polly*, the gypsy would have felt his tea bag and told him that since 1917, when *Polly with a Past* had opened, Ziegfeld had produced three smashing musical successes called *Sally*, *Sunny*, and *Rosalie*. These shows had not only been three variations of the *Polly* plot, but they had starred Marilyn Miller, a great star of the day. Presenting Miss Miller with his usual lavish productions, Ziegfeld had insured the success of her shows by engaging the top comedians — Leon Errol, Jack Donahue, Frank Morgan, Walter Catlett, and others — that money could buy. Following these wonderful shows, Mr. Hammerstein was going into production with June, a star unknown in America, in a regurgitated plot, and with an undistinguished cast.

June arrived from England to great acclaim, which was confined mostly to Mr. Hammerstein's office. The cast — Archie Leach, Inez Courtney, Sid Marion, Olin Howland, myself, and others — were introduced to our star at the first rehearsal. June was small, pretty, demure, gracious, and subdued. She was a great hit with the cast, and for selfish reasons — having to do with a long run — I hoped that she would be as big a hit with American audiences.

As rehearsals progressed, I knew that even if the world were extra dry, this show was not going to set it on fire. An actor, even in rehearsal, can smell a hit. I was in rehearsal and I could smell something, but it wasn't a hit. The names of the show's characters — Mrs. Van Zile, Roy Van Zile, Prentice Van Zile, Sue, Betty, Polly, Arturo (my name was Adelbert Stiles) — sounded like a roll call at a home for passé musical-comedy personnel. The song titles — "Comme Ci, Comme Ça," "Heel and Toe," "On with the Dance," "Pale Little Bo Peep," "Sing a Song in the Rain," "Sweet Liar" — sounded like those you'd expect in a college show. The melodies would never be whistled except by people who were trying to clean their front teeth after a vegetarian dinner. The plot involved a small-town chorus girl who agrees to impersonate a vamping French adventuress in order that a rich society youth may win the hand of his adored one. The chorus girl and the young blueblood fall madly in love with each other, and after a few complications it all ends happily.

My character, Adelbert Stiles, the reporter from Sag Harbor, had not been in the original play. Even in *Polly*, Adelbert wasn't part of the plot. I was always arriving before something had happened, or right after it had. I was always on the verge, or about to, but I never quite did. During most of the show I spent most of my time talking to myself or to other inconsequential characters who were also not involved in the plot. The director was an English gentleman named John Harwood. He was always busy directing June and the other people involved in her scenes; he didn't seem to understand American slang or my type of humor. I was left to my own devices, and proceeded to scatter all the jokes I had been telling with Portland all through the show. After five weeks of rehearsal, my every entrance led with a monologue. Nobody objected. Guy Bolton, the British author, and Mr. Harwood agreed to everything, as long as I didn't bother them. I suspected that not seeing me rehearse with June, Archie Leach, Inez Courtney, and the other plot actors, they weren't really sure that I was with the show.

*Polly* opened at Wilmington, Delaware. There was a rumor that some of the Du Ponts had invested money in the show and that there were so many Du Ponts, the company's efficiency men had proved that it would be simpler to bring *Polly* to the Du Ponts than it would be to bring the Du Ponts to *Polly*. On Wednesday night, before the Thursday opening, a dress rehearsal was to be held at the Wilmington Theatre. Before the rehearsal started, Mr. Hammerstein announced that he had been too busy to read the script or watch rehearsals in New York. He was now going to see *Polly* for the first time. What he saw must have been a shock. After the dress rehearsal Mr. Hammerstein said nothing. He was either speechless, or he was positive that June's personality and talent would surmount her vehicle.

The "World *Première*" was held the next night. After the overture, the curtain went up briskly to expose a solitary colored servant, center stage. The servant was making a mint julep and singing, "Mint julep, don't you dare to touch it!" Chorus girls' heads were popping in and out at the side, whispering, "Sshhh!" The applause was deafening. I looked out from the first entrance and saw the boxes at every level filled with people in evening dress. It was fortunate that all the boxes were filled. The rest of the theater was practically empty. The Du Ponts, making a social evening of it, had bedecked themselves and packed the boxes. The Wilmington general public thought that June was a month, and ignored Mr. Hammerstein's star and his enterprise.

The next week the show went to Philadelphia. Unhappily, the press was not too enthusiastic about June. One critic wrote:

> Whether it was nervousness upon her first appearance before an audience of a new country or some other reason, the much heralded English comedy favorite, June, failed to come up to predictions. She is a decidedly pretty young woman, who dances gracefully and acts with much more skill than the average musical comedy star, and she wears her wardrobe with an air of distinction, but she has not yet learned how to appeal to an American audience. It may be nonappreciation of the best on our part, but there is no question that there was a gulf between the charming visitor and the other side of the footlights last night.

Of another performer, the same critic wrote:

> Archie Leach, as Roy Van Zile, the boyish hero, meets all the requirements for a romantic girl's Prince Charming. He is more than six feet tall, lean, brown, and athletically hard, and his fine cut features, gleaming teeth and curly black hair are well calculated to draw forth feminine admiration. His voice is above average for the male lead in a musical comedy.

I mention Archie's notice because, at the end of the first week, Mr. Hammerstein announced that *Polly* was closing in Philadelphia. The entire cast was to be replaced, with the exceptions of June, Inez Courtney, and me. We were to return to New York. The show was to be rewritten and recast. Rehearsals were to start in two weeks. Out of a job, Archie was disgusted. He told me that he was going to buy a secondhand car and drive out to Hollywood. What Archie Leach didn't tell me was that he was going to change his name to Cary Grant.

*Polly* went into rehearsal a second time. Guy Bolton had revised the book. A German character, who had been played by Sid Marion, had been replaced by a tramp father, played by Frank McCormack; new scenes had been added. Only two revisions affected me: my first name, Adelbert, was shortened to Addie, and I was given a plot comedy scene with Inez Courtney before the show's finale. After frantic rehearsal sessions the show was supposedly ready, and *Polly* opened for its second "World *Première*" at the Alvin Theatre in Pittsburgh. For all the difference it made, we could have stayed in Wilmington. One of the Pittsburgh critics included in his review an arch little social note:

> . . . and right here a little gossip. At the close of the second act, a gay array of roses was presented to June. 'Twas said they were the gift of a Lord — or some such nobleman — from far away England, who followed the actress here and was in the audience last night.

The roses touched off the only excitement the cast saw in Pittsburgh. June, it appeared, was engaged to Lord Inverclyde, of the Cunard family. His Lordship, on an impulse, left London to surprise his fiancée. It turned into a double surprise. When Lord Inverclyde arrived at the stage door in Pittsburgh, June refused to see him. This was a pretty kettle of kippers. The only person Lord Inverclyde knew in Pittsburgh was his intended wife, and she wasn't speaking to him. Until June relented, the lord remained in Pittsburgh, attending every performance of *Polly* and joining some of us after the show for a nocturnal snack and a few drinks at some speakeasy.

But the presence of Lord Inverclyde or that of Oscar Hammerstein could not hold *Polly*. Arthur Hammerstein had sent for his talented nephew in the hope that Oscar could suggest some things that would improve it. I don't know what Oscar told his Uncle Arthur, but *Polly* closed on Saturday night at Pittsburgh. Again it was announced that the show was going to be rewritten, that most of the cast would be replaced, and that those who were being retained would be notified. Mr. Hammerstein was determined to make June a success. Inez Courtney and I had survived two versions of *Polly*. We had rehearsed seven weeks for nothing, and had worked two and a half weeks for which we had been paid. If Mr. Hammerstein could pay to keep closing the show and bringing it back to New York to improve it, Inez and I thought he could pay us for the third set of rehearsals. We went to Equity, the actors' association, and explained the circumstances and our feeling that we should be on salary. The Equity executive promised to call Mr. Hammerstein and told us to return the next day. The following morning Inez and I were ordered to report at rehearsal. We were told that Mr. Hammerstein needed us, and that by rehearsing for nothing we were making it possible for some forty Equity members and chorus people to go back to work. Back we went, and *Polly* this time rehearsed three weeks. Mr. Hammerstein asked me if I could bolster the comedy, and I submitted a newspaper-office sketch and a revamped version of my scene with Inez. Guy Bolton added these to the show. Guy was writing night and day, and had been writing this way since the first version of *Polly*. The trouble was that we had the wrong Guy. We had Bolton — we needed de Maupassant.

The third "World *Première*" was held on December 23, 1928, at the Shubert Detroit Opera House. The Detroit notices weren't bad, but business was. Geography didn't help *Polly*. Every city was Wilmington. It looked like a gruesome Christmas for the cast. We could only hope that if Santa Claus came down the chimney at the theater, he would stay in the theater long enough to see the show. Guy Bolton was still writing furiously. Here in Detroit he contracted a mild case of the flu, and was confined to his hotel room. He continued to write in bed. On two or three occasions, Alonzo Price, the stage manager, and I visited Guy and found him asleep. Rather than awaken him, Alonzo and I would look through the blankets and sheets to see if Guy had written any new scenes before he had dropped off.

Mr. Hammerstein never stopped trying to improve the show. When a new number called "Sing a Song in the Rain" was added to the show, Mr. Hammerstein had a rain effect made in a hurry to have practical rain to insure applause for the first-act curtain. He also brought a dance director from New York to produce a new rain dance for June and the girls. On New Year's Eve, the first-act finale was to be done for the first time. Mr. Hammerstein stood at the back of the theater to get the full effect of the rain and the dance ensemble. It was New Year's Eve and every other theater in Detroit was filled. Our theater had only half a house, but an additional thing disturbed me. One man was sitting, all alone, in the stage box at the right; another man was equally all alone in the stage box on the left. They both sat staring at the stage, but seemed immune to what was going on. Something told me that these characters were not theater lovers. As the drapes parted for the first-act finale, Mr. Hammerstein braced himself against the rail in the back of the orchestra: he was getting ready to enjoy his rain dance. The music started, and two footmen danced on from the left. When the footmen reached the center of the stage, the two men who had been sitting in the boxes suddenly stepped out onto the stage and advanced on the footmen. When they reached them, they presented each footman with a paper, walked back to their respective boxes, and sat down. They had just served each footman with a summons. (It developed that the two footmen were Detroit boys called Gus and Will. Years before, they had taken dancing lessons with some local teacher, and had left for New York, owing the teacher a sizable bill. The bill had subsequently been ignored. When Gus and Will returned to Detroit with a new Broadway show and ignored the dancing teacher's pleas, he went into action, and the result was the summonses.) When Mr. Hammerstein saw his footmen being molested by unrehearsed baggy process servers, he improvised a covey of oaths and, from the back of the theater, announced in a loud voice that he knew the chief of police in Detroit, and he would soon see if any sons of so-and-sos could break up his show. Forgetting all about June, the rain scene, and the new finale, Mr. Hammerstein dashed out of the theater into the night, on his way to the police station.

Also, in Detroit, Guy Bolton was invited out to dinner by a friend. It turned out that the son of the family had a passing acquaintance with Terpsichore. A few nights later, this son was in the show. His name was Leonard Sillman. Leonard was the loudest dancer I have ever heard. He trod the heavy fantastic, and his dancing sounded like a log jam in a dry river. Fortunately, Leonard jilted this muse, and turned to producing. If Leonard had pursued his iron-footed career, he would have beaten holes in every stage from coast to coast, and ruptured the acoustics of every theater in the land.

The middle-aged actor who played the wealthy banker, Prentice Van Zile, in *Polly* always intrigued me. This gentleman had no overcoat. I would meet him on the street during the day, shivering in his business suit. At night, he appeared late in the second act and said, "If all goes well, I'll give two hundred thousand dollars!" His mouth was wealthy at night, but his body was poor during the day.

When fate had exhausted all the tricks it had budgeted to play on *Polly* in Detroit, the show left for New York. Here, on opening day, backstage at the Lyric Theatre was a turmoil. Stagehands were hanging scenery, musicians were rehearsing in the pit, the wardrobe woman and her assistants were carrying costumes from the large wardrobe trunks to hang in the chorus dressing rooms, and the principals, or their maids or valets, were unpacking. I had no valet and was busy hanging up my suits in the dressing room. Suddenly, above the din, I heard Mr. Hammerstein's voice, vibrant and clear, fouling the air with as masterful a display of billingsgate as had ever reached my ears. Mr. Hammerstein's tirade had been occasioned by the stagehands' refusal to hang the pipe for the rain effects. The pipe bore no union label and could not be used in the show. The rain effect had been made hurriedly on the road, and nobody had noticed that it had come from a nonunion shop. Now, a new rain effect would have to be ordered for the opening.

This final blow was too much for Mr. Hammerstein. After the weeks of rehearsals, the openings and the closings, the firings and hirings, the troubles with authors and music writers, he had now come to the breaking point. There was only one way Mr. Hammerstein could get even with *Polly*. Before the show even opened, he took all of the tickets and put them in the cut rate. I felt sorry for him. He had accepted all the buffetings and misfortunes that had been visited on his venture since its inception without ever saying a word. I had tried to help in my small way; when I came back to the theater that night, I found this telegram:

THERE IS ONLY ONE WAY I CAN SHOW MY APPRECIATION FOR ALL YOU HAVE DONE DURING MY TRIALS AND TRIBULATIONS WITH POLLY AND THAT IS IF YOU EVER HAVE NEED OF A FAVOR OR A FRIEND CALL ON ME STOP HERES HOPING YOUR EFFORTS WILL BE COMPENSATED FOR BY POLLY BEING A SUCCESS —
ARTHUR HAMMERSTEIN

It would be nice to record that after *Polly's* misfortunes and adversities, Mr. Hammerstein's hopes materialized, but the opening of the show didn't change his luck. The notices were better than we expected. My additions to *Polly* were fine for me, but they didn't help the show. Steven Rathburn, the critic on the *Sun*, came the closest to the truth. He wrote:

"Polly," Arthur Hammerstein's musical version of "Polly with a Past," made with the help of three librettists, two composers, and a lyric writer, opened last night at the Lyric Theatre before a select audience of Broadway's own four hundred. This large, pretentious production moved along slowly, except when the lively chorus, or the even livelier specialty dancers displayed their gyrations. As the play progressed it became evident that there was some mistake somewhere as the audience was smarter and more brilliant than the show on the stage.

One of the comedians, Fred Allen, who was funny nine-tenths of the time, nearly ran away with the show. Of course that is a popular expression. What he actually did was literally to stop the show whenever he was on the stage. It was Allen versus the rest of the company, and usually Allen won. He was an awful example of what a comedian can do when he is allowed to be as funny as he knows how, as long and as often as possible. Cute Inez Courtney fed him, and he was even fed by aristocratic-looking Isabel O'Madigan, who played the haughty Mrs. Van Zile of Southampton, and June, the attractive prima donna, fed him. He was the best-fed comedian I have seen in years. As a matter of fact, Mr. Allen was quite able to feed himself, a feat that not every comedian can perform. If Joe Cook was the "One-Man Vaudeville Show," then certainly Allen can be called a one-man musical comedy. At least he was almost that last night. But he was very funny, and he prevented more than one theatre-goer from having a dull evening.

*Polly* ran only two weeks. I said good-by to June in January.

# Epilogue

FRED ALLEN died on March 17, 1956. By that date he had completed the part of his autobiography which you have just read, and that part comes fairly close to being the complete book as he intended it. Had he lived, *Much Ado About Me* would have been a longer book, although not much longer, for after 1928, while he continued on the stage for a short time — there were, for example, such successful revues as *The Little Show* and *Three's a Crowd* — most of his years were spent on the radio, and the story of these years he had already told in his earlier book, *Treadmill to Oblivion*. It was not his plan to retell this story in *Much Ado About Me*.

As it stands, however, this autobiography has at least one unity which it could not have had if the radio years had been included. This is the unity of great affection. Fred Allen loved his early years in entertainment. He loved the excitement, the variety, the sheer *fun* of that scrambling, uncertain, and often very difficult life. Radio, which brought him fame, security, and money, was something else again. Its rewards were handsome, but it was big business and hard, grinding work; for it he felt no particular affection, and in it he had no fun at all.

While he was writing *Much Ado About Me* I saw a good deal of Fred Allen. I suppose I was, in a curious sense, his collaborator, although no collaborator ever worked less or with greater pleasure. For one thing, there was no writing to do; Fred took care of that. In an age where the autobiographical "assistant" and the "as-told-to" technique have become commonplaces, it is a pleasure to report that the touch of the ghost is not upon these pages. Every word in this book was written by one man, and that man was Fred Allen.

However, because he had never written in this form or at such length before, he did feel the need of someone to talk to as he was writing, someone with whom he could discuss his plans and roughly block out each of his chapters in advance. I was that someone, and for the last two years we met regularly and Fred talked and I listened. I never had a better time in my life. At the end of each session, I gave him a page or so of notes and suggestions, and we talked about the next chapter; following this, Fred sat down to write.

His work schedule on *Much Ado About Me* was almost unvarying. Although some of it was written in Boston, and a bit of it in Dublin (where Portland, Fred, and I went for a quick and hilarious trip in the fall of 1955), by far the greater part of the writing was done in New York. Fred wrote, not in his apartment, but in a little office he had rented in order to get away from the telephone. He went to this office every morning between ten-thirty and eleven; he came home every afternoon at five, his day's work done. He wrote rapidly and revised thoroughly, and as he went over the years of his life in his memory, and as he talked about them and finally put them down on paper, it was clear that he was doing something that he had always wanted to do, and that he was happy in his task.

And so *Much Ado About Me* was written. It is, I think, a rare and wonderful book by a rare and wonderful man who, in spite of having written the finest comedy in the history of broadcasting, and in spite of having written literally hundreds of the wittiest and most felicitous letters of our time, did not for a moment consider himself to be really a good writer at all. I don't think Fred Allen was wrong in many things, but he was absolutely wrong in this, and the abundant proof is all in *Much Ado About Me.*

EDWIN O'CONNOR

# Index

# Index